"Elegant, insightful, magisterial: Ac [text obscured] instant classic of scholarship, exposir [text obscured] ing legal theories, left and right, and pointing us to a better alternative – one as vibrant and radical as the Western tradition."

Sohrab Ahmari, author of
The Unbroken Thread and *From Fire, by Water*

"You are holding that rarest of books, one that will change minds, change the terms of debate, and change the future. Adrian Vermeule has written the most important and original book on constitutional theory for this generation. Future scholars, lawyers, and citizens will look back at this book for having sounded the death knell of the seemingly unassailable camps of conservative 'originalism' and progressive 'living constitutionalism,' revealing them to be exhausted sides of the same devalued liberal coin. More importantly, this book charts a new and better path – a common good constitutionalism grounded in the classical tradition but repurposed for the revitalization of a declining but redeemable republic."

Patrick J. Deneen, University of Notre Dame,
author of *Why Liberalism Failed*

"This is the most important book of American constitutional theory in many decades. Adrian Vermeule unearths the entirely forgotten classical legal tradition – a mix of Roman law, canon law, and civil law – which dominated judicial thinking from the founding until positivism began to consume constitutional law in the early twentieth century. He exposes the dominant originalist paradigm as an impoverished Johnny-come-lately to the constitutional scene. And he powerfully demonstrates how the classical legal tradition's central idea – promotion of the common good – can inform contemporary public law thinking to promote community flourishing, both domestically and globally. *Common Good Constitutionalism* is a bolt from the blue that challenges conservative and progressive constitutional law paradigms alike. It is destined to infuriate, and to reorient."

Jack Goldsmith, Learned Hand Professor of Law,
Harvard University

"This bold and provocative book challenges the views on constitutional interpretation of both US conservatives and liberals, and reframes the debate by focusing on a substantive concept: the common good. With his characteristic originality and ability to weave the insights of different disciplines, Vermeule puts forward a thought-provoking account of the common good and its legal implications, one which will be of relevance well beyond American debates. Even those who disagree with it will have much to learn from this erudite engagement with one of the main concepts in political thought."

Francisco J. Urbina, Pontificia Universidad Católica de Chile

Common Good Constitutionalism

[I]t is impossible that there can be a right which does not aim at the common good. Hence Cicero is correct when he says in the *De inventione* that laws are always to be interpreted for the benefit of the community. For if laws are not framed for the benefit of those who are subject to the law, they are laws in name only, but in reality they cannot be laws; for laws must bind men together for their mutual benefit.

Dante Alighieri, *De Monarchia* (Prue Shaw, trans. and ed.)

The praetor is also said to render legal right (*jus*) even when he makes a wrongful decree, the reference, of course, being in this case not to what the praetor has done, but to what it is right for a praetor to do.

Digest of Justinian 1.1.11 (Alan Watson, trans.)

Common Good Constitutionalism

Recovering the Classical Legal Tradition

Adrian Vermeule

polity

First published in 2022 by Polity Press

Excerpt from Dante Alighieri, *De Monarchia* (Prue Shaw, trans. and ed.; 1995), reproduced by kind permission of Cambridge University Press.

Excerpt from *Digest of Justinian* 1.1.11 (Alan Watson, trans.; 1985, revised edition 1998), reproduced by kind permission of University of Pennsylvania Press.

Polity Press
65 Bridge Street
Cambridge CB2 1UR, UK

Polity Press
101 Station Landing
Suite 300
Medford, MA 02155, USA

ISBN-13: 978-1-5095-4886-6
ISBN-13: 978-1-5095-4887-3 (pb)

A catalogue record for this book is available from the British Library.

Library of Congress Control Number: 2021946341

Typeset in 9.5 on 14 pt Fournier by
Cheshire Typesetting Ltd, Cuddington, Cheshire
Printed and bound in Great Britain by TJ Books Ltd, Padstow, Cornwall

The publisher has used its best endeavors to ensure that the URLs for external websites referred to in this book are correct and active at the time of going to press. However, the publisher has no responsibility for the websites and can make no guarantee that a site will remain live or that the content is or will remain appropriate.

Every effort has been made to trace all copyright holders, but if any have been overlooked the publisher will be pleased to include any necessary credits in any subsequent reprint or edition.

For further information on Polity, visit our website:
politybooks.com

Contents

Acknowledgments

My debts are many and heavy. First and foremost to my family, Yun Soo, Emily, Spencer, Auntie, Oma, and Bella, who tolerate my foibles and my Amazon addiction. George Owers provided superb editorial guidance and substantive comments at all stages, especially by overcoming my obdurate resistance on the title. For excellent comments on all or part of the manuscript, I am most grateful to Rishabh Bhandari, Conor Casey, Jack Goldsmith, Pedro Jose Izquierdo, Suzanne Smith, William Strench, and three anonymous reviewers. Prof. Casey has been an intellectual companion on this journey and I've been fortunate to learn from him during our co-authored projects. Suzanne Smith straightened my tortured outline and Will Strench provided outstanding research assistance of all sorts, and I can't thank them enough. Dave Owen provided valuable help with the notes.

For more general conversations, insights, and scholarship that infuse the book, or for encouragement and support of the project, thanks and appreciation go to many friends and colleagues, including all those mentioned above and also Sohrab Ahmari, Rafael de Arizaga, Evelyn Blacklock, Evelyn Boyden, Patrick McKinley Brennan, Ricardo Calleja, Yves Casertano, Amy Chandran, Patrick Deneen, Tyler Dobbs, Catherine Feil, Joel Feil, Robin Fennelly, Michael Foran, Jose Ignacio Hernandez Gonzalez, Fr. Carlos Hamel, Fr. Jeff Langan, Fr. Brendon M. Laroche, Jamie McGowan, Ryan Meade, Xavier Menard, Maria Messina, Eli Nachmany, Jake Neu, Fr. Cristian Mendoza Ovando, Christopher Owens, Gladden Pappin, Jeanette Pappin, Christopher Parrott, Darel Paul, Chad Pecknold, Amanda Piccirillo, Anthony Piccirillo, Anibal Sabater, Patrick J. Smith of Bedford, Indiana, Francisco Urbina, Pater Edmund Waldstein, Dan Whitehead, and participants at the Pro Civitate Dei Conference 2021.

At various points, I have heavily adapted excerpts from past articles or blog posts for use in the book. Besides entries on the law blogs *Ius & Iustitium* and *Mirror of Justice*, these include *Common-Good Constitutionalism*, THE ATLANTIC (March 31, 2020); *Rules, Commands and Principles in the Administrative State*, 130 YALE LAW JOURNAL FORUM (Jan. 6, 2021); and *The Unitary Executive: Past, Present, Future*, SUPREME COURT REVIEW (2021) (with Cass R. Sunstein). Thanks to the co-author of the last for his gracious permission to adapt some material for the book.

Introduction: The Return of the Classical Legal Tradition

American public law suffers from a terrible amnesia. Putting aside the work of a few legal historians and other specialists, our law has all but lost the memory of its own origins and formative influences in the classical legal tradition – particularly the *ius commune*, the classical European synthesis of Roman law, canon law, and local civil law.[1] The *ius commune* was heavily influential in England, in a somewhat variant form;[2] both English and continental streams influenced Americans right from the beginning, throughout the nineteenth century and well into the twentieth.

The consequence of this amnesia is that our public law now oscillates restlessly and unhappily between two dominant approaches, progressivism and originalism, both of which distort the true nature of law and betray our own legal traditions. Against both camps, I argue for a view I will call *common good constitutionalism*. On this view, the classical tradition should be explicitly recovered and adapted as the matrix within which American judges read our Constitution, our statutes, and our administrative law. The centerpiece of the classical legal tradition is that law should be seen as a reasoned ordering to the common good, the "art of goodness and fairness,"[3] as the Roman jurist Ulpian put it – an act of purposive and reasoned rulership that promotes the good of law's subjects as members of a flourishing political community, and ultimately as members of the community of peoples and nations. Accordingly, the master principle of our public law should be the classical principle that all officials have a duty, and corresponding authority, to promote the common good – albeit in a manner consistent with the requirements of their particular roles, an important qualification to which I shall often return.

This classical conception embodies the best of our own tradition, the union of well-ordered reason with public authority. And if anything has a claim to capturing the "original understanding" of the Constitution, this does. The classical law *is* the original understanding. In that sense, this book is as much a work of memory and recovery as of theory. So-called "originalism," which in its elaborated theoretical form is a product of the conservative legal movement's particular political and rhetorical situation after World War II, is profoundly anachronistic, indeed counter-originalist.[4] The classical law was deeply inscribed in our legal traditions well before the founding era, and was explicit in legal practice through the nineteenth century and into the twentieth century. Indeed, the classical vision was central to the American legal world until it began to break down, initially in the period before World War I and finally after World War II. The precise timing is immaterial for my purposes, but it is clear that by the 1960s a radical shift had occurred. The so-called "Legal Process" school,[5] which emphasized law as a purposive ordering, represented a last iteration of the classical legal tradition but in a thin, impoverished version, bereft of the rich background of tradition and principle worked out over many centuries by the *ius commune.* The classical tradition, by contrast, is robust. It openly embraces the view that law is ordered to the common good, explains why it is law's nature to be so ordered, and claims that the positive law based on the will of the civil lawmaker, while worthy of great respect in its sphere, is contained within a larger objective order of legal principles and can only be interpreted in accordance with those principles.

I certainly do not advocate a revival of the classical law *because* it is the original understanding. The suggestion is not that, as good originalists deep down, we should adopt the view of the classical legal tradition in a derivative fashion. As we will see, all attempts to combine originalism with the classical view of law are ultimately incoherent, an attempt to mix oil and water. On the contrary, precisely to the extent that American lawyers are genuinely originalist, they should have the courage to discard originalism altogether in favor of the classical law, the fundamental matrix for the thinking of the whole founding generation. The truly principled originalist would immolate his own method and transform himself into a classical lawyer, in an act of intellectual self-abnegation and self-overcoming.

Of course a simple return to the classical legal tradition and its particular legal rules is neither desirable nor even possible. Even were that feasible, which it is not, one would risk simply recreating the conditions that caused the present to come into being. But the core theoretical insights and jurisprudential principles of the classical legal tradition can be recovered, adapted and translated[6] into our world, so as to yield a better interpretation of the past and present of our operative constitutional order. Those insights are scarcely so remote as to preclude recovery; in fact, they are close at hand, if obscured from our current vision. Key elements of the classical view of law remain vital within our law, even as lawyers and judges have ceased to defend or even recognize them.

Rational Ordering for the Common Good

In the classical tradition, law is seen as – in Aquinas' famous definition[7] – an ordinance of reason for the common good, promulgated by a public authority who has charge of the community. Law is seen as intrinsically reasoned and also purposive, ordered to the common good of the whole polity and that of mankind. Classical law treats enacted texts as products of the reasoned deliberation of public authorities who give specific content to the law where background legal principles need specificity or leave relevant issues to discretionary choice. Where at all possible, classical law reads the law of a particular jurisdiction (the *ius civile*) in light of the *ius gentium* (the law of nations or peoples) and the *ius naturale* (natural law), which the civil positive law is taken to specify or "determine" within reasonable boundaries. General principles of law might, for example, say that, at some point, peace and order require that potential defendants should have repose from the risk of being sued; it would then be up to the civil law in such an instance to determine a specific statute of limitations and to resolve the many questions that flow from it.

Put differently, the classical tradition distinguishes, as many European languages do, between two senses of "law," *lex* and *ius*.

(In Spanish, *ley* and *derecho*; in French, *loi* and *droit*; and so on. English, to its misfortune, has no stable version of this distinction and instead uses "law" and "right(s)" in confusing ways.) *Lex* is the enacted positive law, such as a statute. *Ius* is the overall body of law generally, including and subsuming *lex* but transcending it, and containing general principles of jurisprudence and legal justice. Thus *lex* is a source of *ius* but does not exhaust its content. In this tradition, "rights" very much exist, but they are not defined in the essentially individualist, autonomy-based, and libertarian fashion familiar today. Instead "rights" are corollaries of justice, which is the constant aim of giving every man his due. *Ius* is what is due to every person, and in this sense, but only this sense, includes rights. In the classical tradition, both natural and positive are, in somewhat different ways, themselves included within law's larger ordering to the common good.

Today both progressives and originalists either deny the existence of the natural law altogether (the usual progressive view), or deny its relevance to law except in strictly historical terms, as a background belief potentially incorporated into the law laid down by the framers and ratifiers (the now-standard originalist view). Both camps therefore attempt, in different ways, to reduce all law to positive law adopted by officials; for them, all law is in this sense *lex*. But just because *ius* is lost to view does not mean that it has actually been purged from American law – far from it. The classical vision of law as a rational ordering to the common good, embedded in a broader framework of legal principles, has merely been driven underground. Judges and others unavoidably and unmistakably work with some account or other of the common good and of law's ordering to that good. We will see this point over and over again, in disparate areas.

An Interpretive Argument

How does this classical view of law relate to constitutional theory today? I will not offer an argument about jurisprudence in the technical academic sense. Although I draw on jurisprudential ideas as necessary, I have nothing original to say in that regard.[8] Neither is this a work of legal history, although I draw on legal history done by others in order to recover the powerful tradition of the common good in American law. Finally, it is not a work of political theory.

Rather it is written throughout from the lawyer's point of view, as a work of interpretation. From that point of view, I offer an account that aims to put our constitutional order, including the administrative state, in its best possible light, given our whole history – not merely our most recent history. As against the progressives and originalists, I suggest that the best overall interpretation overall of our public law requires us to revive the principles of the classical law, looking backward so that we may go forward. It is a case of *reculer pour mieux sauter*. In terms made famous by Ronald Dworkin,[9] the last few chapters of the chain novel are impossible to square with the arc of what went before. They mar the integrity of the whole, and offer a poor account of our operative constitutional order. The point is not to reclaim the insights of the classical tradition out of nostalgia, but because doing so holds out the greatest promise for a principled and coherent interpretation of our current constitutional order as well as its history.

It does not follow, of course, that the interpretation I offer need be parochial or ignore the contributions of legal traditions outside the United States. Indeed my project is quite the opposite: it is to recover and revive the profound connections between the classical American tradition on the one hand, and on the other the classical Roman and European tradition, the *ius commune*, the latter definitely including the Anglo-American common law as a local variant. The book thus has both a general part and a particular part – a duality that is itself typical of the classical legal framework. It speaks both to general principles of common good constitutionalism and to the specific institutions of the American constitutional order. As such I hope it is of interest to lawyers in the Commonwealth nations, Europe, Latin America, and Asia as well.

Methodologically, this work of interpretation draws not only upon the classical and natural law tradition[10] but also, in limited ways, upon the parts of Dworkin's jurisprudence that are consistent with the classical view of law and that explain and illuminate the latter's commitments. The principal use I make of Dworkin is negative, invoking him as the unsurpassed modern critic of positivism and originalism in Anglophone legal theory. In my view those withering criticisms have never successfully been answered.[11] I illustrate those criticisms of both positivism and originalism with examples from legal and judicial practice: law itself contains general principles,[12] rooted in political morality, whose origins do not seem to depend on any particular act of positive lawmaking; positivism and originalism cannot account for theoretical, as opposed to historical, disagreement in interpretation;[13] and originalism has never successfully coped with the problem of abstraction, the question of the level of generality at which to read the original understanding.[14]

Dworkin used to urge "moral readings of the Constitution,"[15] implemented through his method of fit and justification.[16] Common good constitutionalism shares the view that the positive provisions of the *ius civile*, including at the constitutional level, can only be interpreted in light of principles of political morality that are themselves part of the law. And it urges that the classical law is the best of our tradition, with the emphasis on both "best" (justification) and "tradition" (fit). But it advocates a different set of substantive moral commitments and priorities and a different account of rights from Dworkin's, which were all of a conventionally left-liberal and individualist bent. I emphatically eschew Dworkin's particular, substantively liberal account of justification, which I will take to be detachable. While interpretation necessarily posits some account or other of justification, it need not posit Dworkin's own account. I reject his liberal theory of rights, as trumps over collective interests, in favor of a classical theory of rights as *ius*, founded in the injunction of justice to give to every person what is due to them in a political order devoted to the common good.[17]

In general, nothing in my claims turns on narrow and elaborate debates among professional scholars of jurisprudence about the details and development of Dworkin's thought. I use those of his ideas that have already become part of the common currency of legal theory, in part because they simply describe with great clarity things that are undeniably a part of law (for example, the ubiquity of legal principles). Not coincidentally, those are the ideas that fit like a glove with the classical conception of law that prevailed in America for so long.

The Common Good Defined

Chapter 1 defines the common good, at successively specific levels – conceptually, legally, and constitutionally. In brief, the common good is, for the purposes of the constitutional lawyer, the flourishing of a well-ordered political community. The common good is unitary and indivisible, not an aggregation of individual utilities. In its temporal aspect it represents the highest felicity or happiness of the whole political community, which is also the highest good of the individuals comprising that community.

To give this more specific content, I look to the precepts of legal justice in the classical law – to live honorably, to harm no one, and to give each one what is due to him in justice – and to the related *ragion di stato* tradition in early modern Europe, which articulates the central goods at which constitutionalism should aim. These goods include, in a famous trinity, *peace, justice, and abundance*, which I extrapolate to modern conditions to include various forms of *health, safety, and economic security*. I also elicit from the tradition the key principles of *solidarity* and *subsidiarity*.[18]

The largest point of the tradition is that public authority is both natural and legitimate – rather than intrinsically suspect, as one might infer from certain strands of the liberal tradition. Yet that authoritative rule is bounded and limited by the very condition that gives it legitimacy: that the ruling authority always act through reasoned ordinances conducing to the common good, to public rather than private interest. As we will see, the requirement of reasoned and public-regarding rule leaves ample scope to adjust the law to changing circumstances, but the fundamental nature of law as reasoned ordination to the common good is unchanging.

Common good constitutionalism, then, is not legal positivism, meaning that it does not identify all law with the rules laid down by those authorized to do so by social conventions; on the contrary, it allows that the truth of legal propositions sometimes depends on the truth of moral propositions. Common good constitutionalism draws upon an immemorial tradition that includes, in addition to positive law, sources such as the general law common to all civilized legal systems (*ius gentium*) and principles of objective natural morality (*ius naturale*), including procedural legal morality in the sense used by the American legal theorist Lon Fuller: the inner logic that the activity of law should follow in order to function well as law.[19]

Here it is easy to misunderstand the place of positive law in the classical tradition. Positive law is hardly lacking; it represents a legitimate specification by the public authority of general principles of legal morality that need concrete embodiment, the specification of local rules that take account of local conditions, and is therefore called *ius civile*, literally the "law of the city." Indeed, as we will see, the right and duty of the public authority to determine or specify the content of the positive law imply that the judges or other officials who determine the meaning of law at the point of application are duty-bound to follow a kind of textualism, at least presumptively. But this is not the positivist form of textualism that simply equates law with positive enacted texts; rather it is textualism justified by reference to political morality, the rational ordering of rules to the common good by the public authority. Thus positive enacted texts are always read against the backdrop of, and if at all possible in accord with, the broader legal background of natural law, general and traditional legal principles, and the law of nations. The classical law incorporates positive law, but rejects any commitment to positivism in a jurisprudential sense, regardless of any distinctions between harder or softer, exclusive or inclusive versions of positivism. (As explained later, I follow Dworkin in believing that inclusive versions of positivism and originalism converge entirely with non-positivism and non-originalism; they are essentially ways of saving face at the level of names and labels while abandoning all the important substantive positions.)

The Role of Prudence

The common good, on this view, is a type of *justification* for public action. It does not, by itself, prescribe any particular legal institutions or rules. Leaving aside cases of intrinsic evils, which place deontological side constraints on all public and private action, the common good must be applied to a set of particular circumstances by means of the faculty of prudential judgment – more specifically, the virtue that is called "regnative prudence."[20] This is the prudential judgment, oriented toward justice, of a public authority who is charged with the care of the *res publica*, whether by election, delegation, or some other mode of selection. This prudence is by no means unstructured discretion. It is given shape by an account of the ends for which discretion must be used, that of promoting the good of the whole community as a community – not merely as an aggregation of individual preferences. In other words, discretion may never transgress the intrinsic limitations of legal justice. The obligation of the public authority is to act according to law, meaning that the public authority must act through rational ordinances oriented to the common good.

Of course, nothing in the nature of law guarantees, or could possibly guarantee, that the public authority will in fact always act for the common good. But that is true whatever theory of law we hold; it is to demand too much of law that it exclude the possibility of bad or even tyrannical government. Rather every polity must work out for itself institutional forms and customs that orient public authority toward the common good, at least roughly and on the whole. Legal theory as such, by its nature, necessarily assumes that the prevailing order is at least not wholly tyrannical.

Determination –
Of the Constitution and Within the Constitution

In the classical tradition, regnative prudence is closely linked to the concept of *determination* – the process of giving content to a general principle drawn from a higher source of law, making it concrete in application to particular local circumstances or problems. I will explain this crucial concept in detail in Chapter 1. Briefly, the need for determination arises when principles of justice are general and thus do not specifically dictate particular legal rules, or when those principles seem to conflict and must be mutually accommodated or balanced. Those general principles must be given further determinate content by positive civil lawmaking. There are typically multiple ways to determine the principles while remaining within the boundaries of the basic charge to act to promote the common good – the basis of public authority. By analogy, an architect who is given a general commission to build a hospital for a city possesses a kind of structured discretion. The purpose or end of the commission shapes and constrains the architect's choices while not fully determining them; a good hospital may take a number of forms, although there are some forms it cannot take.

So too at the level of the whole constitutional order. The common good in its capacity as the fundamental end of temporal government shapes and constrains, but does not fully determine, the nature of institutions and the allocation of lawmaking authority between and among them in any given polity. Such matters are left for specification that gives concrete content to the operative, small-c constitution (which is not necessarily the same as the formal written Constitution even in polities that have the latter). Call this determination *of* the constitution.

This agnosticism at the level of institutions, in turn, has two aspects: agnosticism about institutional design, and about the allocation among institutions of authority to interpret the constitutional scheme. Parliamentary and presidential systems, constitutional monarchies and republics, all these and more can in principle be ordered to the common good. Likewise, the common good does not, by itself, entail any particular scheme of (for example) judicial review of constitutional questions, or even any such scheme at all. The common good takes no stand, *a priori*, on the well-known debate over political constitutionalism versus legal constitutionalism,[21] so long as the polity is ordered to the good of the community through rational principles of legality.[22]

This broad agnosticism does not mean that there are no boundaries whatsoever; it just means that the boundaries are set by the nature of law itself, as an ordination of reason to the common good. Certain institutional arrangements, mostly science-fictional and horrific, will be ruled out even if no one set of arrangements is uniquely specified. But they will be ruled out because they are arbitrary and unreasoned, and thus do not participate in the nature of law, not because the common good directly commands particular institutional forms. Likewise, strictly aggregative-utilitarian arrangements will be ruled out by the non-aggregative nature of the common good, an example being a substantial class of invisible-hand arrangements justified as an indirect way of maximizing aggregate utility.[23] But the ruling out of certain arrangements leaves a wide scope for choice that adapts institutional forms to local circumstances.

So far I have been talking about determination of the constitution. At another level, there is also determination *within* or *under* the constitution. Particular sets of institutions (among which authority has been allocated) give further specification to general constitutional principles of the common good, such as principles of solidarity and subsidiarity and others to be discussed here. Indeed, the process of determination is iterative and continues to ever-more detailed levels, as we will see. The legislature and executive, for example, may agree on a general statute giving some specification to a general legal principle, and in turn delegate to administrative agencies the authority to determine the general provisions of the statute. The agency may do so by a binding regulation, which may then require further interpretation, and so on.

General and Particular Claims

An important corollary is that one has to distinguish (1) general claims about constitutionalism ordered to the common good from (2) specific constructive interpretations of a *given* constitutional order that aim to put that order, as it develops over time, in its best light. I have called the former the general part of this book, the latter its particular part. I presuppose here, incorporating previous work by reference, a particular constructive interpretation that fits-and-justifies our own developing constitutional order. In that interpretation, the American small-c constitutional order has come to feature broad deference to legislatures on social and economic legislation and broad delegations from legislatures to the executive. In operation, moreover, lawmaking is effectively centered mainly on executive government, divided in complicated ways between the presidency and the administrative agencies (including both executive agencies and independent agencies). The executive and administrative state can and does act according to the rule of law, constituted in important part by principles of regularity in lawmaking that I will discuss in later chapters. Indeed, by acting through reasoned law, our executive-centered order can be ordered to the common good.

That particular interpretation of our own constitutional order, however, is separable from the general claims about the nature and principles of constitutionalism also offered here. Agreement with the general part does not necessarily entail agreement with the particular part. One may subscribe to the general framework of common good constitutional interpretation without subscribing to the full, particular interpretation of the path of American public law that I have laid out. The failure of some commentators to distinguish general claims about the nature of constitutionalism from specific claims about the determination of the American constitutional order has produced serious confusion, and one of my aims here is to clear that up.

Courts and the Common Good

Throughout the book, I emphasize that *courts* need not be the institutions charged with directly identifying or specifying the common good. A division of institutional roles can, under particular circumstances, itself conduce to the common good. It is not written in the nature of law that courts must decide all legal or constitutional questions. The precise allocation of law-interpreting power between courts and other public bodies is itself a question for determination at the constitutional level.

In America, the classical tradition held that so long as determinations are made within the jurisdictional competence of public bodies, for legitimate ends, and on rational grounds, they are a matter for the public authority, not the courts. A strong legal principle of deference by courts to the determinations of legislatures was part and parcel of our law from the beginning. One of my particular claims is that our small-c constitutional order developed over time to extend this principle to the institutional presidency and administrative tribunals. Today our constitution supports the legitimacy of broad delegations to the executive,[24] shaped and constrained by principles of legality that ensure that the executive acts rationally in ways ordered to the common good.[25] Determination is plausibly the remote ancestor of deference in all sorts of forms that are familiar in the administrative state, such as *Chevron* deference[26] to administrative agencies.

A corollary of the nature of determination is that the public authority – including the executive exercising delegated authority – may, without transgressing its boundaries, engage in what I have called "rationally arbitrary decisions."[27] Because determination involves specification within a range in which reason need not yield a unique answer, some element of irreducible judgment will be required. Should the statute of limitations for a given offense be ten years or fifteen? Or perhaps twelve? The law is not so sophomoric as to demand a first-order reason for the choice of one particular number over another, for it is impossible to give any such reason, at least within a reasonable range of choices. In this sense, reason itself allows a certain degree of arbitrary specification, which will thus not be coded as "arbitrary" in the legal sense for purposes of the common good framework.

Abuse of Power?

Libertarians and liberals find the classical tradition appalling or, worse, irrelevant. Both express, along varying lines, the fear that talk of "the common good" is just a shorthand for the preferences of those in power, and worry above all about abuses of power – although libertarians and liberals tend to focus on different abuses, the former worrying mostly about regulatory abuses, the latter about the imposition of public morality that constrains personal expression and elite "experiments in living." Abuse of power is indeed an evil, and I will have a great deal to say about it in this book. But fear of the common good is mistaken in two ways, institutional and conceptual.

First, we have to take on board the insight of progressives like Dewey that *power is always conserved*.[28] Any claim to "liberty" is a claim for a legal allocation of power to do or not to do or to prevent others from doing or not doing. Hence abuses of power are hardly confined to government actors or the state. Corporations acting under public charters, and nominally "private" actors wielding power under common-law rules of property and contract created and enforced by judges – that is, by a class of government officials – can and frequently do abuse a kind of delegated public power. It is a mistake to focus myopically on direct abuses of power by officials themselves, as opposed to indirect abuses of power made possible by the law.

Second, and more fundamentally, the common good is not "preferences" or "what I like" or "whatever the ruler imposes at whim." It is not an aggregation of individual goods, as in utilitarianism, let alone the interests of the state apparatus, as in certain forms of "Government House utilitarianism."[29] Rather, as I discuss in Chapter 1, the common good is well-ordered peace, justice, and abundance in political community; the flourishing of the political community is also the greatest temporal good for the individual.

The last part is crucial. Libertarians, usually implicitly, read "the common good" as "the good of the collective" or, even worse, "the good of the state apparatus" and then oppose that to the good of individuals. In a utilitarian variant, they interpret the common good as the aggregate utility of individuals summed up according to some social welfare function, and then oppose this aggregate good to the rights of individuals. None of this gets at the truly *common* good of happiness in a flourishing political community, which is unitary, capable of being shared without being diminished, and the highest good for individuals as such.

The Common Good and "the Common Good"

In the end, every legitimate act of government works with some conception or other of the common good; that is inescapable.[30] This point only becomes all the more transparent when – as often happens, especially in the administrative state – courts are called upon to construe legal provisions and clauses that speak in abstract terms of "the general welfare," "the public interest," or other formulations. Such provisions merely make the implicit explicit, writing the common good into the terms of the law itself. Those terms must be construed one way or another. The choices are for the court to give them a substantive construction, which will inevitably require the court to take some view or other of what counts as the public interest, or for the court to defer wholly or partly to political authorities to fill in the provisions' content, perhaps subject to judicial review for reasonableness.

I will argue that the best of our traditions is that the courts should defer to public determination of such provisions, so long as the public authority acts rationally and with a view to legitimate public purposes: the ends of peace, justice, and abundance, and their modern extensions. Construing the "public use" language of the so-called "Takings Clause" of the Fifth Amendment (incorporated into the Fourteenth), the Court once said that "[t]he 'public use' requirement is thus coterminous with the scope of a sovereign's police powers. . . . The Court has made clear that it will not substitute its judgment for a legislature's judgment as to what constitutes a public use unless the use be palpably without reasonable foundation."[31] I argue that this exemplifies a well-ordered scheme of judicial review in our constitutional tradition.

Competitors to the Classical Tradition

As the last point shows, I offer not only a positive account of the common good in public law, but plenty of negative claims as well – critiques of the prominent alternatives. Today, public law and legal theory are dominated by two forces. On the one hand there is progressive constitutional law, which treats the courts as an arena for a liberationist agenda and the law as an instrument for advancing that agenda. On the other hand there is the conservative legal movement, which has largely tied itself to a particular constitutional method, "originalism" – in the version I focus on here, essentially a form of positivism that claims to interpret enacted text according to its original public meaning.[32]

Since its modern inception in the 1960s and 1970s, originalism has never been able to free itself from – or even to acknowledge – the implicit normative assumptions and judgments needed to attribute rationality to legal texts, to determine the level of generality at which the meaning of constitutional texts should be read, and otherwise to make sense of their terms. Thus originalism is, in that sense, an illusion; it proves impossible to avoid interpretation that rests on controversial normative judgments at the point of application, especially in hard cases. The consequence is that even putatively originalist decisions of the Supreme Court turn out to be richly interpretive, richly Dworkinian. They are shot through with implicit and explicit justification in light of claims about political morality – including, where appropriate, deference to other institutions based on political role morality.

Because no law can operate without some implicit or explicit vision of the good to which law is ordered, originalism has no natural immunity against infection from without by whatever theory of the good judges and other legal actors interpolate into the law. Unsurprisingly, then, the illusory positivism of the conservative legal movement has largely been hollowed out and taken over by a substantively libertarian constitutional vision – an extremely well-funded libertarian vision. Originalist-libertarians purport to be horrified by purposive rule for the common good even as they defend the role of common-law judges in defining and protecting property rights. They evince hostility to the administrative state, except for the parts of the administrative state that promote the smooth functioning of financial services and the broader economy, and angrily condemn any departures from the putative original understanding, except in areas such as political free speech rights for corporations, gun rights, and "takings" of property rights, in which the law propounded by conservative judges is either expressly or arguably non-originalist. On social matters, originalist judges have written expressly originalist opinions, such as the decision in *Bostock v. Clayton County*,[33] reaching results that almost no one alive at the time of the law's enactment would conceivably have thought desirable or even defensible. It is a strange originalism indeed that would be unanimously voted down by the enacting generation.

The larger significance of all this is methodological: both progressivism and originalism (in the version I focus on here) are positivist approaches, albeit in somewhat different ways:

[T]he terms of many debates in American jurisprudence ... generally oscillate between two mostly positivistic poles: progressive moralism and conservative originalism. In the mainstream one can only choose between the revolutionary positivism of the progressive, who denies substantively the normative claims of the natural law in the name of the liberation of the individual will, and the academic, genteel positivism of the originalist, who denies methodologically the normative claims of the natural law in the name of preserving the will of semi-mythical lawgivers. The U.S. Supreme Court's decision in *Bostock v. Clayton County* has revealed a late fruit of this brambled garden: progressive originalism, the method of the conservative, now perfected at the service of the progressive's ends.[34]

Later I will illustrate and explain the convergence that produces an originalism indistinguishable from progressive living constitutionalism. For now, the key methodological point is just that originalism and progressivism both stand on the same side of a gulf that separates them from the classical legal tradition.

Vices and Virtues

None of this means that progressivism and originalism are wholly valueless. Just as vices may sometimes be deformations or exaggerations of virtues, so too progressivism and originalism are themselves both deformations of legitimate insights and legitimate parts of the overall scheme of classical legalism. Progressivism exaggerates the entirely legitimate idea that doctrine may develop over time, not because principles of constitutionalism change, but because circumstances do, so that the application of permanent principles in new circumstances may require a development of doctrine. Progressivism goes wrong by extending this idea to the principles themselves, proposing to update and even discard them in the service of the endless advance of human liberation. In what follows, I will distinguish legitimate development from the vices of legal progressivism.

So too, originalism rests on the entirely legitimate insight that the public authority may establish rules of municipal positive law, the *ius civile*, that vary from place to place and time to time, and that interpreters should respect the lawmaker's aims and choices when they implement a reasoned determination of the civil law for the common good. The problem arises when originalism attempts to liberate itself from the larger framework of the law overall, which includes both general principles of legal justice (*ius*) and particular written laws (*lex*), and which interprets the *ius civile* to harmonize with the broader background principles and commitments of the legal system, including the natural law (*ius naturale*) and the law of nations (*ius gentium*).

Properly speaking, the classical approach to law is not an opponent or alternative to originalism or textualism. Rather it *includes* its own properly chastened versions of those ideas, because it includes the *ius civile* as part of a larger scheme of law, and because it respects the authority that determines the content of the positive law. Yet it also limits and orders that law, and the duties of its interpreters, by binding it to the common good. The positive civil law is a good servant, but a bad master. The classical conception of *ius civile*, in other words, can be summed up as *positive law without jurisprudential positivism*.

Shibboleths Dispelled

Beyond my positive and negative claims, a final aim of this book is to dispel some commonly heard, but erroneous, assumptions or shibboleths about common good constitutionalism.[35]

- It is entirely question-begging to say that interpretation in the classical tradition "departs from the meaning of the text" or "substitutes morality for law." Rather the classical tradition, in appropriate cases, looks to general principles of law and the *ius naturale* precisely in order to understand the meaning of the text, as a mode of interpretation. It claims that while there are powerful arguments of political morality to respect *lex* as law, it is also true that *lex*, precisely because it is law, must be interpreted in light of *ius*. The classical tradition thus claims that principles of political morality are themselves already part of the law and internal to it.

• Relatedly, the classical tradition does not substitute "preferences" for law; it claims that there are objective principles of legal justice accessible to the reason, that it is entirely possible to "find" rather than "make" law.[36] That claim may or may not be correct, but it is utterly tendentious to take it for an entirely different claim which no one makes, that interpreters are licensed to enforce their own arbitrary "preferences." Even purportedly positivist arguments are informed by some conception or other of the common good, and it is entirely legitimate to examine, in the light of reason, whether any given conception of the common good is a plausible one.

• The classical tradition does not, at least not primarily, see the point of natural law as overriding the positive civil law (a view created by excessive focus on the natural rights strand of the classical tradition). Rather it mainly draws upon the natural law both to construe the civil law and to justify action for the common good on the part of the political authority.

• The classical tradition, in itself, does not license judges in particular to rule as they see fit for the common good. It takes no *a priori* position on questions like the appropriate scope of judicial review, the exact balance between political and legal constitutionalism, or the importance of "democracy" (somehow understood) vis-à-vis judicial review. Many different institutional allocations of decision-making authority can be ordered to the common good and be consistent with it. The liberal mind finds it hard to process that the whole focus of the theory is not on advocating for particular forms of institutional technology or particular institutional arrangements, but instead on the purposes or ends to which law is aimed. A range of institutional technologies can in principle be ordered to the common good. Whether they can be so in practice is a function of particular conditions in particular constitutional orders, and thus a matter for prudential arrangement, not a matter of conceptual necessity.

In our own system, judges are generally, or presumptively, bound to respect reasonable determinations in the public interest by the legislature and the executive, perhaps under legislative delegation. Again, this is not a necessary claim about constitutionalism; it is an interpretive claim about the American constitutional order. And it also happens to hold true for other constitutional orders, such as the system of European human rights law, one of whose fundamental principles is the "margin of appreciation"[37] – very roughly, an appropriate margin of discretion for member states and public authorities to decide how best to implement legal respect for human rights.

• It is irrelevant that there was, is, and will be disagreement between classical lawyers over the content of the common good and the natural law, in hard cases. The same is chronically true of the positive civil law, indeed of any body of law (whether *lex* or *ius* or both) that is more than trivial. Disagreement, by itself, is neither here nor there, and it is hardly unique to the natural law or the common good. Every June, the Supreme Court gives ample illustration that a body of nine lawyers may split almost down the middle as to the meaning of positive laws, yet without undermining the belief of any of the Justices that there is nonetheless a right answer. As Richard Helmholz puts it, partial indeterminacy "is true of virtually all fundamental statements of law – Magna Carta, the Bible, the United States Constitution, for instance. They have not lost their value or forfeited their respect among lawyers despite long continued variations in the conclusions to be drawn from their contents."[38] And, Helmholz continues, "natural law itself did not claim to provide definitive answers to most legal questions that arose in practice."[39] Rather it provides general principles that must be rendered concrete by determination.

In short, the possibility of "disagreement" is often cast as an objection to classical constitutionalism by those who ignore profound disagreements over the positive constitutional law, and over the best conception of abstract constitutional concepts embodied in that law, such as "liberty" and "equality." This arbitrarily selective emphasis on disagreement is an infallible sign of ideology, a kind of myopia. These and other points will be explicated in what follows.

Plan of the Book

Chapters 1 and 2 together lay out a positive vision of common good constitutionalism, both generally and as an approach to our own constitutional order in particular. Chapter 1 offers a general, positive definition of the common good, a sketch of common good constitutionalism, and an account of its basic contours, premises, and commitments. Chapter 2 then turns to our own constitutional order, beginning with the *ius commune* – the rich stew of Roman law, canon law, and other legal sources that formed the matrix within which European legal systems developed – and its relationship to Anglo-American law. That relationship is much closer than many American lawyers realize, partly because of a tradition in Anglophone legal theory of cheerleading for the exceptionalism of the common-law tradition.

Chapter 2 then turns to a series of demonstration projects involving both justification and fit. They aim both to put common good constitutionalism in its best light, and also to show how deeply influential the classical tradition has been on the foundations of our constitutional order. I discuss the law of due process and economic regulation in detail, arguing that the first Justice Harlan's dissent in *Lochner v. New York* (1905)[40] amounts to a model judicial opinion for common good constitutionalism, and that the Court's deferential due process jurisprudence in the area of social and economic regulation generally embodied the classical idea of determination. I then turn to Dworkin's favorite interpretive chestnut, *Riggs v. Palmer*,[41] the "Case of the Murdering Heir," showing that a certain type of interpretive textualism is itself justifiable in terms of the common good, and that such textualism is in fact built into the classical legal tradition. That classical version of textualism has built-in limits, however: general legal principles drawn from the *ius naturale* and the *ius gentium* may be used to clarify and construe ambiguous positive texts. Finally, I examine the famous opinion in *United States v. Curtiss-Wright Export*

Co.,[42] showing that and how the Court drew upon the classical legal tradition to interpret the fundamental nature of American sovereignty, the powers of the presidency, and the role of the *ius gentium* in our constitutional order.

Chapters 3 and 4 turn to recent American law and legal theory. I examine the main competitors of common good constitutionalism: originalism, until recently the all-but-official view of the conservative legal movement, and progressivism, still the dominant ideology of the legal academy by sheer weight of numbers. Chapter 3 argues that originalism, the main competitor to common good constitutionalism on the American scene, is an illusion. It exists primarily as a rhetorical posture and an implicit, but only intermittently acknowledged, set of normative commitments. Originalism lacks the internal theoretical resources required even to identify meaning without normative argument at the point of application, most obviously and explicitly in hard cases, but necessarily in all cases. In courts, for example, originalist decisions are pervaded by commitments of political morality that judges use to decide legal questions. It follows that originalism, in this sense, does not actually exist. I illustrate the point with recent decisions from our putatively originalist Supreme Court, including *Bostock v. Clayton County, Georgia*,[43] which interpreted Title VII of the 1964 Civil Rights Act[44] to cover sexual orientation and gender identity, and *Seila Law v. CFPB*,[45] which invalidated the independence of the Consumer Financial Protection Bureau. These decisions can only be described as Dworkinian, despite the contrary self-conception of their originalist authors. The Justices are speaking fit-and-justification without knowing it.

Chapter 4 turns to progressivism. Here my basic aim is to show that progressivism presupposes a particular and contestable vision of the good, and to show that a non-originalist, common good approach to constitutionalism need not presuppose that vision. Like originalism, progressivism emphatically works with an unacknowledged vision of the good, but the progressive illusion takes a different form; progressives take themselves to simply be liberating individuals from the unchosen bonds of tradition, family, religion, economic circumstances, and even biology. This is, of course, just another very particular account of human flourishing, and it is a wildly implausible account. The answer to progressivism's liberationist theory of the good is not to pretend that the law can be identified independent of morality, the answer given by originalism. Instead the answer is to understand that law flourishes *as law* when it incorporates, not liberationism whether of the economic or sexual varieties, but genuine concern for the common good at ever higher levels – individual, family, city, nation, and commonwealth of nations.

I also rebut the widespread assumption that an organic, developmental vision of constitutionalism must be a progressive vision. A tendentious slogan of originalists is that "classical constitutionalism is just another type of living constitutionalism." But it is perfectly possible to have a developing constitution that adapts basic principles to changing situations in order to promote the common good over time, without subscribing to a Whiggish "living constitutionalism" that promotes individualism, radical autonomy, and identitarian egalitarianism – the aims of the progressive movement in the Anglophone world.

Accordingly, I draw upon John Henry Newman's idea of the "development of doctrine" to distinguish developing constitutionalism from progressive constitutionalism. Under developing constitutionalism, natural legal principles remain constant even as interpreters unfold the implications of those principles and apply them to new circumstances over time, whereas under living constitutionalism the law is instrumentalized to promote an ongoing agenda of progress. To illustrate both possibilities I offer a trio of examples: *Obergefell v. Hodges*,[46] *Euclid v. Ambler Realty*,[47] and an international declaration of pro-life principles from 2020 called the Geneva Consensus.[48] The first is a paradigm of progressive instrumentalization of the law. The second and third illustrate healthy doctrinal development in the direction of solidarity and community. The key point here is that nothing in a developing, organic account of constitutionalism necessarily presupposes or requires a progressive theory of the good for human beings, with a paramount emphasis on individual autonomy.

Chapter 5 offers illustrative applications of common good constitutionalism in various domains: the administrative state and deference to agencies; problems of subsidiarity and federalism; and then finally the theory of rights, such as the freedom of speech. I approach these topics partly as a matter of normative justification but partly also as a matter of fit[49] – suggesting, in other words, that our law is and always has been susceptible of being read in light of the common good. The amnesia of our law about the classical tradition does not at all mean that law's intrinsic nature has been wholly abandoned. On the contrary, I suggest that the centerpiece of our operative constitutional order, the administrative state, is structured and suffused by principles of legality that order it to the common good.

I take particular pains to dispel the mistaken assumption that common good constitutionalism is incapable of recognizing rights. Under common good constitutionalism, rights very much exist, but are grounded and justified in a different way than under standard autonomy-based liberal theories. Common good constitutionalism does not aim to maximize the autonomy of each person or citizen, subject to the like autonomy of all; that is antithetical to the idea of a genuinely common good. But the classical legal tradition has a rich account of rights, rooted in the basic idea of *ius* as what is due to each. On this account, rights exist to serve, and are delimited by, a conception of justice that is itself ordered to the common good. It is definitely not that the common good "overrides" rights; rather it defines their boundaries all along. Liberty on this conception is taken to be a bad master, but a good servant. Common good constitutionalism makes no fetish of Liberty, but protects liberties as component parts of the common good and contributors to it.

In the brief conclusion, I return to the relationship between common good constitutionalism and the fissure that developed in American public law sometime after World War II, becoming especially marked in the 1960s. I argue by analogy: we must do through a reorientation of thought, and on a large scale, what courts do on a smaller scale when they overturn a recent deviant precedent in order to revert to an earlier, long-standing line of precedent that is better justified in principle, and that fits better with the legal landscape as a whole.

Scope and Ambitions

This is the sort of book that might be done in either seventy thousand words or seven hundred thousand. I have opted for the former, on both circumstantial and methodological grounds. My intended audience is neither the student of first-order policy questions, nor the professional student of jurisprudence. (In the Anglophone world, at least, the latter have mainly opted to immure themselves in a sterile research program of hard positivism.) Rather my audience is the intelligent observer of the law, whether or not a lawyer, who intuits that something has gone very wrong with our law and our legal academy, but isn't sure exactly how or why. At present, there is widespread and increasing dissatisfaction with establishment progressive rights-talk and establishment originalism. Thus timeliness is a consideration, and the book seemed more likely to make a contribution if it appeared sooner rather than later.

The methodological point is that sometimes a broad sketch of a distant scene helps the unfamiliar observer apprehend it more clearly than does a detailed landscape. The thesis that the classical heritage of our law can be recovered and adapted for current and future conditions is sufficiently unfamiliar, and, when first ventilated, provoked such strangely violent reactions from both progressives and originalists,[50] that it may be better to introduce it by degrees. I therefore provide an overall sketch of a view and a program, with illustrative applications, rather than a comprehensive treatise on the implications of common good constitutionalism in area after area. The notes are kept light, with no pretense of historical or doctrinal completeness. I hope to spark enough interest that others will explore similar themes; indeed they have already begun to do so.[51] A model and inspiration for the book is Charles Black's short work on *Structure and Relationship in Constitutional Law*[52] – on a per-word basis, among the most influential works of legal theory.

Chapter 1
The Common Good Defined

What is the common good? I begin with some antonyms, and then turn to a series of positive characterizations of increasing specificity, discussing the common good generally, the common good in law, and the common good as a constitutional concept.

Antonyms of the Common Good

Let me first approach the common good along the *via negativa*, mentioning some antonyms to define the notion by contrast, before turning to a positive characterization.

Aggregation. The sum of separate private utilities, no matter how large, can never add up to the common good, which is the good proper to, and attainable only by, the community. To be sure, it is important that the common good is also a good for individuals, indeed their highest good, but the common good is not produced by the summation of individual goods. When the Roman jurist Papinian says that "public law cannot be changed by private pacts,"[53] this is to say that the *res publica* that is the locus of the common good is something that rises above the mere conjunction of interests, in which you decide what is good for you and I decide what is good for me. This is so even if our decisions may happen to coincide in an agreement, and even if the decision is equally to all of our advantage.[54] Obviously one way that the public authority may promote the common good is by maintaining an institutional system for enforcing private contracts, perhaps by arbitration, but that system itself ultimately sets the bounds of enforceable arbitration and is not properly subject to change by private pacts, so Papinian's point is preserved.

Tyranny and Faction. Another antonym to the common good is ruling for private benefit. In classical constitutional theory, there are three types of rule, each divided into good and bad forms, yielding six categories in total. Rule by one, few, or many are each subdivided into either rule ordered to the common good or for private benefit, the latter being considered tyrannous. The resulting category-pairs are monarchy and tyranny (in a more specific sense), aristocracy and oligarchy, polity and democracy. Thus self-interested rule can take any of three forms: the tyrannous rule of the one, the corrupt rule of the few (oligarchy), or the oppressive rule of the many (democracy).[55] In the last two cases, especially, we may speak of rule by faction, whether a minority or majority faction, as the antonym of the common good.

Rule for private benefit is obviously bad, but rule by faction more specifically also features a kind of restless instability. Democratic theorists praise the partisan alternation in power, but there is also a nightmarish version of the alternation in power in which there is an indefinite cycle of successive victories and defeats by factions locked in an endless struggle for rule. The most vivid depiction here is perhaps Machiavelli's *Florentine Histories*, a vision of the faction-ridden city in which any sense of the *bonum commune* is lost.[56]

"Monstrous Government." Finally, related to but different from rule in the service of private interest, another antonym for the common good is *the confusion of public and private functions*. Bartolus (Bartolo de Sasseferrato), the great fourteenth-century commentator of the *ius commune*, identified a sort of anti-type of the common good that he called the "Monstrous Government," one that went beyond the usual six categories of government in classical theory. The defining feature of the monstrous government is a multiplicity of quasi-independent private tyrants dominating a weak public authority:

There is a seventh mode of government, the worst one, which now exists in the City of Rome. There are many tyrants there so strong that one [can] not prevail against the other. For there is a common government of the whole city so weak that it cannot [prevail] against any of the tyrants, nor against anyone adhering to the tyrants, except only so far as they allow it. Aristotle did not discuss (*posuit*) this government, and fittingly so, for it is a monstrous thing. What, indeed, if someone sees one body having one common

[and] weak head, and many other common heads stronger than it, and all opposed to one another? Certainly it would be a monster.[57]

This sort of regime is tossed restlessly between domination by private actors, often abusing their legal entitlements, on the one hand, and on the other hand futile attempts at reassertion of ruling authority by public actors. In such conditions, any possibility of purposive public action for the common good is lost.

The Positive Common Good in Politics and Law

So much for the negative side. Let me now turn to a positive characterization of the common good in politics and law. I begin with some general conceptual points, and then turn to the legal common good specifically.

In the classical account, a genuinely *common* good is a good that is unitary ("one in number") and capable of being shared without being diminished.[58] Thus it is inherently non-aggregative; it is not the summation of a number of private goods, no matter how great that number or how intense the preference for those goods may be. Consider the aim of a football team for victory, a unitary aim for all that requires the cooperation of all and that is not diminished by being shared. The victory of the team as such cannot be reduced to the individual success of the players, even summed across all the players.

In the classical theory, the ultimate genuinely common good of political life is the happiness or flourishing of the community, the well-ordered life in the *polis*. It is not that "private" happiness, or even the happiness of family life, is the real aim and the public realm is merely what supplies the lawful peace, justice, and stability needed to guarantee that private happiness. Rather the highest felicity in the temporal sphere is itself the common life of the well-ordered community, which includes those other foundational goods but transcends them as well. Nor is this the same as the good of the state. On the classical account, the state is merely one part of the larger political community, and the good of the community is itself the good for individuals – a crucial point emphasized by the great theorist of the common good, Charles de Koninck.[59]

Put differently, human flourishing, including the flourishing of individuals, is itself essentially, not merely contingently, dependent upon the flourishing of the political communities (including ruling authorities) within which humans are always born, found, and embedded. This is not at all to say, of course, that the individual should be absorbed into the political community or subjected to it; that is the opposite error of the one the libertarian commits. The end of the community is ultimately to promote the good of individuals, but common goods are real as such and are themselves the highest goods for individuals.

I have referred to "the temporal sphere" because the account I offer here is limited to the ends of natural or temporal happiness. As the theologian Walter Farrell, O.P., observes in a classic study of the structure of the natural law:

> The final end of man is his happiness; a supernatural happiness, it is true, but not all communities have to do with leading man to his supernatural end directly. Nevertheless they have at least to do with the attainment of his secondary ends of natural or temporal happiness, which are a means to the supernatural final ends.[60]

Just as not all communities must concern the supernatural end, so too not all books must do so. In what follows I limit my account to the secondary ends of the political community: its temporal felicity, the order of nature rather than the order of grace. I do this not only for substantive reasons, out of respect for the legitimate autonomy of the temporal power within its proper sphere, but to limit myself to the terms of my professional competence, the ordinary work of the civil lawyer. For present purposes, therefore, I neither need advance, nor do advance, any particular account of ultimate ends, and nothing in my claims depends on such an account.

The Common Good in Law

With these general points in the background, let me now turn to the theory of the common good in law, a subject with both substantive and institutional aspects. From the lawyer's standpoint, the common good is a centerpiece of our legal traditions, in both the continental and Anglo-American variants, rather than the alien irruption of a new-fangled or ominous idea. It appears in different versions in different streams or applications of the tradition, but with a shared thrust and intention. Whether as the object of the *ius commune*'s concern for the *bonum commune* (common good) and the *utilitas rei publicae* (public interest), or in the form of the "general welfare," "public good," and "public interest" so often cited in modern constitutional, statutory, and regulatory law, the concept has long served as the normative locus and foundation of law.

A good place to begin is with Ulpian's dictum on the precepts of legal justice, one of the most famous in the classical law: *Iuris praecepta sunt haec: honeste vivere, alterum non laedere, suum cuique tribuere*. "The basic principles of right are: to live honourably, not to harm any other person, to render to each his own."[61] Versions or descendants of these precepts were commonly cited in American caselaw throughout the founding era and the nineteenth century; they were, and even today still are, part and parcel of our law. American nuisance law, as we will see shortly, was substantially constructed around the maxim *sic utere tuo ut alienum non laedas*, a common-law descendant of Ulpian's second precept. In subsequent chapters, I offer illustrations of the pervasive influence of the classical conception of *ius* on American law.

The temporal common good can then be described this way for the purposes of the civil lawyer: (1) the structural political, economic, and social conditions that allow communities to live in accordance with the precepts of legal justice, combined with (2) the injunction that all official action should be ordered to the community's attainment of those precepts, subject to the understanding that (3) the common good is not the sum of individual goods, but the indivisible good of a community ordered to justice, belonging jointly to all and severally to each. The conditions that allow communities to live in accordance with justice define the legitimate ends of civil government. To specify those conditions is to specify the ends to which civil authority is rightly ordered and that it should promote.[62]

What are those conditions? The central strand of the *ragion di stato* tradition, originating with Giovanni Botero,[63] argues that the interest of the state and the authority that rules the state is to promote the common good; political authorities that govern in accordance with the common good will both promote the flourishing of their peoples and secure their own state. The *ragion di stato* tradition then spoke of the *bonum commune* as comprising, more specifically, a triptych of "justice, peace and abundance."[64] This became both the standard list of the legitimate ends of government and an idealized description of the polity in which it is possible to live honestly, to do no harm to others, and to render to each his due. There are all sorts of things that can be said about the logical and temporal order of these goods – for example, one might ask whether peace is itself a precondition for justice, or the reverse, or whether the two are mutually reinforcing. But questions of that sort are asked *within* the project of common good constitutionalism; the point of the project is to work out answers to them over time.

Justice, peace, and abundance, or recognizable modifications and descendants of these, became standard constitutional subheadings of the common good. In the Commonwealth tradition, one standard formulation of the common good is that of the British North America Act (or Constitution Act) of 1867: "peace, order, and good government."[65] So-called "POGG" clauses appear in many treaties and constitutional instruments and have elaborate histories. On the continent, "public order" clauses have been ubiquitous in constitutions and other legal instruments.[66] To this day, European human rights law features "public order" provisions. An example chosen almost at random is ECHR Article 9 (2): freedoms of thought, conscience, and religion are subject to "such limitations as are prescribed by law and are necessary in a democratic society in the interests of public safety, the protection of public order, health or morals, or for the protection of the rights and freedoms of others."[67]

In the United States, similar provisions appear at both federal and state levels, in both enacted texts and judge-made doctrine. The federal Constitution, in both its Preamble and text, refers to "the general welfare," as I will discuss later, and a number of state constitutions contain clauses referring to the general welfare, the common good, or similar concepts.[68] At the level of jurisprudence, the state courts early developed a standard conception of the so-called "police power," which is the power to legislate for "the protection of the health, morals, and safety of the people," as the Court put it in 1887 in *Mugler v. Kansas*.[69] Note here that "health" and "safety" just as squarely presuppose a substantive conception of human flourishing in political community as "morals" does.

Many of these decisions are quite express that the police power exists to address violations of Ulpian's conditions. In *Commonwealth v. Alger* from Massachusetts in 1851,[70] for example – widely cited as a cornerstone of American police power jurisprudence – one of the holdings is that the police power allows regulation when private owners commit a nuisance by violating the maxim *sic utere tuo ut alienum non laedas*, a standard modification of the second precept of legal justice.[71] The Court connected that idea to the interpretation of the due process clause of the Fourteenth Amendment in cases like *Munn v. Illinois*,[72] in 1877, which expressly drew upon the classical maxim:

> [T]he very essence of government . . . has found expression in the maxim *sic utere tuo ut alienum non lædas*. From this source come the police powers, which . . . "are nothing more or less than the powers of government inherent in every sovereignty, . . . that is to say, . . . the power to govern men and things." Under these powers the government regulates the conduct of its citizens one towards another, and the manner in which each shall use his own property, when such regulation becomes necessary for the public good.[73]

There is a complication here – one that is, however, chronically exaggerated by originalists and libertarians – because of the distribution of powers between national and state governments. As of 1870,

in *United States v. DeWitt*, the Court officially denied that the federal
government, as a government of enumerated powers, held a general police power.[74] Yet that principle was always in tension with the
McCulloch v. Maryland[75] principle that enumerated powers should
be expansively construed over time to accommodate changing circumstances; the whole point of the latter principle is that rigid limits
on the scope of federal power could not be laid down in advance.
Over time, the difference between the state police power and federal
enumerated powers became more theoretical than real. "Legal and
political developments between 1877 and 1937 made that federal
police power – an essential attribute of modern, centralized states – a
practical if not a technical reality."[76]

Today, the scope of federal powers has become all but equivalent to a general police power in substance, despite occasional and
largely ineffectual protests to the contrary, and despite very occasional
invalidations of statutes of secondary importance.[77] In a series of
crucial decisions in the 1930s and 1940s, the Court began to develop
and adapt the principles underlying the scope of national powers
– and the basic principle of *McCulloch v. Maryland*, under which
the Constitution was "intended to endure for ages to come, and consequently to be adapted to the various crises of human affairs" – by
all but expressly equating national powers with state police powers.[78]
By the time the Court upheld broad ratemaking authority for the
Federal Power Commission in *FPC v. Hope Natural Gas Co.*,[79] decided
in 1944, the Court was openly drawing upon police power decisions
arising under the due process clause of the Fourteenth Amendment,
like *Munn v. Illinois*, to define the scope of federal legislative power.
As the Court put it,

> When we sustained the constitutionality of the Natural Gas Act
> in the *Natural Gas Pipeline Co.* case, we stated that "the authority
> of Congress to regulate the prices of commodities in interstate
> commerce is at least as great under the Fifth Amendment as is
> that of the states under the Fourteenth to regulate the prices of
> commodities in intrastate commerce." Rate-making is indeed but
> one species of price-fixing. *Munn v. Illinois*. . . . The fixing of prices,

like other applications of the police power, may reduce the value of
the property which is being regulated. But the fact that the value is
reduced does not mean that the regulation is invalid. *Block v. Hirsh*
[a police power case that upheld wartime rent control legislation in
the District of Columbia].[80]

In recent decades, the Court has twice invalidated relatively
marginal statutes as exceeding Congress' enumerated powers,[81] but
ultimately flinched from invalidating the only major legislation it
has examined, the Affordable Care Act.[82] Meanwhile, all the major
statutes that emerged from the later New Deal and Great Society and
the environmental revolution, many of which modern libertarians and
localists condemn as constitutionally dubious, remain in place and
have no real prospect of being challenged. Despite the high volume of
chatter in originalist and libertarian circles, the federal government
for all intents and purposes has acquired by prescription, over time, a
de facto police power.

To be sure, all this represents a development and translation of the
original constitutional scheme to new circumstances, but as argued
in Chapter 4, it is a development that preserves the principles of
the common good and general welfare that always underpinned that
scheme, and is therefore valid. Nor should we overstate the extent
of the development. What has changed is not the permissible ends
to which governmental power –– state or federal –– may be put. At
any level of government, the "general welfare" or the common good
defines the permissible aims of the exercise of public authority; the
state police power cases just explicate and make more concrete, in
one particular setting, what that general aim has always encompassed
according to the tradition. Rather the development has solely been
in the scope rather than permissible aims of federal power. And that
scope has increased because the subjects on which federal power
was always paramount –– for example, commerce among the states
–– have themselves developed over time, outside any law books, to
encompass ever-greater domains.

Finally, similar common good provisions and clauses are absolutely ubiquitous in the statutory frameworks of the administrative

state. For American administrative lawyers, the two most famous examples are probably (1) the clause that has historically defined the sweeping authority of the Federal Communications Commission to regulate broadcast media "as public convenience, interest, or necessity requires,"[83] and (2) the Administrative Procedure Act's provision allowing agencies to issue binding rules without even informal rule-making process, so long as the agency "for good cause finds" that the usual procedure is "impracticable, unnecessary, or contrary to the public interest."[84] Conversely, the same Act authorizes judges to review and set aside administrative action that is "arbitrary and capricious [or] an abuse of discretion." All these provisions are fraught with implicit normative content; there is no escape, for interpreters, from the duty to answer, one way or another, the questions whether government is acting in the public interest and whether government action is adequately reasoned.

The lawyer who is skeptical or hostile to the idea of the common good fails to understand not only the history but also the present practical reality of the law. Provisions that make reference to "the public interest" or any of its many variants must be given some reading or another (including, among the possibilities, deference to the readings of other officials); they cannot simply be wished away. For lawyers, it simply will not do to become excessively skeptical about the common good, or to take the possibility of disagreements about the common good as fatal objections to drawing upon the concept or its cognates in legal interpretation. The ancient and exceedingly rich history of legal provisions invoking, in one way or another, the common good and its subsidiary principles of public order, justice, peace, and abundance is a history that is very much still with us.

A Framework, Not a Blueprint

The classical triptych of justice, peace, and abundance is a kind of framework orientation, not a blueprint or a set of position papers. It is not intended to provide specific answers to questions about the proper level of the minimum wage, the circumstances under which abortion should or should not be legal, or whether there should be *de novo* judicial review of administrative action. It is a category mistake, a misconception of the nature of the enterprise, to demand that specific answers to such questions be provided at the analytic level of the definition of the common good and its major headings. Rather the enterprise is to, first, specify the major aims or ends of constitutionalism that serve the flourishing of the political community, and then apply those general aims through the lens of prudential judgment to specific circumstances (what we have called determination). To outline the enterprise is to initiate a project that will unfold over time in a community of interpreters who share that framework orientation, even as they disagree, perhaps bitterly, over implementations and details.

In this respect, if no other, it is parallel to more familiar legal projects that treat constitutional law as an engine of continual liberation, or of equalization. In such projects, it is not taken as a fatal or even important objection that the high-level commitments of the framework do not, by themselves, decide future issues and cases. Rather it is said, with a kind of faith and trust, that the future will witness the unfolding and full flowering of the enterprise as circumstances warrant. And indeed, no constitutional framework can or should aim to provide more specificity, right at the outset, than the nature of the enterprise permits. To demand more than this of the classical law's orientation to the common good is unjustifiably selective; it is to betray an ideological hostility, masquerading as a question.

Common Good Constitutionalism

Against this background, common good constitutionalism is classical constitutionalism that, although not enslaved to the original meaning of the Constitution, also rejects the progressives' overarching sacramental narrative, the relentless expansion of individualistic autonomy.[85] Instead it reads constitutional provisions to afford public authorities latitude to promote the flourishing of political communities, by promoting the classical triptych of peace, justice, and abundance, and their modern equivalents and corollaries. These include health, safety, and a right relationship to the natural environment. In a globalized world that relates to the natural and biological environ-ment in a deeply disordered way, a just state is a state that has ample authority to protect the vulnerable from the ravages of pandemics, natural disasters, and climate change, and from the underlying struc-tures of corporate power that contribute to these events.

Constitutional law should also elaborate subsidiary principles that help public authorities direct persons, associations, and society gen-erally toward the common good. These principles include respect for legitimate authority; respect for the hierarchies needed for society to function; solidarity within and among families, social groups, and workers' unions, trade associations, and professions; appropriate subsidiarity, or respect for the legitimate roles of public bodies and associations at all levels of government and society; and a candid willingness to "legislate morality" – indeed, a recognition that all legislation is necessarily founded on some substantive conception of morality, and that the promotion of morality is a core and legitimate function of authority. Promoting a substantive vision of the good is, always and everywhere, a proper function of the political authority. Every act of public-regarding government has been founded on such a vision; any contrary view is an illusion.[86] Liberal and libertarian con-stitutional decisions that claim to rule out "morality" as a ground for public action are incoherent, even fraudulent, for they rest on merely a particular account of morality, an implausible account.

The main aim of common good constitutionalism, then, is not the liberal goal of maximizing individual autonomy or minimizing the abuse of power – an incoherent goal in any event, as multiple risks of abuse of power by multiple actors, private and public, chron-ically trade off against one another.[87] Instead it is to ensure that the ruler has both the authority and the duty to rule well. A corollary is that to act outside or against inherent norms of good rule is to act tyrannically, forfeiting the right to rule, but the central aim of the constitutional order is to promote good rule, not to "protect liberty" as an end in itself. Constraints on power are good only derivatively, insofar as they contribute to the common good; the emphasis should not be on liberty as an abstract object of quasi-religious devotion, but on particular human liberties whose protection is a duty of justice or prudence on the part of the ruler because protecting them promotes the flourishing of the community.

Finally, common good constitutionalism does not suffer from a horror of legitimate hierarchy, because it sees that law can encourage those subject to the law to form desires, habits, and beliefs that better track and promote communal well-being.[88] The subjects' own perceptions of what is best for them may change over time anyway, as the law teaches, habituates, and re-forms them. This point outrages liberals and libertarians, yet it is a routine feature of policy-making even in liberal constitutional states. Consider policy initiatives such as cigarette taxes and other "sin taxes," motorcycle helmet laws and seatbelt laws, and waiting periods for marriage licenses and gun purchases – laws whose aim is, in whole or in part, explicitly to change preferences for the better, or at least to reduce the influence of hasty and ill-considered action influenced by passions. Consider also civic obligations and structures such as mandatory public education, mandatory jury duty, or mandatory national service or military service. These are calculated, in part, to shape and improve the political beliefs of the citizenry. There has never existed, in the history of the world, a polity that took no stand on which preferences and beliefs are normatively proper – emphatically including the subset of polities that aim to inculcate and enforce liberal beliefs and preferences in the name of "tolerance."

Moral Readings of the Constitution

How, if at all, are these principles to be grounded in the constitutional text and in conventional legal sources? The sweeping generalities and famous ambiguities of our Constitution afford ample space for substantive moral readings that promote peace, justice, abundance, health, and safety, by means of just authority, solidarity, and subsidiarity. These highly general and abstract clauses have to be given some content or other, and it is – by their terms – impossible to do so without considering principles of political morality, which may of course include principles of role morality that allocate lawmaking authority among institutions.

Consider the Preamble to the Constitution, which provides that "We the People of the United States, in Order to form a more perfect Union, establish Justice, insure domestic Tranquility, provide for the common defense, promote the general Welfare, and secure the Blessings of Liberty to ourselves and our Posterity, do ordain and establish this Constitution for the United States of America." Libertarian-originalists have rather notoriously emphasized only the "blessings of liberty" (and, I will suggest later in discussing the question of rights, a false conception even of those "blessings"). Note, however, that the Preamble's account of the purposes of government is otherwise entirely substantive, and the reference to "liberty" must be read *in pari materia*. On the classical conception, "liberty" is no mere power of arbitrary choice, but the faculty of choosing the common good.[89] The aim of recognizing liberty is not to maximize individual choice, subject to the like liberty of all, but instead teleological and ordered to the ends of the good, in exactly the same way the classical tradition of *ragion di stato*, specifying the substantive aims and purposes of government, is teleological.

Only when we read the Preamble against the backdrop of the classical tradition can we see that, properly understood, it aims to constitute a political authority for the purpose of promoting justice, peace ("tranquility"), and the flourishing of the *res publica* (the "general welfare").[90] These are of course just the classical trinity of peace, justice, and abundance, merely stated and ordered in a different form, but not essentially different. The fundamental teleological aims of government identified by the classical tradition are also the aims of our constitutional order. The text and structure of the Constitution itself should always be read in light of those aims, and construed so as to promote them.

Within the operative sections of the written Constitution itself, consider also the General Welfare Clause, which gives Congress power to "lay and collect Taxes, Duties, Imposts and Excises, to pay the Debts and provide for the common Defence and general Welfare of the United States."[91] This is an obvious place to ground principles of common good constitutionalism. Because of its obvious semantic ambiguity (exactly how many powers does it confer?), the precise meaning of the Clause has always been a locus of contest between more and less expansive conceptions of the aims of government and of federal power in particular.[92] In *United States v. Butler*,[93] decided in 1936 at the height of the Supreme Court's resistance to the New Deal, the Court invalidated the Agricultural Adjustment Act and along the way construed the Clause to deny Congress a freestanding power to "provide for the general Welfare."[94] In the Court's view, that interpretation would make "the government of the United States . . . in reality a government of general and unlimited powers, notwithstanding the subsequent enumeration of specific powers."[95] The conclusion hardly follows, however, as we can see once we understand the teleological structure of the classical conception of governmental power. On the construction rejected in *Butler*, the power to provide for the general welfare does not mean whatever the federal government wants it to mean. Rather it would be taken to refer to, and incorporate, an elaborate tradition specifying the legitimate ends or purposes of government in light of the common good, itself defined by the tradition. On this view, the subsequent enumeration of specific powers would represent concrete determinations and illustrations of the general power, but not an exhaustive list.

Despite the cramped reading unnecessarily given to the Clause in *Butler*, the spirit of the more expansive, classical reading of the Clause has certainly triumphed in other forms. The expansive reading of the Commerce Clause given in *McCulloch v. Maryland*[96] – and even more importantly, the general principle of developing constitutionalism that *McCulloch* embedded in our law, saying that our Constitution was "intended to endure for ages to come, and, consequently, to be adapted to the various crises of human affairs"[97] – did much of the same work. As we will see, the Court developed the law of federal powers over time to, in practice, all but equate federal power with the expansive police power of the states to promote health, safety, and morals – a conception drawn straight from the classical law.

So too with provisions in the Bill of Rights. Constitutional concepts such as liberty and equality need not be given libertarian or originalist readings. Instead, as I argue in Chapter 5, they can be read in light of a better conception of liberty, as the natural human capacity to act in accordance with reasoned morality ordered to the common good.[98] It is not as though such provisions can escape being given some moral content or other; the only question is what that content will be, and which institutions will have the authority to specify it. Although Dworkin had a bad theory of rights, he was absolutely correct to argue that

> in constitutional adjudication ... the pertinent constitutional standards are ... explicitly moral: They declare rights of free expression, treatment as equals, and respect for life and dignity, and sometimes make exceptions for constraints "necessary in a democratic society," for example. [In constitutional adjudication] cases are often hard not because they lie at the borders of doctrine, but because they call for a fresh understanding of the most basic underlying underpinnings of the doctrine.[99]

The broad generalities of our own constitutional texts will inevitably be saturated with principles of political morality, with some conception of the common good, of one sort or another.

More important still, thinking that the common good and its corollary principles have to be grounded in *specific* texts is a mistake; they can be grounded in the general structure of the constitutional order and in the nature and purposes of government. The Supreme Court, like Congress and the presidency, has often drawn upon broad structural postulates and background principles, derived from the classical tradition and the natural law, to determine the just authority of the state.[100] "Police power" is nowhere mentioned in the written Constitution at the federal level, yet is broadly recognized as a matter of federal law, including due process, as the measure of state authority. America's real, "efficient" Constitution[101] is largely unwritten or uncodified, as is true of constitutions everywhere.[102]

The succeeding chapters will flesh out how constitutional law might change under this approach, but a few broad strokes can be sketched. The Court's jurisprudence on free speech, abortion, sexual liberties, and related matters will prove vulnerable under a regime of common good constitutionalism.[103] The claim, from the notorious joint opinion in *Planned Parenthood v. Casey*, that each individual may "define one's own concept of existence, of meaning, of the universe, and of the mystery of human life" should be not only rejected but stamped as abominable, beyond the realm of the acceptable forever after.[104] So too, the libertarian assumptions central to free speech law and free speech ideology – that government is forbidden to judge the quality and moral worth of public speech, that "one man's vulgarity is another's lyric," and so on – will fall under the ax.[105] Libertarian conceptions of property rights and economic rights will also have to go, insofar as they bar the state from enforcing duties of community and solidarity in the use and distribution of resources – although, as we will see, non-libertarian conceptions of rights are very much available to justify certain rights ordered to the common good, including property as a secondary right.

As for the structure and distribution of authority within government, as I have argued elsewhere, our own constitutional order has developed to center on a powerful presidency, reigning and in part ruling over a powerful bureaucracy with quasi-independent elements.[106] In the best constructive justification of these arrangements, our executive-centered government acts through principles of administrative law's inner morality, with a view to promoting solidarity and subsidiarity. The bureaucracy will be seen not as an enemy, but as the strong hand of legitimate rule. The state is to be entrusted with the authority to protect the populace from the vagaries and injustices of market forces, from employers who would exploit them as atomized individuals, and from corporate exploitation and destruction of the natural environment. Unions, guilds and crafts, cities and localities, and other solidaristic associations will benefit from the presumptive favor of the law, as will the traditional, multigenerational family. In virtue of subsidiarity, the aim of rule will be not to displace these associations, but to help them function well. In general, elaborating on the common good principle that no constitutional right to refuse vaccination exists,[107] constitutional law will define in broad terms the authority of the state to protect the public's health and well-being, protecting the weak from pandemics and scourges of many kinds – biological, social, and economic – even when doing so requires overriding the selfish claims of individuals to private "rights" conceived as trumps protecting a zone of autonomy, rather than as ordered to the common good.

Who Decides?

Let me now focus in more detail on a crucial question mentioned above: "who decides?" One sometimes encounters an odd assumption that common good constitutionalism entails that judges should decide everything. This isn't right; it confuses two distinct issues, one of interpretive method and one of institutional allocation. It is one thing to say that the right interpretive method for all officials, not merely judges, is common good constitutionalism. Legislators and executive agents as well as judges ought to interpret constitutional principles in light of the common good. But the allocation, across different officials, of authority to ascertain the content of the common good is a separate question.

Put differently, while the promotion of the common good is a duty incumbent upon all officials in the system, legislators and executive officers as well as judges, as a logical matter it does not follow that each official or institution in the system, taken separately, must make unfettered judgments about the common good for itself; the political morality of the common good itself includes role morality and division of functions. How the Constitution should be interpreted and how judges should decide cases are not necessarily the same question. A system that conduces to promoting the common good overall may do so precisely *because* there is a division of roles across institutions, such that not every institution aims directly to promote the common good.

In fact, the best interpretation of our constitutional practices, as I will discuss in Chapter 2, is that judges do and should broadly defer to political authorities, within reasonable boundaries, when legislative and executive officials engage in such specifications. We have here simply two complimentary aspects of common good constitutionalism: giving the public authority sufficient scope to allow it to promote the common good, and judicial respect for the legitimate roles of other public bodies constituted by that authority, when those other actors are engaged in reasonable specifications of legal principles – what the classical tradition calls *determinationes* or determinations.

What exactly is a determination? We need to start with some fundamentals about the relationship between natural and positive law. In his remarkable and underappreciated book on *Natural Law in Court*, Richard Helmholz observes that when moderns turn to the subject of the relationship between natural law and positive law, they immediately focus on the question whether the former in some sense "trumps" the latter in cases of irreconcilable conflict.[108] To the classical lawyer, however, that question was not central. To be sure, as early as the *Institutes of Gaius* it was said that "considerations of civil law can destroy civil but not natural rights."[109] But natural right and natural law had many other roles detailed by Helmholz, roles much more central in actual practice, such as supplying interpretive principles and default rules for construing statutes, supplying principles of just procedure, and suggesting remedies.[110]

More broadly, for the classical lawyer, the whole framework within which to discuss the relationship between natural and positive law was different, centering on their complementary roles rather than on potential conflict. The positive law, the *ius civile*, was understood as a set of rational ordinances promulgated by the public authority for the common good – that is, in order to give more specific content to the general principles of the natural law. In a famous passage, Aquinas distinguished two ways in which positive law might be derived from the natural law:

> It must be noted, however, that something may be derived from the natural law in two ways: in one way, as a general conclusion derived from its principles; in another way, as a specific application of that which is expressed in general terms. The first way is similar to that by which, in the sciences, demonstrated conclusions are derived from first principles; while *the second way is like that by which, in the arts, general ideas are made particular as to details: for example, the craftsman needs to turn the general idea of a house into the shape*

of this or that house. Some things are therefore derived from the principles of the natural law as general conclusions: for example, that "one ought not to kill" may be derived as a conclusion from the principle that "one ought not to harm anyone"; whereas *some are derived from it as specific applications: for example, the law of nature has it that he who does evil should be punished; but that he should be punished with this or that penalty is a specific application of the law of nature. Both modes of derivation, then, are found in the human law.* Those things which are derived in the first way are not contained in human law simply as belonging to it alone; rather, they have some of their force from the law of nature. But those things which are derived in the second way have their force from human law alone.[111]

This public "determination" (*determinatio*) of the natural law, making it more concrete in application, has two important features. First, "those things which are derived in the second way have their force from human law alone." They are law only because of the command of the legitimate public authority. In this sense, a special kind of legal positivism – very different than its current versions – is embedded within the *determinatio* framework, as a special case. I have said that classical legal theory is opposed to positivism; it rejects the claim that law may be defined stipulatively and exclusively in historical and descriptive terms, as whatever norms have been issued by a source authorized to do so by a conventional rule of recognition. But another way of understanding the issue is that modern positivism is merely the myopic view that part of the framework of classical law should be broken out and treated as though it were the whole of law. It is a case of a part trying, quite impossibly, to break free of the framework and become the whole. In a proper perspective, by contrast, the classical framework itself builds in an account of both the authority and limits of the positive law.

Second, the public authority fits the general precepts of the natural law to varying local circumstances; as Aquinas puts it, "[t]he general principles of the natural law cannot be applied to all men in the same way because of the great variety of human circumstances; and hence arises the diversity of positive laws among various people."[112] This means that determination will inevitably be discretionary within bounds; in the limit, it may even call for a decision of the sort I have elsewhere called "rationally arbitrary."[113] The basic purpose of making general precepts of the natural law concrete in particular circumstances is like a vector; it sets a broad direction for the public authority, but does not say exactly how far to go, without further specification. Always subject to the nature of lawmaking in the classical conception – reasoned ordination to the common good – there is an irreducible discretion to choose. And that discretion, Aquinas suggests elsewhere, may be exercised through the kind of inarticulate or intuitive judgment that the artifex uses.[114] As John Finnis puts it,

> [t]he kind of rational connection that holds even where the architect has wide freedom to choose amongst indefinitely many alternatives is called by Aquinas a *determinatio* of principle(s) – a kind of concretization of the general, a particularization yoking the rational necessity of the principle with a freedom (of the lawmaker) to choose between alternative concretizations, *a freedom which includes even elements of (in a benign sense) arbitrariness.*[115]

The basis for deference, then, is that deference is how law respects the discretionary space of the public authority to engage in determination. Obviously legal context must be taken into account, and in what follows I will speak separately and more specifically to both constitutional and administrative contexts. But the fundamental structure of relationships is clear. Deference is essentially that favorite tool of the classical lawyer: the rebuttable presumption of authority. It can be overcome, of course, when the public authority acts in such a way as to forfeit its claim to be implementing law at all, either because (1) a particular body acts outside its sphere of legal competence, or (2) it pursues aims that have no imaginable public purpose, or (3) it acts in an unreasoned manner, arbitrarily and capriciously. Because law is an ordinance of reason for the common good by one charged with care of the community, fulfillment of any of these conditions puts the act of the public authority outside of law and thus forfeits its claim to be engaged in determination of the natural law. But the presumption is important nonetheless.

A Note on "Democracy"

Sometimes, deference to the reasonable judgments of public authorities is said to be grounded in "democracy." In what sense is this sort of argument available within the classical legal tradition? Is "democracy" good, on the classical view? The answer is that it depends what "democracy" means and, even more importantly, to what ends it is put and how it is justified.

The Introduction explained that determination can operate *on* as well as *within* the constitutional order. That is, the common good, as such, takes no particular stand, *a priori* and across the board, on the nature of the best political regime in the circumstances of a particular polity. (This proves difficult for the liberal mind to process, obsessed as it is with institutional technologies and the question "what is the best form of regime?") On the classical view, a range of regime-types can be ordered to the common good, or not. If they are, then they are just, and if they are not, they are tyrannical, but their justice is not defined by or inherent in any particular set of institutional forms. Democracy – in the modern sense of mass electoral democracy – has no special privilege in this regard. A democracy, in that sense, may or may not be oriented to the common good; one has to see whether it is, and the answer will depend upon circumstances.

The same point operates *within* the general family-resemblance category "democracy." Democracy is not an all-or-nothing package; there can be varying packages of democratic elements that may or may not be present in a polity ordered to the common good. One polity may make broad use of referendums and other tools of direct democracy, another might have a highly indirect system of representation. One might have first-past-the-post voting based on districts, another national party-list voting. One might have a strongly parliamentary system of the classic Westminster variety, another might have a separation of powers. One might employ representation only for individual citizens as such, while another recognizes representation of civil society groups, professions, trade associations, and other forms of corporatism. And so forth. The crucial point is that the common good need not justify itself before the bar of democracy, but the reverse: democracy, like any other regime-form, is valuable only insofar as it contributes to the common good, and not otherwise.

To be sure, as a prudential matter, independent of the classical theory of the common good as such, there may be good reason in particular circumstances to think that small-d democracy – consultation and representation of persons, cities, professions, civil society groups, and others affected by the acts of public authority – is often a useful technique of government and of lawmaking. Polities without mass electoral democracy use small-d democratic elements of representation and consultation – what one might call *democracy without voting* – to obtain information about popular preferences and to generate solidarity. More broadly, the mixed government beloved of classical lawyers contained popular elements intended to balance monarchical and aristocratic elements, and a late version of this sort of arrangement influenced the United States Constitution. This sort of representation was defended by Aquinas on the ground that while kingship is the best form of government, it is also true that "all should have some share in the government; for an arrangement of this kind secures the peace of the people, and all men love and defend it."[116]

An issue sometimes conflated with the value of "democracy" is the value of representative legislatures as lawmaking bodies. As we will see, the classical tradition identifies good reasons to respect, within a broad range of determination, the law produced by legislatures, because that law takes into account a broader range of central cases, resting on a broader base of information and a more impartial basis, than does the judgment of any fallible individual in particular cases. For similar reasons, the common good will often require that judges defer to the reasonable and public-oriented judgments of legislatures, within their constitutional competence, as I discuss throughout. Such points, however, are only contingently and prudentially related to democracy, especially in its modern mass-electoral form. Legislatures long predate modern democracy, and their value as lawmakers is not necessarily bound up with democracy as such.

The Constitution of Risk and "Abuse of Power"

Finally, let me address a stock concern about political rule, under robust authority directed to the common good: abuse of power. One approach to constitutional design aims to give this concern a sort of constitutional priority, in one form or another. The idea takes various forms, but the idea is that competing views of the good can be bracketed in favor of agreement on a common view of the bad; even political actors or groups who cannot agree on the positive aims of the constitution can agree that minimizing the risk of abuse of power by the state is common ground. As Karl Popper put it, the question "who should rule?" should be replaced by the question "How can we so organize political institutions that bad or incompetent rulers can be prevented from doing too much damage?"[117] On this conception, a liberal society should "[w]ork for the elimination of concrete evils rather than for the realization of abstract goods."[118] Concretely, Popper proposes, the master "principle of a democratic polity" (he actually means a liberal polity) should be to "create, develop, and, protect, political institutions for the avoidance of tyranny."[119] Judith Shklar's "liberalism of fear" runs along similar lines.[120]

There are two basic objections to this sort of theory. The first is that to speak of "abuse of power" is, necessarily, to assume some picture, explicit or implicit, of what goods power may or must legitimately aim to promote. It assumes, necessarily, a theory of the legitimate ends of government. Without agreement on the good, it is impossible even to find agreement on the bad either; "abuse" is ill-defined unless one has an account of the legitimate ends of good government. The Popper-style theorist believes these two are detachable, and that we can find consensus on what we don't want even as we have very different positive life plans built around different values. The better view, however, is that the bad is privative and thus defined by the good. Hence it is not possible to agree on an account of bads, of "abuses," while bracketing the question of what counts as the good and legitimate ends of government. I have stated the classical account of the legitimate ends of civil government earlier; the point here is just that there can be no coherent talk of "abuse of power" without specifying an account of such ends.

The second basic objection is that the approach focused on abuse of power by the state is often myopic about other constitutional risks. As I have argued at length elsewhere, the "Constitution of Risk" should constitute an order of public law that does not obsess over particular risks, but that should rather take a broad view, considering the risks of inaction as well as action, and the risks posed by the exercise of power by corporations and other "private" actors under delegated legal powers.[121] Myopia here means that the theorist urges constitutional precautions devoted to minimizing one sort of risk, while ignoring that the precautions may themselves create or exacerbate risks elsewhere.

In particular, constitutional theory often takes a libertarian form that becomes obsessed with the risks of abuse of power created by state organs in particular, while overlooking the risks of abuse of power that public authorities prevent through vigorous government. Those countervailing risks are erroneously coded as "private," overlooking that they are created by economic actors whose power necessarily depends on the protection afforded by legal rules and entitlements. The emphasis on prevention of tyranny in the name of protecting autonomy overlooks that tyranny may itself arise in the very name of protecting autonomy.[122] As John Dewey and Robert Hale pointed out in different ways, a claim that one's "liberty" should be protected by law is itself, necessarily, a claim to exercise coercive power over others.[123]

In general terms, then, the problem with these libertarian approaches, a problem of greater or lesser degree depending on how strongly the approach gives priority to avoiding abuses of power, is that a robust government acting for the common good can itself avoid or eliminate abuses of power. The state, narrowly understood as the official organs of government, is hardly the only source of abuses. Actors empowered directly or indirectly by law – including the property entitlements of corporate law and common law – may abuse their power throughout the society and economy.

The abuse of power by market actors is only one possibility, one illustration of countervailing risks. In general, for essentially historical rather than theoretical reasons, liberal theory tends to focus myopically on the risks of abuse by legislatures and (especially) executive actors. But the true calculus should consider all relevant risks of abuse of power, from whatever quarter, and take into account the countervailing risks of the precautions themselves. In this spirit, some countervailing risks of particular concern are: (1) the abuse of economic power, including the powers to engage in costly litigation and lobbying, by corporations wielding common-law rights of property, tort, and contract; (2) the abuse of power by the judiciary, especially when invoking "the risk of abuse" in order to abusively impose limits on the power of other actors attempting to prevent or remedy abuses; (3) the abuse of power by state and local governments, especially when abusively resisting attempts by the federal government to prevent or remedy abuses; and (4) governmental abuse of the power of inaction, especially in areas where governments could act to prevent or remedy abuses elsewhere on this list.

Again, the point here is definitely not that abuse of power is of no concern. In the subsequent chapters I will discuss the mechanisms the classical law uses to police the risk of such abuses – most importantly, the insistence on legal reason, on the rational intelligibility of the laws, of administrative procedures, and of exercises of official discretion. But the simplest rejoinder to the libertarians is that robust governance for the common good prevents or cures abuses as well as risking their occurrence. It is high time we turned to concrete examples to illustrate these points; the next chapter takes them up in the setting of American public law.

Chapter 2

The Classical Legal Tradition in America

This chapter aims to illustrate, with a series of demonstration projects, how pervasive the classical law has been in American law; to examine the structure of judicial review under (our particular determination of) classical constitutionalism; and to explain the sense in which the classical law is not opposed to textualism and other staples of legal conservatism, but instead includes them, as part of a larger scheme of law harmonized and ordered to the common good.

To make these claims concrete, the chapter begins with a brisk sketch of the main elements of the classical legal regime that prevailed in America from before the founding through the nineteenth century, and then examines a series of cases – embedded in broader lineages of doctrine – that illustrate the role and uses of the classical tradition within our public law. The first is *Lochner v. New York*,[124] a focal point for discussion of the basic doctrinal structure of judicial review under common good constitutionalism, of the crucial classical idea of determination and its connection to judicial deference, and of Justice Harlan's dissenting opinion – a model of common good constitutional interpretation. I then use *Riggs v. Palmer*[125] to illustrate the importance and role of enacted text in the classical tradition, which couples a version of textualism with the understanding that text as law (*lex*) is always embedded in larger structures of law (*ius*). Finally, I turn to *United States v. Curtiss-Wright Export Corp.*,[126] a foundational case on sovereignty, presidential power, and the *ius gentium*. *Curtiss-Wright* scrambles our current categories; it is neither an originalist nor a progressive, living-constitutional decision, but rather a classical decision. It reads the very nature of the United States as a concrete order, an embodied, living sovereignty that exists apart from and prior to the written large-C Constitution. In this context, then, one finds at the very foundation of the American polity the *ius gentium*, not the positive will of We the People embodied in the constitutional text enacted in 1788. Nor was there some other, unwritten, act of sovereign choice that brought that concrete order into being as a matter of positive law.

Taken together, these three cases – from disparate areas and eras of our law – illustrate how deeply the classical legal tradition has always infused our law; it is hardly some sort of alien intrusion. Originalism is in fact an extreme latecomer. It is a recent doctrine that has tried to graft itself onto our organic, developing – but not progressive – legal tradition, and it has fit very uneasily with that tradition. But that is veering into my negative case; this chapter is meant to be largely positive and interpretive, aiming to outline what common good constitutionalism actually is, how it works, and the principles on which it rests.

American Law as Classical Law: An Overview

The principles of the classical legal tradition are our own principles, written into our own traditions. Right from the beginning, long before the Constitution of 1789 was written, the classical legal tradition structured and suffused our law. It has since been displaced by progressive living constitutionalism and by originalism, approaches that – despite their differences – are from my standpoint co-conspirators. Both reject key premises of the classical law. More accurately, they imagine that they reject those premises. As we will see, the official commitment to legal positivism that is the main common characteristic of the reigning approaches is itself consistently belied by the actual behavior of judges and other interpreters, who are far more classical than they know.

The cumulative effect of these developments is that the classical legal tradition and its influence on American law have been largely lost to view. Law students are somewhat bewildered, for example, to discover that Blackstone's *Commentaries*, the main legal resource for many of the Constitution's framers and ratifiers, is organized around a scheme addressing the rights of persons, the rights of things, and wrongs, both private and public.[127] The reason for that seemingly odd scheme is that it is, in one form or another, a venerable mode of organization for legal textbooks in the tradition of Roman law and then in the *ius commune*; it descends ultimately from the great introductory text of the Roman law, the *Institutes of Gaius*.[128] Despite some typical asides fulminating against Romish absolutism,[129] Blackstone structures his exposition around divine law, natural law, and civil or "municipal" law – the ordinary cosmology of the classical law. (Note that "municipal" law only makes sense as a contrast to a larger legal community of nations, the *ius gentium*.) Reading Blackstone as some sort of post-World War II positivist, as many originalists implicitly do, is a bizarre category mistake and a telltale symptom of our legal culture's amnesia.

The same law students who puzzle over Blackstone also typically read *Pierson v. Post*,[130] the English fox-hunting case, which relies heavily on an ur-text of the classical law, the *Institutes of Justinian*.[131] The case illustrates nicely that "the decisions of English common law courts [drew] upon non-English authorities from the natural law and Roman law traditions. To the *Pierson* court, these traditions were part of the common law, broadly understood."[132] Yet that substantial unity of the common law and the *ius commune* is not typically developed in legal education.

The classical legal tradition in America, like any living tradition, was no monolith; it was constituted by a series of internal debates held within a common framework. Blackstone himself was criticized by leading American jurists of the founding era as having been insufficiently faithful to the classical tradition.[133] And indeed two strands of that tradition co-existed, sometimes uneasily, in the founding era and well beyond. One emphasized the common good and the inherently political and social nature of man, whose law is ordered to the good of particular political and social communities. The leading representatives of this sub-tradition were jurists such as James Wilson, Chancellor Kent, and Nathaniel Chipman. The other sub-tradition, more social-contractarian in its premises, and represented by Blackstone among others, tended to emphasize natural rights and saw human nature as intrinsically individualistic rather than social and political. But both traditions, despite reasoning in somewhat different ways, afforded broad scope for public authorities to act in service of the common good. Even more importantly, both shared the classical legal cosmology in which civil positive law gives specification to, and is interpreted in light of, general background principles of natural law and the law of nations, understood as enduring commitments of the legal order. Just as Blackstone's *Commentaries* were structured around Gaius' categories, so too the law lectures of one of his American critics, James Wilson, were organized in part around the classical categories of divine, natural, and municipal law.[134] The classical legal tradition contained disagreements and differences in emphasis, but within a common set of categories. It formed the matrix in which American law grew.

We are fortunate to now be able to draw upon excellent recent, or fairly recent, secondary overviews of the classical legal tradition in America by professional legal historians and scholars of the classical law. Some examples include Richard Helmholz's profoundly learned treatment of *Natural Law in Court*, which ranges over the medieval *ius commune* of the continent, the local variant of the *ius commune* that we call English common law, and American law of the eighteenth and nineteenth centuries;[135] William Novak's explanation of *The People's Welfare* (*salus populi*) as a master principle of the eighteenth- and nineteenth-century constitutional and legal tradition in America, itself underwritten by natural law, contrary to the libertarian versions of natural law most often discussed;[136] Stuart Banner's overview of the pervasiveness of natural law themes in American law;[137] and an important critique of originalism by Jonathan Gienapp.[138] Furthermore, these accounts are as it were folded within a body of comparative work at a higher level of generality, by Tamar Herzog,[139] Helmholz,[140] and other figures, that has corrected overly strong claims about the distinctiveness of the Anglo-American common-law tradition relative to the classical law of continental Europe. These and other works do not all pursue the same aims, or even necessarily speak with one voice as to details. Yet together, they create a broad, clear picture that is indisputable in its basics. Without purporting to summarize the whole picture, let me just offer a few key points:

- The *ius commune* was influential throughout continental Europe, England (and later Britain and its overseas possessions), and the American colonies. The exceptionalism of the Anglo-American common law should not be overstated; it is best seen as a local variant of the *ius commune*, which shares the basic classical framework of *ius* and *lex*, of *ius naturale*, *ius gentium* and *ius civile*, and so on.

> [B]oth English and continental law formed part of the very same legal tradition. Their specific technologies or solutions might have varied to some degree or the other, but they shared a common genealogy that bound them together more strongly than that which drew them apart. . . . Rather than being foreign to each other, English common law and continental civil law formed part of a single European tradition from which they both drew as well as contributed.[141]

- The same is true of *ius naturale* in particular. As Helmholz puts it, "the law of nature was a common possession of lawyers in the world of Western jurisprudence. In the course of investigating European, English, and American case law, remarkably few points of difference related to the applications and teachings of the law of nature emerged."[142]
- The tradition itself had multiple strands and was internally complex. For one thing, it contained both an older natural law strand embedded in the *ius commune*, and a newer, Enlightenment-influenced strand focused primarily on "natural rights." Moreover, the two strands tended to be justified in different ways as a matter of high political theory, with the natural rights strand resting on a social contract theory that was at least arguably a departure from the tradition's more Aristotelian premises. Here there are many debates at the level of political theory that I need not engage, for the *operational* difference between these strands should not be overstated at the level of constitutional law. Relative to the modern and currently reigning approaches, originalism and progressivism, the two strands of the joint natural law and natural rights tradition displayed substantial similarities.

In particular, we would go very wrong to imagine that the natural rights strand of the tradition supported anything like the sort of robust judicial review and scrutiny of legislation we see in the modern caselaw. That is a kind of anachronism, originated after the Civil War by property rights libertarians. Instead the natural rights tradition itself recognized broad scope for public authorities to make reasonable determinations as necessary to balance and reconcile competing natural rights or to override them for the general welfare.

Consider, for example, constitutional free speech rights – beloved by Justices who putatively identify as originalist. The problem is that free speech in the founding era was subject to pervasive public regulation. In a useful piece on the natural rights tradition in early free speech law, for example, Jud Campbell shows that judicial review was sharply limited, not as a contingent matter, but by the very terms of the natural law and natural rights theories themselves:

[[W]hether inherently limited by natural law or qualified by an imagined social contract, retained natural rights were circumscribed by political authority to pursue the general welfare. Decisions about the public good, however, were left to the people and their representatives – not to judges – thus making natural rights more of a constitutional lodestar than a source of judicially enforceable law. Natural rights, in other words, dictated *who* could regulate natural liberty and *why* that liberty could be restricted, but they typically were not "rights" in the modern sense of being absolute or presumptive barriers to governmental regulation.[143]

- Contrary to a pervasive modern assumption, the main point of invoking the *ius naturale* was not to "strike down" statutes contrary to the natural law. Indeed, such an approach was extremely rare. Rather the pervasive assumption of the classical framework was that the civil law, the natural law, and the law of nations served different roles in the legal system, came to the fore at different stages, and could be harmonized with one another. The natural and positive law, for example, work together in a larger framework, in which the positive law specifies and gives concrete form to general principles established by the natural law. The main vision is not one of contradiction, but of harmonious cooperation. As Helmholz puts it:

> An unfortunate accident of the dominance of the modern practice of judicial review in American courts has been to suggest that "striking down" legislative acts was the main purpose natural law was meant to serve. The American case of *Calder v. Bull* has also had the unhappy "side effect" of suggesting that courts were faced with an either/or choice. One choice was the Constitution, and the other was the law of nature; the majority of the courts chose the former. In reality, however, they were always meant to work together. The American Constitution stated rules of positive law, some of which were derived from the law of nature or were at least consistent with it. Lawyers who made reference to both natural and positive law in submissions to courts of law were not confused. They were relying on traditional learning. It taught that the two laws were in harmony and should be used together.[144]

- The largest and simplest point may also be the most important: the classical law was central to our legal world (not exclusive, but central) during the founding era and through the nineteenth century. "In understanding the law this way, Americans were following a long English and continental European tradition."[145] A change happened around the end of the nineteenth and beginning of the twentieth centuries – well after not only the adoption of the Constitution itself, but the adoption of its most important amendments, such as the Reconstruction Amendments. Of course there were controversies and changes within this classical legal framework over time; it was a living tradition, as much rife with internal disagreement as are the currently dominant approaches. And it is unmistakable that positivist notes began to be sounded over time, at first quietly, later as a swelling chorus. But for a surprisingly long time, the classical law provided the organizing framework for our legal world.

These points show that large chunks of the canonical constitutional theorizing of recent decades rest on mistaken assumptions. Here is an illustration. It is sometimes suggested – for example, by John Hart Ely – that the "natural law" tradition in America should be associated only with the Declaration of Independence, and that the Constitution itself abandoned that tradition.[146] Not infrequently, this sort of view is based on a wild overreading of *Calder v. Bull*[147] as a rejection of natural law. But this kind of view just isn't right. It overlooks that according to the classical conception itself, the positive law of the Constitution determines the background natural law, and would always be interpreted in light of its background principles.

In fact the natural law was used in two major ways after the Constitution's enactment: first, to interpret texts, reading them where fairly possible to square with traditional background principles and the objective order of justice; and second, to ground the authority of government in the pursuit of the common good. The latter idea has been almost completely lost to view in American law, to the point that even non-libertarian scholars who are not wholly positivist refer to natural rights, rather than natural law. But a primary role of the natural law, perhaps the primary role, was to underwrite the legitimacy of political action by authorities on behalf of the legitimate ends of government – peace, justice, abundance, health, and safety – as aspects of the common good:

> Perhaps surprisingly for a source of law so often cited by modern critics for its broad defense of property rights, the law of nature was rarely called upon successfully to limit the validity of social legislation in the years before the Civil War. It was used in cases involving the requirement of governmental compensation for outright takings of property, but rarely extended beyond that. More often it was used to promote principles of sociability and peace.

In the great majority of cases, statutes that regulated conduct and commerce were regarded as serving that legitimate purpose.[148]

Moreover, even at the artificially narrow level of natural rights, there is no question that Edward Corwin was largely correct to observe that the *ius naturale* was incorporated into the interpretation of the Bill of Rights in the American tradition over time.[149] "Then [i.e. at the time of the adoption of the Constitution], and for many years afterward, it was sometimes said that the constitutional provisions were 'declarative of natural law,' and that has always been true in a sense. They gave more definite shape to certain natural law principles."[150] And that function of giving more definite shape to background legal principles, adapting them to local circumstances and changing conditions, is precisely the function of positive law in the classical conception.

The same is true even after the classical law as such drops out of the consciousness of American lawyers. The natural law still appears today, in substantive due process and equal protection cases, cloaked in the language of "fundamental fairness" and similar formulations. It does not follow, of course, that all of the cases implicitly invoking natural rights and natural law in these guises are correct; it is just as possible to be mistaken about the natural law as about the positive law. But it is not the case that the *ius naturale* dropped out of American law. Rather it went underground and changed into a kind of disguise. Or to change the metaphor: just as the onset of amnesia does not mean that the sufferer's actual biography changes, so too our history has not changed. We have just become unaware of it, victims of a kind of illusion.

Lochner v. New York

It is high time we turned to particulars. I will begin by examining the Court's economic due process caselaw after the adoption of the Fourteenth Amendment, and in particular Justice Harlan's dissenting opinion in *Lochner v. New York* (1905), a case in which the majority invalidated a law setting maximum hours and minimum wages for bakers.[151] I have two purposes in doing so. One is to show how the classical framework operated in the cauldron of judicial practice. The other is to start to build up my interpretive argument. Harlan's dissent is a model opinion for common good constitutionalism – in sharp contrast to both the Court's opinion and Justice Holmes' more famous dissent, which both depart from the framework of common good constitutionalism, albeit in different ways.

Due process, determination, and the common good

Harlan's opinion draws upon a central stream of law within American constitutionalism, not a foreign grafting. If one simply searches for "common good" in the Supreme Court database in Westlaw, the centrality of this stream is made readily apparent, as the roughly 130 results immediately pick up the main line of the due process caselaw after the Civil War (and this is even without looking at adjacent terms such as "general welfare" or "public interest"). Among these are *Munn v. Illinois* (1876),[152] upholding maximum rates for grain warehouses and elevators; *Mugler v. Kansas* (1887),[153] in which Harlan wrote for the Court to uphold state regulation of the manufacture and sale of intoxicating liquors; *Holden v. Hardy* (1898),[154] upholding an eight-hour maximum day for miners; and *Jacobson v. Massachusetts* (1905),[155] another famous Harlan opinion, decided the same year as *Lochner*, that upheld a scheme of mandatory vaccination, and that has taken center stage in recent litigation arising from the Covid-19 pandemic.[156]

Along the way, the Court upheld a surprising variety of regulatory and administrative measures; indeed, a cursory acquaintance with this caselaw is enough to dispel any notion that the administrative state is a twentieth-century creation.[157] Although there were occasional decisions invalidating government action as entirely beyond the bounds of the defensible, the strong tendency of this body of law was to support capacious public authority to regulate property, economic activity, and even personal liberty for public purposes.

This body of law used the concept of the common good to define the "police powers" of government, a term whose contemporary usage referred broadly to the power of government to "enact and enforce public laws regulating or even destroying private right, interest, liberty, or property for the common good (i.e., for the public safety, comfort, welfare, morals, or health)."[158] The "common good" or "general welfare" is what the exercise of police powers should aim for, as the cases say over and over again.[159] The basic conception is purposive and teleological; the legitimacy of authority is defined in terms of the aims it pursues. An infallible diagnostic symptom that an American legal theorist is in the grip of an invented libertarian tradition is horror, or professed horror anyway, at the thought that promotion of public morality is an ordinary and indeed essential component of political rule; in American law, nothing is more venerable than the morals head of the police power.

In the economic due process caselaw,[160] the main application of police powers is to state governments, rather than the federal government. As David Currie has observed, one effect of the police powers framework was to treat state governments as governments of defined powers akin to the federal government – an approach in some tension with the written Constitution.[161] On the other hand, the police power framework hardly defined the powers of state governments in a rule-bound way. Rather it indicated a broad set of legitimate purposes for government action, and thereby created a loose-fitting garment allowing the exercise of broadly reasonable discretion by government to promote the common good over time, very much in line with Chief Justice Marshall's capacious approach to the power of the federal government in *McCulloch v. Maryland* in 1819.[162] In this sense our law, as it developed over time, applied to all levels of government a unified framework ultimately drawn from the classical legal tradition.

I shall call this "the common good framework." An excellent summary comes from Harlan's opinion in *Mugler v. Kansas:*

Nor can it be said that government interferes with or impairs any one's constitutional rights of liberty or of property, when it determines that the manufacture and sale of intoxicating drinks, for general or individual use, as a beverage, are, or may become, hurtful to society, and constitute, therefore, a business in which no one may lawfully engage. Those rights are best secured, in our government, by the observance, upon the part of all, of such regulations as are established by competent authority to promote the common good. *No one may rightfully do that which the law-making power, upon reasonable grounds, declares to be prejudicial to the general welfare.*[163]

The main elements of the framework, as Harlan explains, are that (1) the public authority acting within its constitutional sphere of competence (2) may act on a reasonable conception of the common good (defined in the police power caselaw by reference to the legitimate ends of government – health, safety, and morals) by (3) making reasonable, nonarbitrary determinations about the means to promote its stated public purposes. When it does so, then (4) judges must defer.

Judges, then, are to review the determinations of public authorities on three grounds: to see whether the authority has acted within its sphere of competence, whether it has pursued a reasonable public purpose, and whether the means it has chosen are rational. If the determinations of authority exceed public jurisdiction, are aimed at no reasonably conceivable public benefit, or adopt plainly arbitrary means, then judges should invalidate them. This approach is analogous, in some important respects, to the approach taken in American administrative law, in which – speaking very generally – agencies are often treated as having broad delegated power to act for public purposes, but must justify their actions on the basis of nonarbitrary reasons. Under this sort of approach, arbitrariness review does much of the critical work.

The common good framework flows from a straightforward account of the constitutional text and structure, including the Constitution's express commitment to the "general welfare" and the tacit postulates of the constitutional plan, as to both the federal government and the states.[164] Ultimately, it derives from the whole teleological conception of the aims of government and of constitutionalism in the classical tradition – a conception widely shared by American lawyers until quite recently, in historical perspective. The common good was the ordinary and original framework of American public law right from the beginning. As Blackstone observed, natural liberty could be "so far restrained by human laws . . . as is necessary and expedient for the general advantage of the public." Or, as a modern scholar of natural rights in the founding era puts it, "[d]ecisions about the public good . . . were left to the people and their representatives – not to judges."[165] Blackstone emphasized the role of determinations, observing of municipal laws (another term for civil laws, as opposed to the laws of divine revelation, of nature, or of international society) that

> sometimes, where the thing itself has its rise from the law of nature, the particular circumstances and mode of doing it become right or wrong, as the law of the land shall direct. Thus, for instance, in civil duties; obedience to superiors is the doctrine of revealed as well as natural religion: but who those superiors shall be, and in what circumstances or to what degrees they shall be obeyed, is the province of human laws to determine.[166]

Lochner and the common good

We are now in position to turn to *Lochner* itself. Justice Peckham's opinion for a bare majority of five justices invalidated a law that prohibited bakers from working more than sixty hours in a week or ten hours in a day.[167] Peckham argued that the law interfered with individual liberty of contract, and that it could not be justified as a labor law because it would be paternalistic to override the free choice of the bakers, who were "in no sense wards of the state" – a view that overlooked inequalities of bargaining power, the social externalities created when people work themselves half to death, the problems of labor-side collective action that allow employers to play divide-and-conquer in labor markets, and, most simply, the numerous precedents before *Lochner* that allowed authorities to override individual choices.[168]

To mention only the period of 1902–03, shortly before *Lochner*, Justices Brewer, Harlan and Holmes respectively had written for the Court to uphold prohibitions of prepayment to sailors of their own wages,[169] speculation in grain futures,[170] and margin sales,[171] all of which showed that public authorities may promote the common good by regulating the putatively free choices of market participants. As for justifying the law as a health measure, Peckham stated in brief and conclusory fashion that "the trade of a baker, in and of itself, is not an unhealthy one to that degree which would authorize the legislature to interfere"[172] – an approach that evaded the only question relevant under the long-established doctrine, which was whether the legislature *could reasonably find* maximum hours regulation to be a useful means of protecting the bakers' health. Any work under the wrong conditions can be "unhealthy . . . to that degree which would authorize the legislature to interfere." People doing any job can be overworked or underpaid.

The *Lochner* majority opinion was fundamentally a case of *mala fides*, of bad faith – an indisputable deviation from the settled framework of the caselaw, with its heavily deferential standard of review. It was easy for Harlan, in dissent, to show all this and to reassert (as he had written for the Court in *Jacobson*) that "there are manifold restraints to which every person is necessarily subject for the common good," to be reasonably determined by public authorities.[173] Harlan was clearheaded about the Court's own limited role and about the need for an authoritative determination of the competing principles of health and liberty:

> What is the true ground for the state to take between legitimate protection, by legislation, of the public health and liberty of contract is not a question easily solved, nor one in respect of which there is or can be absolute certainty. . . . What the precise facts are it may be difficult to say. It is enough for the determination of this case, and it is enough for this court to know, that the question is one about which there is room for debate and for an honest difference of opinion.[174]

Harlan's unanswerable dissent should have been the majority. It is pointless to try to show, as Peckham hinted obscurely and some libertarians have argued, that despite the legislation's aims, the legislature may in fact have had "other motives" and that the law might be seen as "class legislation" intended to favor unionized bakeshops, rather than a measure to benefit the common good of the whole community.[175] Although such efforts are unconvincing on their own terms, the main problem with them is that the long-standing common good framework ruled out probing judicial scrutiny of facially plausible legislative justifications; the same arguments necessary to justify the *Lochner* majority would also entail that a dozen cases before *Lochner* were wrongly decided, including the trio of cases from 1902–03. As Currie, no progressive himself, observed with some asperity:

> In light of the precedents it is not surprising that four Justices dissented. . . . Harlan, joined by White and Day, graphically demolished the Court's unsubstantiated conclusion on the health question by documenting the dangers of constant physical exertion. . . . The Court made only the most perfunctory attempt to deal with precedent, and it was obvious that it was applying a far stricter level of scrutiny than it had applied in previous cases.[176]

Lochner, then, was wrong the moment it was decided, not because of some paradigm shift after 1937.

The reason why *Lochner* was wrong, in Harlan's view and in my own, is that it represented a betrayal, in bad faith, of the common good framework. Justice Holmes' more famous dissent pointed out the flagrant inconsistency between the majority opinion and the precedents, but also offered a categorically different approach that rejected the common good framework itself, the framework that the majority purported to share with Harlan (although Peckham applied it in bad faith). In Holmes' view, the Court ought to defer not to public authority, charged with care of the community and acting for the common good, but rather to "the natural outcome of a dominant opinion" – meaning whatever opinion proves victorious via some mechanism, more or less "democratic," for aggregating opinions.[177]

Lost here is the classical idea of a genuinely common good that transcends preference aggregation and that is entrusted to the care of the public authority. As Dworkin observed,[178] Holmes' positivism – manifested most clearly in his famous critique, in diversity cases, of the general law as a "brooding omnipresence in the sky"[179] – is not the analytic positivism of the post-World War II era, but a positivism that underwrites deference by appealing to a democratic theory of political morality. But Holmes' conception of democracy is impoverished; it has lost sight of the rational ordering of law to the natural moral ends of the community. In contrast, then, to both Peckham's tendentious majority and Holmes' morally skeptical dissent, Harlan's dissent kept the faith, applying the common good framework with real integrity – with a fair-minded appreciation of the point and justification of the preceding caselaw, with appreciation for the limits of the judicial role in an overall institutional system of common good constitutionalism, and with an appropriate conception of the true ends of government, the classical and American conception.

Progressives and libertarians

Put differently, the capacious scope of public discretion to promote the common good is often neglected in discussions of the constitutional world of *Lochner*. In a conjunction of interest based on opposite motives, progressives and libertarians tend to portray that world as highly restrictive of governmental authority – progressives because they want to emphasize the need to break with the past, libertarians because they want to disguise as originalist and traditional their attempt to sharply restrict the ruling power of the state, an approach that is in fact innovative and modernist.

The progressive and the libertarian are twins, mirror images of one another, despite their mutual enmity. They are, in fact, on the same side of the fault line that separates the constitutional common good from modernism.[180] Hence their shared tendency to panicky, bewildered outrage at the thought that government might be charged with care for the morals and welfare of the community.[181] In contrast to these twin modernist approaches, the police power framework has firm roots in the classical legal tradition.

Comparison to modern approaches

We can understand the methodology of Harlan's opinion better by comparison and contrast with modern approaches. It is not originalism. Most of the background due process caselaw makes at most cursory reference to the founding era, and even then only for broad points about the traditional purposes of government. Harlan's dissent contains no reference to the framers or founders (or ratifiers), whether of 1789–91 or of 1868, nor is there any mention of the "original public meaning" of the Constitution. Rather the basis for the dissent is legal principles reflected and explicated by caselaw over time. In that sense it is closer to "living-tree constitutionalism" or "common-law constitutionalism," but it lacks the animating spirit of those approaches in their modern forms, which is a Whiggish faith that liberty and equality work themselves pure over time. (I expand upon this point in Chapter 4, which offers a distinction between developing constitutionalism that applies unchanging background principles to new circumstances, and progressive or living constitutionalism, in which Whiggish progress is understood to extend to indefinite improvement in the principles themselves.) Whig constitutionalism is also deeply reluctant to allow the point – unquestionable for millennia – that morality is obviously a sound and, indeed, an unavoidable basis for public lawmaking.

Harlan's dissent and the common good framework generally find later, imperfect echoes in certain versions of Legal Process rational purposivism that recognize the crucial role of background norms and principles (*ius*) in deciding even what enacted law (*lex*) should be taken to mean, but that also recognize the importance of role divisions across institutions. As Hart and Sacks put it, on one approach, "the law rests upon a body of hard-won and deeply-embedded principles and policies – such, precisely, as the principle that one should not be allowed to profit by his own wrong; [and] this body of thought about the problems of social living is a precious inheritance and possession of the whole society."[182] They go on to urge a principle of interpretation that would read statutes not to depart lightly from this "body of principles and policies" – the same approach the classical law takes with respect to background principles of the *ius naturale*, the *ius gentium*, and the municipal legal system. More generally, Hart and Sacks' teleological account of the aims of government and the legal system is a definite holdover from the classical law. Yet somehow, by the Legal Process era, the *content* of the common good, the rich theory worked out over time by the *ius commune*, has been largely forgotten. All that remains is a pallid invocation of "the fact of . . . interdependence with other human beings and the community of interest which grows out of it."[183] The basic ends of government, on this view, turn out to be "the satisfaction of wants" in light of "common interests" – implicitly, a thin and inadequate conception of the common good in utilitarian and aggregative terms.

More promisingly, one might see the common good framework as Dworkinism-plus-deference, just with a better account of justification than the one Dworkin offers.[184] In line with Dworkin's law-as-integrity, combining "fit" and "justification," the common good framework attempts to "fit" the developing law while also providing justifications for that law in light of a political morality of the common good, understanding political morality to itself include a morality of institutional roles that commits primary competence for promoting the common good to political authorities. On this view, the coherence and integrity of law include arguments from political morality for deference to nonjudicial decision-makers, within reasonable boundaries. Which is just to say that Dworkin reinvented a version of the classical legal tradition without knowing it, especially when toward the end of his career he categorized law as a department of political morality – albeit a distinctive department, itself including distinctive moral considerations such as qualified continuity with past decisions and respect for institutional roles.[185] That framing would have both Aquinas and the classical lawyers nodding in approval.

Arrogance and skepticism

Against the backdrop of the classical legal tradition and its common good framework, there are two distinct ways in which a judge can go wrong. The first of these two, Peckham's mistake, is rooted in arrogance. It is to assume that ascertaining the common good is entirely committed to the judgment of the courts, overlooking the legitimate scope for public authorities to determine (in the classical sense) the import, relationship, and weight of competing principles, within reasonable boundaries. In the nature of things there is no metric or algorithm for determining the boundaries of the reasonable, but a hallmark of maturity is the realization that the absence of such a metric is hardly a decisive objection. The classical tradition rests, in the end, on the overarching principle of *bona fides*, good faith. Where such good faith is systematically absent, the law may misfire, but in such a scenario the misfiring of the law would be the least of the polity's problems.

The other mistake, Holmes' mistake, is skepticism, which comes in two distinct forms. (These need not be combined, necessarily, but Holmes did suffer from both forms.) The first is to be skeptical that there exists an objective common good that transcends human will. The natural tendency of this view is to identify the political good with whatever results from voting procedures that aggregate subjective preferences, and then, as parliamentary legal positivists like Bentham and Austin argued, to identify law with the willed command that emerges from that aggregation procedure, or from the commands of representatives installed by the aggregation procedure, and so on. It is familiar that this skeptical form of positivism underlies much of Holmes' jurisprudence.

The second form is skepticism that the public authorities can successfully act on behalf of the common good, even if the latter exists. On this view, the common good can only be attained indirectly, through invisible-hand mechanisms such as the "marketplace of ideas,"[186] another of Holmes' pet notions. These two forms of skepticism share a crucial negative commitment: a horror of purposive rule directing and coordinating the polity toward the common good – precisely what the classical legal tradition envisions as the central or ordinary case of rule by and through law. That classical picture is central to the American legal tradition, which thus sets its face against both the arrogance of judicial libertarianism and the moral skepticism of Holmesian positivism. It assumes that there is a common good that political authorities can, should, and usually will act purposively to attain through reasonable determinations of (potentially competing) principles. In the words of a brilliant formulation by the Spanish theorist Ricardo Calleja, the injunction of classical governance for the common good is *imperare aude* – "dare to command!"[187]

The great mistake of the modernist is to assume that such imperative rule can only be a matter of will, not reason (here projecting the modernist's own will to power). But the whole point of the classical view is that governance and law are themselves suffused with and constituted by reason. In the nature of things, the resulting law requires reasoned argument in the spirit of Dworkin's fit and justification – with integrity. It requires courts to make reasonable judgments, in good faith, about whether public authorities have themselves made reasonable judgments, in good faith.

It is no accident that Harlan's dissent in *Lochner* is longer than both the majority and Holmes' dissent. The former is comparatively brisk because it ignores, minimizes, or arbitrarily sweeps aside perfectly sensible arguments for the reasonableness of the legislation at issue; the latter is brisk because it strikes a bored pose of skeptical detachment that requires no engagement with reason at all. Only Harlan does reason right, asking why the relevant legislation might plausibly make sense as a purposive measure aimed at the common good. The other opinions stray from the true path in one direction or the other. Hence only Justice Harlan could truly boast *"non declinavit ad dextram sive ad sinistram"*[188] – that he had strayed neither to the right nor the left.

Riggs v. Palmer

So much for the basic framework of common good constitutionalism and judicial review. Let me now turn from substantive constitutional law to methods of legal interpretation. I focus on a famous chestnut, perhaps the most famous chestnut, of American legal interpretation: *Riggs v. Palmer*,[189] the "Case of the Murdering Heir," which posed the question whether a grandson who murdered his own grandfather could inherit under a will made valid by the relevant statutes. Law students are conventionally taught *Riggs v. Palmer* as a case about the choice between "textualism" and "purposivism," or sometimes a choice between "following the statute" or "departing from the statute in extraordinary circumstances." Any such frame, however, is both wrong and anachronistic. In fact one cannot understand *Riggs v. Palmer* without understanding something about the classical legal tradition, or so I will argue. Both the majority and the dissent in the case are firmly embedded within that tradition, and their disagreement is entirely internal to the tradition. Indeed, until quite recently in historical perspective, the classical tradition supplied the framework of interpretive principles by means of which American courts commonly organized their agreements and disagreements about what the law requires.

Two versions of textualism

Before turning to the case, I need to offer some background about the relationship between "textualism" and the classical tradition. At least since Justice Antonin Scalia began to influence the thinking of law professors and judges about interpretive method in the 1980s, the debate over interpretive method has often centered on a stock opposition between "textualism" on the one hand and "purposivism" on the other,[190] with "textualism" taken to mean "following the ordinary meaning of statutory text" and purposivism taken to mean "departing from the ordinary meaning of statutory text when it diverges from apparent legislative purpose."

That opposition is somewhat parallel to the paired opposition between "originalism" and "living constitutionalism" that dominates our constitutional law.[191] I've suggested in the latter case that the opposition is entirely misleading when one realizes that the two approaches are mirror images of one another and lie on the *same* side of a gulf separating them from the classical legal tradition. So too here. Textualism equates "following the law" with "following the ordinary meaning of the statutory text," but that equation presupposes a very particular, positivist way of understanding law. On the classical approach, however, the "law" (*ius*) itself includes consider-ations beyond the enacted text (*lex*). The background principles of *ius* themselves enter into and help to determine the meaning of *lex*. Enacted texts deserve great respect as a determination of the legiti-mate public authority, but the law is broader than their temporary and local commands, and it is presumed that those commands can be and will be harmonized with the background *ius*.

This does not at all mean that the classical tradition "ignores the text" or anything of that sort. Rather, "textualism" itself can be said to work in two different ways. One version, the modern version, is incompatible with the classical legal tradition. Another version, how-ever, is entirely compatible with the classical legal tradition; indeed it is Aquinas' own view.

In the first version of textualism, a positivist version, textualism is justified analytically and stipulatively, as an exclusive claim about what counts as "law." On this view, there is nothing outside the text – meaning, in law, that there is no law outside enacted positive texts. Any considerations adduced from beyond the text are not-law and thus lie beyond the office of the judge to consider. This view was on display, for example, in Justice Neil Gorsuch's opinion for the Supreme Court in the recent *Bostock* case, which I will discuss in Chapter 3. There Justice Gorsuch wrote that "[o]nly the written word is the law."[192]

In a second version, however, textualism is justified not analytically but by reference to substantive goods of political morality, as Ronald Dworkin put it in a closely related discussion of "analytic" and "polit-ical" justifications for positivism.[193] Those goods may include legal generality, certainty, predictability, and other distinctive desiderata of a legal system that textualism is claimed to produce.[194] (Whether it does *in fact* produce such goods is not my concern here.) Nothing in the structure of this second version requires or presupposes that the relevant goods lie "outside" law, whatever that means, or that only the text counts as "law." Since, on Dworkin's view, law is a distinctive department of political morality, it is perfectly possible to speak of promoting goods of political morality *within* law. The relevant goods are goods inside the law, as it were – internal to its activity. It is the practice and reasoning of officials within the legal system, emphatically including judges, that identify the goods as such.

This second version is classical textualism. It rests, not on a stipulative claim about the nature of law, but on an institutional claim: for a certain class of decision-makers, under given circumstances, certain goods are best attained by requiring those decision-makers to stick closely to the ordinary, conventional meaning of text. In other words, the common good promoted by law in its extended classical sense, including general principles rooted in the law of nations and the natural law, might itself best be served if judges were generally to stick to the ordinary meaning of texts of civil law enacted by public authorities who, having been charged with stewardship of the community, were to enact those texts as rational ordinances intended to serve the common good.

Under what conditions might this be true? Why might judges or other decision-makers conceivably do better by, in effect, refusing to consider elements of law that lie outside enacted texts? The basic answer is that if the decision-maker at the point of application is limited in some way, prone to error, it may be better that they should not attempt to consider anything beyond the ordinary meaning of the text, at least presumptively. Aquinas explains:

As the Philosopher says (Rhet. i, 1), "it is better that all things be regulated by law, than left to be decided by judges": and this for three reasons. First, because it is easier to find a few wise men competent to frame right laws, than to find the many who would be necessary to judge aright of each single case. Secondly, because those who make laws consider long beforehand what laws to make; whereas judgment on each single case has to be pronounced as soon as it arises: and it is easier for man to see what is right, by taking many instances into consideration, than by considering one solitary fact. Thirdly, because lawgivers judge in the abstract and of future events; whereas those who sit in judgment of things present, towards which they are affected by love, hatred, or some kind of cupidity; wherefore their judgment is perverted. Since then the animated justice of the judge is not found in every man, and since it can be deflected, therefore it was necessary, whenever possible, for the law to determine how to judge, and for very few matters to be left to the decision of men.[195]

Aquinas here argues, as the legal scholar Fred Schauer later put it,[196] that "cases make bad law"; decision-makers at the point of interpretation may often go wrong precisely because they are aware of the particulars of the application of the law at issue. The generality and formalism of textualism (in the second of the two senses I have identified) attempt to combat this by subjecting the decision-makers to a general rule.

To be clear, Aquinas does not mean that the interpreter of the law should *never* depart from the ordinary meaning of the text. At the operative level, Aquinas' approach is an example of what we might call presumptive textualism[197] – textualism that is defeasible when an unusual circumstance falls outside the core central case that was within the rational ordination of the law. On the classical view, departing from the text is not the same as departing from the law; the law is the lawmaker's reasoned ordination for the common good, which may be imperfectly expressed by the enacted text. Because the lawmaker, too, is imperfect and subject to limited foresight, cases may arise that fall outside the central case of the lawmaker's rational ordination. When this occurs the text, if followed according to its plain meaning in that deviant case, will no longer track the common good that the lawmaker meant to promote. Aquinas again:

It happens often that the observance of some point of law conduces to the common weal in the majority of instances, and yet, in some cases, is very hurtful. Since then the lawgiver cannot have in view every single case, he shapes the law according to what happens most frequently, by directing his attention to the common good. Wherefore if a case arise wherein the observance of that law would be hurtful to the general welfare, it should not be observed. For instance, suppose that in a besieged city it be an established law that the gates of the city are to be kept closed, this is good for public welfare as a general rule: but, if it were to happen that the enemy are in pursuit of certain citizens, who are defenders of the city, it would be a great loss to the city, if the gates were not opened to them: and so in that case the gates ought to be opened, contrary to the letter of the law, in order to maintain the common weal, which the lawgiver had in view. Nevertheless it must be noted, that if the observance of the law according to the letter does not involve any sudden risk needing instant remedy, it is not competent for everyone to expound what is useful and what is not useful to the state: those alone can do this who are in authority, and who, on account of such like cases, have the power to dispense from the laws. If, however, the peril be so sudden as not to allow of the delay involved by referring the matter to authority, the mere necessity brings with it a dispensation, since necessity knows no law.[198]

Aquinas is here carrying a certain sort of institutional claim – of the sort I have tried to explain in other work – as far as it will go.[199] The obligation of the interpreter is to distrust his own first-order judgment about whether the apparent meaning of the text has diverged from the common good – so long as there remains any possibility of recourse to interpretation by the authorized lawgiver. Where there is no time for such recourse, however, so that a genuine emergency has arisen, what else can an interpreter do but rely upon his own judgment? On any account of interpretation, this must be true; the strictest injunctions to textualism can never exclude the question arising, for the official on the spot in a genuine emergency, whether the command at issue has or has not gone terribly wrong in application.

What about the separation of powers? A standard response offered by textualists goes as follows. Aquinas' view does not exactly envision a modern separation-of-powers system,[200] in the sense that the highest public authority is implicitly envisioned by Aquinas to hold both lawmaking and law-interpreting power.[201] In a separation-of-powers system, the argument runs, the interpreter allocated a confined role, such as a judge, should never directly consult the common good. As a would-be defender of Justice Scalia's textualism put it, it is a perfectly consistent position to hold that lawmakers have a moral obligation to legislate in accordance with the natural law *and* to hold that judges possess only the limited authority to inter- pret those laws according to the lawmakers' original meaning. In fact, this perfectly consistent position was precisely the position of Justice Scalia, who, on more than one occasion, expressly stated his belief in the Catholic doctrine of natural law even while warning that such a doctrine does not provide a good basis for interpreting laws.[202]

This is, however, a position that no or almost no real judges hold, least of all Justice Scalia. In fact Scalia consistently held that judges should apply an interpretive doctrine of "absurd results,"[203] under which judges may depart from the apparent meaning of text to avoid egregious outcomes that no reasonable legislator could be thought to have intended, in light of fundamental general background principles of the legal system – precisely the view of the majority in *Riggs v. Palmer*. This is, in essence, the doctrine of the "equity of the statute," which I will consider shortly.

The point in terms of separation of powers, however, is that it is question-begging to assume that this sort of presumptive textualism is inconsistent with the allocation of lawmaking powers to legislators. No one denies that allocation under our constitutional scheme; the problem is that it is a truism, a generality. The question at issue is to decide what the law means, the core of the judicial function, and the presumptive textualism of the classical law offers an account of precisely that. The question as to whether that account is right or wrong may not be answered satisfactorily by abstract invocation of the separation of powers.

Epikeia

Aquinas' account of interpretation, following the standard view of the *ius commune* (and stemming ultimately from Aristotle) looks to the virtue of *epikeia* or "the equity of the statute." *Epikeia* is a virtue per- taining to legal justice[204] that adjusts the application of the law from its literal text to track a reasonable account of the common good. The most typical cases involve narrowing the strict literal terms of the statute to cover only central cases within the aim of the lawgiver, but it is also possible to include cases not covered by the literal terms, yet presenting the same evils the lawmaker addressed.

The old chestnuts of the *ius commune* are familiar, such as the Bolognese surgeon who bled an epileptic to treat a seizure, and was exempted by *epikeia* from punishment under a statute that forbade the "drawing of blood" in the streets. But recent American cases feature the same idea, just under other names. Consider *United States v. Smith*,[205] a famous dissent of Justice Scalia in which he argued that a statute enhancing sentences for those who "use a firearm during and in relation to . . . a drug trafficking crime"[206] did not cover a defendant who traded his gun for drugs.[207] Scalia cast his argument mainly in terms of the distinction between literal and ordinary meaning, but this is often just a way of pursuing *epikeia* without saying so. The tipoff is that what counts as "ordinary meaning" is not determined by any actual empirical assessment of what most speakers of the language would think; typically no linguists are consulted, nor are polls done. Rather the judges simply consult their own natural intuitions, themselves partly formed by the virtue of *epikeia*.

Another example is *Yates v. United States*,[208] in which the question was whether a criminal prohibition on the destruction of any "record, document or tangible object" to obstruct a federal investigation covered the destruction of fish to avoid a charge of unlicensed fishing.[209] By a 5–4 vote, the Court – properly in my view – held that the apparent context and purpose of the whole statute, in all its provisions, was to cover only objects used to record or preserve information.[210] In both cases, the Justices exercising *epikeia* attempted to discern the central case or common case covered by the law and to exclude applications outside that core.

In contrast, a famous failure of *epikeia* is the dissenting opinion of Justice Powell in *TVA v. Hill*,[211] which argued that the Tennessee snail darter should be read to be exempt from the facially unqualified operation of the Endangered Species Act. Powell thought that applying the statute would produce absurd results by requiring that a dam project would be shut down, at great cost. Yet Powell did not give any convincing reason to think that the snail darter was outside the central case laid down by the Act, which did not in any way tie its strictures to the size, charisma, or economic importance of the species at issue or the federal actions that might threaten it. Nor was there any reason in background principles of the *ius naturale* to think that the kind of monetized cost-benefit analysis Powell suggested is written in the nature of things. On the contrary, as I will discuss later, principles of man's duty of stewardship to nature are close to the heart of the common good,[212] and are themselves the highest interest of individuals. *Epikeia* is *not* the use of individualistic standards of value to trump the central case of a statute ordered to the common good.

The broader debate over the equity of the statute is familiar to students of American statutory interpretation from a controversy between William Eskridge and John Manning over the importance of equity in the founding era.[213] Although I will not review the debate here, in my view there is no question that *epikeia* held a central place of honor in the classical legal tradition in America. But *epikeia* is hardly the same thing as "dynamic interpretation"; it is bad faith to strip *epikeia* of the limits that cabin it in the classical tradition. *Epikeia* is bounded by the very terms on which the classical law recognizes it.

The basic constraints are twofold. First, as we have seen, if it is reasonably feasible to secure an authoritative interpretation from the lawgiver, then that course should be pursued unless the lawgiver has itself instructed otherwise, delegating to interpreters on the ground, as it were, the authority to engage in *epikeia*. In modern legal systems, the latter case is typical; the lawgiver is typically understood to entrust its commands to authorized interpreters, such as agencies or judges (and there is then a separate question how to allocate interpretive authority between those agents, a question I take up later).

Second, *epikeia* is bounded by its own intrinsic limits. *Epikeia* is the virtue that discerns the command of the lawgiver *more* accurately than does a wooden literalism, because it understands what the lawgiver laid down as the central or standard case and the theory of the common good underlying that decision. As Justice Harlan put it in

Jacobson, "the spirit of . . . a constitution[] is to be respected not less than its letter; yet the spirit is to be collected chiefly from its words."[214] The virtue of *epikeia* does not license arbitrary overrides of the text at the individual whim of the interpreter. Rather it is a virtue for discerning the reasoned choice that the public authority, as an authority, truly made in and through the text, in light of background principles of the *ius naturale*, the *ius gentium*, and the common good to which that authority is rightly ordered.[215] It executes a famous injunction of the Digest: "Knowing laws is not a matter of sticking to their words, but a matter of grasping their force and tendency."[216]

Much more could be said about this, and the full structure and nuance of Aquinas' view could be drawn out at greater length. All that is for further work that adumbrates the classical theory of interpretation in modern contexts. But I trust my main point is clear enough: there is a sense of (at least presumptive) textualism, bounded by appropriate exercises of *epikeia*, that is entirely compatible with the classical legal tradition. It should be clear that no global condemnation of "textualism" is adequate, from the standpoint of the classical lawyer, if we risk sweeping Aquinas' view into the net.

The opinions

We are now in a position to understand the opinions in *Riggs v. Palmer* and what, exactly, the majority and dissent disagreed about. Simplified, the grandson had poisoned his grandfather in order to inherit under a will. The will was validly executed and the relevant statutes provided that an inheritance under a valid will should pass as designated, without qualification.[217] Today the case would be governed by so-called "murdering heir" statutes, and the inheritance probably subjected to a constructive trust for the benefit of third parties. In the actual case, however, the majority held that the murdering heir should not inherit, while the dissent argued that he should.

The majority's reasoning started with a crucial proposition of the classical legal tradition: "It is a familiar canon of construction that a thing which is within the intention of the makers of a statute is as much within the statute as if it were within the letter; and a thing which is within the letter of the statute is not within the statute, unless it be within the intention of the makers."[218] On this proposition, the dissent agreed. What then did the two opinions disagree about? The majority thought that "the statute" should be read in light of what the majority called "general, fundamental maxims of the common law."[219] The key maxim was that "[n]o one shall be permitted to profit by his own fraud, or to take advantage of his own wrong, or to found any claim upon his own iniquity, or to acquire property by his own crime."[220] For the majority, "[t]hese maxims are dictated by public policy, have their foundation in universal law administered in all civilized countries, and have nowhere been superseded by statutes."[221] This was an explicit appeal to the *ius gentium*, itself reflecting the *ius naturale*. Importantly, the majority did not think that the civil law and the common law diverged in any way on this point. Indeed the court thought that the common law naturally, as it were, incorporated the civil-law rule without need for statutory enactment:

> Under the civil law, evolved from the general principles of natural law and justice by many generations of jurisconsults, philosophers, and statesmen, one cannot take property by inheritance or will from an ancestor or benefactor whom he has murdered. Dom. Civil Law, pt. 2, bk. 1, tit. 1, § 3; Code Nap., § 727; Mack. Rom. Law, 530, 550. . . . [S]o far as I can find, in no country where the common law prevails has it been deemed important to enact a law to provide for such a case. Our revisers and law-makers were familiar with the civil law, and they did not deem it important to incorporate into our statutes its provisions upon this subject. This is not a *casus omissus*. It was evidently supposed that the maxims of the common law were sufficient to regulate such a case, and that a specific enactment for that purpose was not needed.[222]

The dissent did not argue that the majority went wrong by considering "extralegal" sources, or offer any other version of a positivist account. Indeed the dissent is just as deeply engaged with the classical tradition as the majority is, including both the positive civil law (*lex*) and general principles of law found in the tradition (*ius*). Rather the dissent argued that the competent civil authority had considered the relevant questions and made a valid determination, resting on substantial reasons ordered to the welfare of society. The case did not fall within the category of the unforeseen exception because the legislature had for deliberate reasons excluded the matters to which it pertained from consideration under that rubric:

> Modern jurisprudence, in recognizing the right of the individual, under more or less restrictions, to dispose of his property after his death, subjects it to legislative control, both as to extent and as to mode of exercise. Complete freedom of testamentary disposition of one's property has not been and is not the universal rule, as we see from the provisions of the Napoleonic Code, from the systems of jurisprudence in countries which are modeled upon the Roman law, and from the statutes of many of our states. . . . The reason for the establishment of such rules, we may naturally assume, consists in the purpose to create those safeguards about these grave and important acts which experience has demonstrated to be the wisest and surest. That freedom which is permitted to be exercised in the testamentary disposition of one's estate by the laws of the state is subject to its being exercised in conformity with the regulations of the statutes. The capacity and the power of the individual to dispose of his property after death, and the mode by which that power can be exercised, are *matters of which the legislature has assumed the entire control, and has undertaken to regulate with comprehensive particularity.*[223]

What of the majority's appeal to fundamental public policies, embodied in general legal principles common to all civilized nations? The dissent by no means denied that such principles were part of the law. Rather it argued that the majority had focused on the wrong one: "Public policy does not demand [an exemption]; for the demands of public policy are satisfied by the proper execution of the laws and the punishment of the crime. . . . [T]o concede appellants' views would involve the imposition of an additional punishment or penalty upon the respondent."[224] The dissent here appeals to one of the law's immemorial maxims, *nulla poena sine lege*. This is just as firmly a part of the classical tradition as the majority's principle that no man shall profit from his own wrong.

In consulting the *ius naturale*, however, the dissent partly undercut its own position. No determination can entirely block out, as it were, consideration of background principles, for on the classical view consideration of such principles is necessary even to understand the scope and point of the determination. This does not mean that the determination collapses, or has no effect; the law is different after it is made than it would be if it had never occurred, and the issue left to full first-order decision by the judges themselves. But it does mean that on the classical view, the positive law can never entirely exclude consideration of the law in its broader sense of *ius*, especially in hard cases. I return to this point later.

Let us step back. The core analytic structure of *Riggs v. Palmer* – common to both majority and dissent – is easily misunderstood and often misrepresented by positivists. The point is emphatically not that the enacted text is irrelevant in itself, and that if the judges could gather the "intention" some other way – for example, by interviewing the legislators – they could then simply implement that intention. The intention has always to be *embodied* in an ordinance and promulgated to count as law; recall the classical definition of law as an ordinance of reason for the common good, promulgated by one in authority. Rather the point is that statutes are to be read, not as cryptic collections of words dropped from the sky, but as rational ordinances that aim to promote the common good of the community.

As we have seen, the common good itself includes role morality and division of functions. That is, judges are not to directly decide for themselves, in an all-things-considered way, what the common good requires; that is for the public authority in the first instance. The structure of the judicial inquiry is different. It is primarily to ask what the public authority has done by ascertaining what the authority has said; and secondarily to ask whether the court faces the nonstandard case in which the authority's rational ordering for the common good has been imperfectly captured by what the authority said, read in light of larger background principles.

The disagreement in *Riggs v. Palmer*, then, is not at all a dispute over "textualism" versus "purposivism," or "whether to follow the law" versus "departing from the law due to extraordinary circumstances," or anything of that sort. Rather the disagreement between majority and dissent is entirely *internal* to the classical legal tradition. Both opinions see law as including enacted texts while not being limited to them. Both think the law includes enduring general principles. The disagreement between them is just over whether the presumption of textualism should or should not hold; over whether, on Aquinas' view, the court was or was not facing a noncentral case. If so, then practice of civilized nations, itself reflecting the natural law, shows that the court should read the meaning of the enacted text (*lex*) in light of the whole law (*ius*).

For our purposes here, the main issue is not which opinion in the case was correct, although in my view the majority has much the better of the argument. What *Riggs v. Palmer* mainly illustrates is that, and how, the classical legal tradition pervaded the law even in the later nineteenth century, thereby providing a structured framework for legal interpretation. The judges in *Riggs* simply swam, like fish, within the classical tradition, drawing at will upon civil and Roman law and the *ius commune* generally in the form of general maxims and principles, and seeing no conflict between those sources and the common law. It is a rank modern misreading to describe the case as some sort of conflict or choice between "textualism" and "purposivism." Rather both opinions in the case are premised upon a different kind of textualism than the positivism of later interpreters, a textualism that takes the enactments of legitimate public authority seriously and reads them as embedded within a broader set of legal principles and sources. Indeed, as we will see next, those principles themselves *constitute* the legitimate public authority.

Curtiss-Wright and the *Ius Gentium*

Finally, I turn to structural constitutional law and the relationship between our constitutional order and the unwritten law and international law. The Supreme Court's 1936 decision in *United States v.*

Curtiss-Wright Export Corp.[225] will, I hope, illustrate that the American constitutional order rests, not upon positive written law, but upon the *ius gentium.* Only the classical perspective can explain this, which amounts to a grave problem for positivist originalism. Thus this final example begins the segue into the next chapter, in which I shift from the positive sketch of common good constitutionalism to the negative critique of its competitors.

Curtiss-Wright upheld the validity of a joint resolution authorizing the president, by proclamation, to make illegal the selling of arms to combatants in a conflict between Bolivia and Paraguay.[226] Justice Sutherland's opinion for the Court framed the issue by assuming, for the sake of argument, that the delegation would be invalid if it only involved internal affairs, and then asking whether the foreign relations context made a difference. His answer to that question was that it made all the difference, for two main reasons. First, the government as a whole possessed the relevant powers as inherent concomitants of external sovereignty.[227] Second, the context was one of concurrent presidential authority over external affairs, in which the president enjoys special powers to act as "sole organ of the federal government in the field of foreign relations."[228] These points both implied that the standards of valid delegation were more capacious than in domestic affairs.

Curtiss-Wright is familiar, I hope, to every well-trained American lawyer; it must appear on any short-list of cases about presidential power, delegation, and the sovereignty of the United States. It is, however, usually discussed substantively, from the standpoint of its holdings and arguments about the subjects it touches upon. I want to ask a few questions about its method: what sort of opinion is *Curtiss-Wright?* Is it originalist, resting on the original meaning of constitutional text? (We are reliably informed, after all, that originalism has long been "our law.") Is it living-constitutionalist? Something else?

Our current constitutional debates are usually framed around this choice between originalism and living constitutionalism and their variants, but neither description really rings true with respect to *Curtiss-Wright.* First, *Curtiss-Wright* is hardly an originalist decision; indeed it stands as a direct and rather flagrant affront to originalism, and to the positivism of which the currently reigning version of originalism is a species. *Curtiss-Wright* says squarely that the sovereignty of the United States, and the foreign relations powers that flow from sovereignty, was not created by the written Constitution of 1789, but arose even before the enactment of the Constitution, through *translatio imperii* – by transfer of sovereignty from the British Crown according to pre-existing general principles of international law, the *ius gentium*. The Court rejects, emphatically and memorably, the view that the relevant foreign relations powers flow from the adopted written Constitution:

> The broad statement that the federal government can exercise no powers except those specifically enumerated in the Constitution, and such implied powers as are necessary and proper to carry into effect the enumerated powers, is categorically true only in respect of our internal affairs. . . . [S]ince the states severally never possessed international powers, such powers could not have been carved from the mass of state powers but obviously were transmitted to the United States from some other source. . . . As a result of the separation from Great Britain by the colonies acting as a unit, the powers of external sovereignty passed from the Crown not to the colonies severally, but to the colonies in their collective and corporate capacity as the United States of America. . . . Rulers come and go; governments end and forms of government change; but sovereignty survives. A political society cannot endure without a supreme will somewhere. Sovereignty is never held in suspense. When, therefore, the external sovereignty of Great Britain in respect of the colonies ceased, it immediately passed to the Union. . . . *The Union existed before the Constitution.*[229]

This approach is historical without being originalist. It draws upon history to prove the chain of legitimate title to sovereignty, for purposes of the *ius gentium*, but not to interpret the meaning of constitutional provisions. Other passages in *Curtiss-Wright* can be read, more narrowly, to offer a separate alternative rationale according to which the sovereign foreign relations powers of the United States do stem from the written Constitution, but that point does not undermine anything I discuss here.[230] In any event, in 2004 the Court cited *Curtiss-Wright* with approval for the critical proposition: that there are "preconstitutional powers necessarily inherent in any Federal Government."[231]

In Justice Sutherland's opinion, no trace may be found of the view that law is exhausted by the past positive enactments of authorized lawmakers; indeed, for the majority, there is far more to "law" than the enacted written text. As the Court put it:

> It results that the investment of the federal government with the powers of external sovereignty did not depend upon the affirmative grants of the Constitution. The powers to declare and wage war, to conclude peace, to make treaties, to maintain diplomatic relations with other sovereignties, if they had never been mentioned in the Constitution, would have vested in the federal government as necessary concomitants of nationality. . . . [A series of foreign relations powers], none of which is expressly affirmed by the Constitution, nevertheless exist as inherently inseparable from the conception of nationality. This the court recognized, and in each of the cases cited found the warrant for its conclusions *not in the provisions of the Constitution, but in the law of nations.*[232]

It thus seems unsurprising that the great foreign relations scholar Louis Henkin underscored the anti-originalist character of *Curtiss-Wright*, noting that the claim that "the new United States government was to have major powers outside the Constitution is not intimated in the Constitution itself, in the records of the Convention, in the Federalist papers, or in contemporary debates."[233]

The shockingly anti-originalist idea that "[t]he Union existed before the Constitution" may be one of the most consequential sentences ever to appear in the United States Reports – at least for those who overlook the difference between our small-c constitutional order and the written text of the Constitution and its original understanding. Our constitutional order is and always has been a concrete set of real, extratextual, political institutions, arrangements, and ever-changing norms, unwritten in crucial respects – a concrete order never fully captured by positive law. (There is, by the way, no tension whatsoever between this point and the Court's observation that every political society features a sovereign "supreme will." Relative to any other civil authority, the sovereign is ultimately supreme over the *ius civile*, but it does not follow that the sovereign is unlimited by the law of nations, the natural law, and the divine law. Bodin, who originated or crystallized the theory of absolute civil sovereignty, also thought that the sovereign was bound by the natural and divine law, by fundamental customs of the polity, and by treaties and international law.)[234]

Second and conversely, there is nothing particularly living-constitutionalist about the Court's opinion – and nothing about the progressive unfolding of the law that suggests that the Court's conclusions would have been different in, say, 1836 rather than 1936. Nor do the Court's own precedents feature centrally in the opinion; they are invoked *en passant*, only to confirm a conclusion that has already been reached by reasoning on the basis of the general principles of the *ius gentium*.[235] The same is true of a series of statutes that created similar delegations, which the Court took to have, either by practice or by "liquidation," put a gloss of custom on the written Constitution.[236]

The best way to understand *Curtiss-Wright* – and the reason it is puzzling today – is that it is a decision that sounds in and draws from the classical legal tradition. For the classical tradition, the written law does not exhaust the law. Although written positive enactments (*lex*) are undoubtedly part of the law, the law in a broader sense as a body of general principles (*ius*) includes the *ius gentium*, the (often) unwritten customary law of nations – even when not adopted into our legal system by positive enactments. Those principles not only inform the interpretation of our written instruments, but operate as sources of law in their own right, vesting sovereignty in the Union before the written Constitution even comes into being. This is why the main discussion in *Curtiss-Wright* is focused neither on the original public meaning of particular texts, nor on the Court's precedents as they developed over time, but on general principles of constitutionalism accessible to the reason, or at least to the well-trained reason of the informed lawyer. *Curtiss-Wright* reasons, not so much from the formation of the Constitution, as from the formation of the constitutional order; it is interested in the purposes for which our government was formed, but not in the putative "original meaning" of specific texts.

This account has several important implications. Substantively, if the government of the United States is a creature of international law, it is also limited by that law as a domestic constitutional matter in certain respects. For the United States to contravene international law not only violates that law itself on the international plane, but might also violate the domestic constitutional order, at least with respect to questions bearing on war, territorial control, and other attributes of sovereignty. Our sovereignty, in other words, would be itself both constituted and regulated by principles of international law, by the *ius gentium*. That law is both enabling and constraining, simultaneously; it both empowers and controls public authority in our constitutional order. As Henri de Bracton put it, "law makes the King."[237]

The most important implication, however, is methodological. There is a world that lies beyond our exhausted opposition between progressive living constitutionalism and originalism: the world of the classical legal tradition, drawn from Roman law and the *ius commune* of Europe and still very much living today. That tradition was, for a century and a half, an explicit and central component of our law, which explains why one of the cornerstones of our law of foreign relations and of presidential power is a powerfully, indeed profoundly, counter-originalist decision. Originalism, paradoxically, flattens and even erases the rich legal world of the classical tradition that the founders originally inhabited. *Curtiss-Wright*, then, is merely one example of the lost classical tradition in American law, erased by originalism's rewriting of our history, and desperately in need of recovery.

The Classical Tradition as Our Law

This chapter has emphasized that the classical legal tradition, the matrix that gives rise to common good constitutionalism, was our law, right from the inception. It is not some sort of intrusion into the American scene; indeed, it is originalism that is a latecomer to the American scene. Claims to the contrary are "invented traditions."[238]

Of course it is possible to take passages out of the larger overall context of the classical law, passages that sound originalist standing alone, and then claim, on that basis, that our law has always had (at least) an originalist strand. But on a proper conception of the classical legal tradition, the existence of such passages is unsurprising. The classical conception of law itself explains the authority of the *ius civile* as a deliberate ordering of positive law to the common good, within the space of determination. Of course if we are trying to understand the commands of the public authority, we will want to pay attention to the words used by that authority, and the meanings attached to them when produced. None of that is or should be controversial. But the larger structure of the classical law ensures that these insights do not become hypertrophied or exaggerated, distorting the whole. The *ius civile* enjoys its authority as a specification, and adaptation to local circumstances and to changing circumstances over time, of background norms with which the positive law must be harmonized. In this way, the classical legal tradition aims to read law as *lex* to preserve the larger structure of law as *ius*. In the next two chapters, we will see the distortions that occur when one or another element of this framework is broken out and given exaggerated importance.

Chapter 3
Originalism as Illusion

In recent years, allegiance to the constitutional theory known as originalism has become all but mandatory for American legal conservatives. Every justice and almost every judge nominated by recent Republican administrations has pledged adherence to the faith.[239] At the Federalist Society, the influential association of legal conservatives, speakers talk and think of little else. Even some luminaries of the left-liberal legal academy have moved away from speaking about "living constitutionalism," "fundamental fairness," and "evolving standards of decency," and have instead justified their views in originalist terms.[240] One often hears the catchphrase "We are all originalists now."

Originalism comes in several varieties, and baroque debates about key theoretical ideas rage among its proponents. Underlying these debates is the common view that constitutional meaning was fixed at the time of the Constitution's enactment (or that of relevant amendments), and that this fixed meaning ought to constrain constitutional practice by judges and other officials. Under this umbrella assumption, originalists of various stripes typically offer some version of a further distinction between two stages of the theory: (1) *interpretation*, the ascertainment of meaning, and (2) the *construction* of constitutional or statutory provisions where meaning is equivocal or indeterminate. I will argue, however, that this distinction is illusory, and that it is impossible even to ascribe "meaning" to a constitutional text without some explicit or implicit conception of basic preconditions for meaning such as the rationality of the authority that enacted the text, and the level of generality at which the text should be read – conceptions that will inevitably be laden with normative assumptions.

We also have to distinguish between two distinct uses of originalism: as a full-fledged *normative theory* of how judges and other officials ought to interpret the Constitution and execute their offices, or, alternatively, as a *rhetorical posture* arising out of a particular legal and political struggle. The latter was the "context of discovery" for originalism, while the former is its "context of justification."[241] That is, like all legal theories of real interest, originalism arose out of a concrete political and rhetorical context in which it struggled with an enemy, an antonym – in this case, the progressive legal theorizing of the Warren and Burger Courts. Later, theorists arrived, from the academy and elsewhere, to lend the rhetorical posture intellectual refinement. Originalism is now in a decadent phase in which the elaborate theoretical structure propping it up dominates the landscape of the American legal right. Yet cracks in the edifice have now appeared, and a kind of simmering, widespread discontent is undeniable.

I will begin with originalism as a rhetorical posture (the context of discovery), and then turn to originalism as a theory (the context of justification). The former, I argue, was extremely successful in its time, but is now floundering in very different circumstances. The latter, I argue, is untenable. Originalism as a theory is an illusion. As Ronald Dworkin argued decades ago in a devastating review of Robert Bork's effort to lay out a coherent version of originalism, originalism only purports to have a theory of meaning that stands apart from thick interpretation in light of the principles of political morality. In fact, any determination of "meaning" always already requires interpretation in light of those principles.

Context of Discovery

Alternatives to originalism have long existed on the right, loosely defined. One is libertarian (or "classical liberal") constitutionalism, which emphasizes principles of individual freedom that are often in uneasy tension with the Constitution's original meaning and the founding generation's norms. The founding era was hardly libertarian on a number of fronts that loom large today, such as freedom of speech and freedom of religion;[242] consider that in 1811, the New York courts, in an opinion written by the influential early jurist Chancellor James Kent, upheld a conviction for blasphemy against

Jesus Christ as an offense against the public peace and morals.[243] Important recent work has shown that blasphemy prosecutions occurred regularly throughout not only the founding era but the whole nineteenth century,[244] a point to which I return in Chapter 5. There is no originalist discourse defending blasphemy prosecutions, however. One of the telltale features of originalist jurisprudence, which shows its libertarian leanings and the invented traditions on which it rests, is that the justices who practice it are often the most fervent advocates of expansive free speech protections, far more expansive than could possibly be underwritten by their originalist theory.

Another alternative is Burkean traditionalism, which tries to slow the pace of legal innovation. Here, too, the difference with originalism is clear, because originalism is sometimes revolutionary; consider the Court's originalist opinion declaring a constitutional right to own guns, a startling break with the Court's long-standing precedents.[245] I will return to this disruptive, occasionally even revolutionary quality of originalism shortly. Suffice it to say that the attempt to conflate Burkean traditionalism with originalism repeatedly runs headlong into cases in which originalism, at least without some overriding and entirely external theory of precedent stapled onto it, unsettles long-standing legal traditions. This is no accident; originalism was initially created in order to unsettle the evolving doctrine of the Warren and Burger Courts, which conservatives despised. Disruption was baked into originalism from the beginning.

The alternative schools of thought still have scattered adherents, but originalism has prevailed, mainly because it has met the political and rhetorical needs of legal conservatives struggling against an overwhelmingly left-liberal legal culture. After initially having been developed in the 1970s and 1980s, the theory of originalism enjoyed its initial growth because it helped legal conservatives to survive and even flourish in a hostile environment without fundamentally challenging the premises of the legal liberalism and positivism that dominated both the courts and the academy. It enabled conservatives to oppose constitutional innovations by the Warren and Burger Courts, appealing over the heads of the justices to the putative true meaning of the Constitution itself. When, in recent years, legal conservatism won the upper hand in the Court and then in the judiciary generally, originalism was the natural coordinating point for a creed, something to which potential nominees could pledge fidelity.

Context of Justification

So much for the context of discovery. I turn now to the context of justification. Here we need to make clear the structure of modern (or "new") originalism, which gives itself two different degrees of freedom. First, there is the question of the level of generality at which the original public meaning is specified. Is the "meaning" the specific applications the relevant actors expected would result from the enacted language (call this "specific expectations originalism"), or instead the abstract semantic content of the words they enacted ("abstract originalism")? As we will see, originalism has no internal theoretical resources with which to pin down the choice between these two. That lack of theory allows originalists to tack between applications and semantic content at will according to the dictates of opportunism. A second degree of freedom is afforded by a typical positivist distinction between "interpretation" and "construction," according to which the semantic meaning of the text is first identified, and normative argument is relegated to a "construction zone"[246] when semantic meaning is indeterminate. This is, in essence, the standard positivist distinction between "rules" and "zones of discretion" when rules are ambiguous, vague, or silent on a certain issue.

For prominent cases supposed to be originalist in method, originalism of this kind does not actually take place; it is an illusion, mere talk.[247] What actually happens is that judges recur to implicit or explicit normative principles of political morality – which the judges take to be part of the law – even to determine meaning and to choose the level of generality at which meaning is specified. Importantly, this is not merely some process of "construction." It is not as though judges first determine the meaning, find it ambiguous or otherwise indeterminate, and then introduce principles of political morality. Rather they call upon such principles *even to understand what texts mean*. To attribute meaning to a text requires some conception of the authors' rationality and of the subject they are addressing, at what level of generality, and such a conception is always normatively laden.

I will actually explore two related versions of this argument. Dworkin's argument is that originalism is necessarily illusory, for jurisprudential reasons. A weaker version of the argument is that originalism is in fact illusory in our world, for systematic reasons involving the limited capacities of interpreters, even if one can posit a logically possible world in which originalism actually exists. Let me call these stronger and weaker arguments the *theoretical* and *pragmatic* versions of the thesis that originalism is an illusion. In what follows I will discuss both versions; my claim will be successful so long as *at least* the pragmatic version holds. But I also happen to think the theoretical version holds as well.

Dworkin's Critique

Ronald Dworkin initially developed his critique of originalism in a review of Robert Bork's *The Tempting of America*,[248] and then worked it out over many years, including in a review of Justice Scalia's book *A Matter of Interpretation*.[249] In my view it has never been successfully answered. Dworkin poses a dilemma for originalists; by and large, they tend to confidently grasp one horn or other of the dilemma and offer reasons for doing so, not realizing that by offering this sort of response they are illustrating, not evading, the force of Dworkin's critique.

Dworkin observed that originalism is committed to "public meaning," but that "public meaning" is itself ambiguous, and that originalist judges and other interpreters constantly toss uneasily between the two accounts of meaning; the choice between them can only be made, explicitly or implicitly, on the basis of normative principles of political morality. In one version of originalism, meaning is based on expected applications; in another, meaning is based on the principles embodied in semantic content. A stock illustration is the notion of "cruel and unusual punishment." Should this be taken to refer to a particular set of punishments that, according to the expectations of ratifiers and framers – perhaps every single one of the founding generation – the provision would cover and thus outlaw? (This would seem to follow from the adoption of the expected applications version of meaning.) Or should it be taken at a higher level of generality to refer to an abstract principle, somehow defined (at the highest level of abstraction, a principle against morally unjustified punishments)? Dworkin argued that the choice between these two versions of meaning could not possibly be made from *within* originalist premises. Rather the originalist would always and necessarily – even if implicitly, without admitting it – have to make the choice between the two conceptions of meaning on the basis of normative principles of political morality, not given by the theory itself.[250]

Put differently, the choice between expected applications and semantic principle poses a dilemma for originalists that cannot be resolved simply by insisting on "ordinary meaning," on the fixation of ordinary meaning at the time of enactment, or the putative distinction between "interpretation" and "construction." On either the specific or abstract version of originalism, the putative original meaning of the text has been fixed as of the time of enactment; the dilemma is precisely how to determine which version of meaning is in play.

The dilemma is a serious one because neither the expected applications approach nor the semantic meaning approach is wholly satisfactory. The approach based on expected applications has seemed objectionable to many originalists, and the trend over time has increasingly been to reject it, for two main reasons. On the one hand, specific expectations provide no theoretical criterion for resolving new cases over time that differ from the particular expected applications. Which features of the expected application are legally relevant, and which irrelevant? The moment that one begins to generalize, one needs a theory, and that theory will inevitably be normative, a theory about the *point* of creating the category in the first place. The relevant features can't simply be read off the facts in the way one would read a menu. But if the interpreter is trying out various normative theories for generalizing the expected applications, and testing them for justificatory appeal and fit with surrounding legal doctrines and principles, this is already the Dworkinian project.

Furthermore, if one takes expected applications to be the touchstone of meaning, one seems artificially to constrict what texts *say*, which often outruns the particular applications in the heads of anyone involved in the process of their creation. The enactors themselves may even understand that future interpreters may decide that the enactors' expected applications did not, even at the time the texts were created, capture the full scope of the principle the enactment embodied. This is especially so when new circumstances are apparent or new information has come to light. Enactors who did not think that hanging was a "cruel and unusual" punishment, for example, might expect and even welcome future interpreters deciding otherwise if the advance of knowledge, scientific and moral, showed indisputably that it should be so considered.

On the other hand, however – and this is the other horn of the dilemma – if the approach based on expected applications is rejected, the startling consequence is that the provision might someday come to be understood to bar punishments that *none* of the ratifiers or the public or anyone else in the founding or enacting generation understood to be covered by the relevant language, or would have wanted to be covered, no matter what future interpreters might come to believe. (We will shortly see an example, in the *Bostock* case, of an application that would almost certainly have been vehemently rejected by almost every one of the enacting legislators.) In the latter sense, one wants to ask, what exactly is the force of calling the method "originalism"? As should be immediately apparent, where this sort of conceptual ascent that contradicts the unanimous expectations of the enacting generation is possible, the "original" meaning is "fixed" in only the most nominal sense. No amount of appealing to the "fixation" of original meaning can prevent that sort of conceptual ascent, however.

Living Originalism

Put differently, this second horn of the dilemma embodies the problem of "living originalism," a term propounded by the Yale scholar Jack Balkin, who urges very general readings of the principles underlying constitutional provisions.[251] Likewise, originalists such as

Steven Calabresi have adopted similar versions of originalism that allow principles to be read at dizzyingly high levels of generality.[252] All this creates an "originalism" that is difficult to distinguish from the program of the American Civil Liberties Union or the American Constitution Society. Living originalists, for example, read the Equal Protection Clause as embodying an "anti-caste principle," from which they extrapolate abortion rights and rights of same-sex marriage.[253]

Needless to say, such conclusions have irked many originalists who, after all, turned to the theory as a weapon against precisely this sort of outcome from the judiciary. Here the political and rhetorical point of originalism is turned against its theoretical claims. As Nelson Lund puts it witheringly, "[a] founder of the Federalist Society, Calabresi clerked for Judge Robert H. Bork and Justice Antonin Scalia. He was a special assistant to Attorney General Edwin Meese III and a speechwriter for Vice President Dan Quayle. He went on to become one of the most frequently cited academic originalists of his generation." And, Lund says, "Calabresi has unmistakably abandoned originalism, perhaps unknowingly."[254] This "convergence" of living constitutionalism and originalism, rightly identified as such by Balkin and others,[255] is like the convergence of a predator and its prey.

Note here that, despite Balkin's (impishly subversive) phrase "living originalism," the core problem in this context is *not* whether words possess fixed and durable meanings over time, or instead "living" and changeable meanings. Rather the issue is how, at what level of generality, to determine those (fixed and durable) meanings in the first place. The level of generality at which to interpret "the meaning of the words" is the main problem in and for originalist interpretation, even if we attend *solely* to the meaning of the words as of the time of enactment. When living originalists argue that the founding generation enacted texts whose original meaning embodies general principles of political morality ("ordered liberty," "anti-subordination," or what have you), from which these originalists proceed to deduce rights that would make the founders and modern conservatives alike stare in horror, they aren't arguing against the durability of meaning, nor are they stepping outside the boundaries of the originalist method – as evidenced by their participation in the community of professional originalists. (Balkin is an originalist in good standing who often speaks to the Federalist Society, although one suspects he also propounds his theory of "living originalism" with a certain mischievous intention to subvert originalism. In this he has been supremely successful, by showing that originalism prohibits very little that the progressive jurist would otherwise want to do.)

When stated at a high level of generality, originalism becomes a vacuous commitment that allows interpreters to implement abstract concepts written into the Constitution, such as "liberty" and "equality," in ways that are pragmatically indistinguishable from the progressive constitutionalism that originalism was created and designed to oppose. Because originalism lacks the resources, from within its own premises, to specify the level of generality at which meaning is determined – the resources, in other words, theoretically to justify the choice between specific expectations originalism and abstract semantic originalism, as Dworkin repeatedly argued – there is no way to exclude the possibility of this sort of transformation.

Examples

So far the discussion has been abstract. Let me now turn to the concrete to show, in cases where one ought to find originalism, that at key moments the interpretation (not the construction) of the relevant texts turns on implicit or explicit normative principles. The courts and decisions that claim to be originalist turn out to be, in fact, Dworkinian. They interpret the "meaning" of law by seeking the best constructive interpretation in light of principles of political morality taken to be themselves part of constitutional law, and in light of the meta-principle that today's decision should fit with previous ones and put them in their best possible light. These twin features – what Dworkin calls "fit" and "justification" – will turn out to be what originalist judges actually do. Originalism, in this sense, does not exist. Over and over again, originalism turns out to be a kind of Dworkinian interpretation that dare not speak its own name.

To illustrate the illusory character of originalism, I will use three recent examples from the Roberts Court – a Court that at the relevant time had at least five justices who identify as originalist, and which now has at least six. If originalism is not to be found here, it is not to be found anywhere in real space, whatever the logical possibilities might be. And in fact it is not found here; in all three cases, the Court's decision, purporting to be originalist, is in fact Dworkinian.

Independent agencies

The first example is *Seila Law LLC v. Consumer Financial Protection Bureau*,[256] a 2020 decision in which the Court, per Chief Justice Roberts, held that the Director of the Bureau (hereafter the CFPB) could not be an independent officer, removable only for cause, because the Constitution does not allow agencies to be headed by single-member officials who are independent officers in the legal sense – in contrast to standard independent agencies with multiple heads.[257] The Court held that the CFPB's structure was incompatible with the constitutional design, which "scrupulously avoids concentrating power in the hands of any single individual," except in the case of the president, "the most democratic and politically accountable official in Government . . . elected by the entire Nation."[258] The CFPB's unitary structure, on this view, threatened the core structural principles of self-government and liberty. The Court went on to suggest that in a multimember agency, the members check each other in some way, and that this produces a kind of mutual accountability, an additional safeguard for constitutional liberty:

> The CFPB's single-Director structure contravenes this carefully calibrated system by vesting significant governmental power in the hands of a single individual accountable to no one. . . . [T]he Director may *unilaterally*, without meaningful supervision, issue final regulations, oversee adjudications, set enforcement priorities, initiate prosecutions, and determine what penalties to impose on private parties. With no colleagues to persuade, and no boss or electorate looking over her shoulder, the Director may dictate and enforce policy for a vital segment of the economy affecting millions of Americans.[259]

At critical points in *Seila Law*, the analysis turns on contestable interpretations of abstract principles and uses them to decide what the Constitution means. The majority's opinion is all but frankly Dworkinian; it rests on an effort to read the existing fabric of law in the best constructive light, by reference to considerations of political morality. The point of the Court's arguments is not that, somewhere in the text and original understanding of Article II, a distinction is drawn between single-member-headed agencies and multiple-member-headed agencies. It is that the Court is attributing to the "structure" of the whole constitutional order broad principles, and then arguing for a particular conception of those principles. Justice Kagan characterized the Court's conception of "liberty," for example, as one of "anti-power-concentration."[260] The Court's particular conception is not some straightforward exercise in originalism; it is more like political philosophy. It is contestable and premised on a thick, normative view of constitutional liberty. In that respect, *Seila Law* can be illuminatingly understood as a response to emphatically contemporary concerns. The decision reflects anxiety about the powers of unaccountable bureaucrats, freed from the constraining arm of the president (and hence We the People). As Justice Kagan wrote in dissent, acutely:

It is bad enough to "extrapolat[e]" from the "general constitutional language" of Article II's Vesting Clause an unrestricted removal power constraining Congress's ability to legislate under the Necessary and Proper Clause. It is still worse to extrapolate from the Constitution's general structure (division of powers) and implicit values (liberty) a limit on Congress's express power to create administrative bodies. And more: to extrapolate from such sources a distinction as prosaic as that between the SEC and the CFPB – *i.e.*, between a multi-headed and single-headed agency. That is, to adapt a phrase (or two) from our precedent, "more than" the emanations of "the text will bear." By using abstract separation-of-powers arguments for such purposes, the Court "appropriate[s]" the "power delegated to Congress by the Necessary and Proper Clause" to compose the government.[261]

The point here is not that Justice Kagan is necessarily right or the majority necessarily wrong. It is that the majority is engaged in a process of reasoning from abstract principles of constitutional-political morality – what the Court calls "first principles"[262] – and adopting contested conceptions of those principles, in ways that can only be called Dworkinian. If this is originalism, one wonders what is not originalism. It is not surprising, therefore, that the dissent discusses at some length Dean John Manning's argument[263] that the Constitution contains no general, abstract principles such as "the separation of powers." Nor is it surprising that the Court majority squarely rejected that argument, stating that although "there [is neither] a 'separation of powers clause' [nor] a 'federalism clause' [in the express constitutional text,]" "[t]hese foundational doctrines are instead evident from the Constitution's vesting of certain powers in certain bodies."[264] For the Court, the text's distribution of certain powers to certain bodies is in fact evidence of true, underlying, subsistent constitutional principles that are themselves part of "the law." If this is not Dworkinian, it isn't clear what would be.

The Electoral College

The second example is *Chiafalo v. Washington*,[265] in which the Supreme Court ruled that states may subject "faithless electors" – members of the Electoral College who vote for a candidate other than the one to whom they are pledged – to statutory penalties such as a monetary fine.[266] The opinion for the Court was written by Justice Kagan, but joined by the Chief Justice and Justices Alito, Gorsuch, and Kavanaugh. (Justice Thomas concurred in the judgment, in an opinion that Justice Gorsuch joined as well.) If, as Justice Kagan said, "we are all originalists [now],"[267] one should expect it to show here, if anywhere. In fact, however, *Chiafolo* looks to our developing small-c constitutional practices over time as the touchstone of constitutional legality. (In a moment, I will show that this is entirely consistent with Kagan's point, and that her oft-quoted dictum has been widely misunderstood.)

The main basis for the Court's opinion was what it called "our whole experience as a Nation."[268] The framers may have expected electors to make independent judgments, but alas, "[w]hether by choice or accident, the Framers did not reduce their thoughts about electors' discretion to the printed page."[269] And "established practice," developed since the nineteenth century, authorizes states to reduce electors to a pass-through mechanism.[270] As early as 1864, the English barrister J. F. Stephen had observed acidly that

> the election of the President by electors chosen by the people at large was supposed to be a security for the appointment of men of high character and ability. The security turned out to be worthless, inasmuch as for many years past, the electors have always been so completely pledged before their election that they might as well be dispensed with altogether.[271]

Of course "faithlessness" is ambiguous here; fidelity to the state-enforced pledge might be seen as infidelity to the original conception of the Electoral College itself, which as Stephen noted was intended by its creators and explained to the ratifiers[272] as an independent body[273] of notables deliberating in the public interest. Indeed, the whole line of development that culminates in *Chiafalo* would certainly startle the members of the Convention. As Max Farrand said of the Electoral College scheme in 1913, "of all things done in the convention the members seemed to have been prouder of that than of any other, and they seemed to regard it as having solved the problem for any country of how to choose a chief magistrate."[274]

If originalism is "our law," it is apparently so in some very special, epicyclical sense that does not bar the Nation's developing norms and traditions from so "informing" the interpretation of the written law as to essentially reverse the framers' and ratifiers' publicly stated expectations about a central mechanism of the constitutional plan. One may say all sorts of things to square such a result with originalism – heroic work can be and has been done with concepts like "construction" and "liquidation," and the Court gestures briefly at the latter phrase[275] – but the sheer amount of work one has to do merely raises questions about the value of the originalist enterprise itself, just as one might question the value of a car that must constantly be repaired. In a world in which *post hoc* developments can undo what was, in any rationally purposive sense, thought to be a linchpin of the constitutional plan, it is at best unclear what the force of calling oneself an "originalist" really is, or indeed what it means to say that originalism exists at all.

The same is true if we take "originalism" at a sufficiently high level of abstraction, as do leading originalist scholars like Balkin and Calabresi. Originalists, who tend to take Justice Kagan's famous dictum out of context and treat it as a declaration of surrender to originalism, should by their own lights consider what she actually meant by it. In the full context, the point of saying "we are all originalists [now]" was that, at a high level of abstraction, originalism is indistinguishable from a living form of constitutionalism, because the original understanding will supply only an abstract principle that interpreters will have to apply to changing circumstances over time, according to their best contemporaneous understanding of the principle. Here is what Kagan actually said:

[T]he Framers were incredibly wise men, and if we always remember that, we will do pretty well, because part of their wisdom was that they wrote a Constitution for the ages. And this was very much in their mind. This was part of their consciousness. You know, even that phrase that I quoted yesterday from the Preamble of the Constitution, I said the Constitution was "to secure blessings of liberty." I did not quote the next part of that phrase. It said "blessings of liberty for themselves and their posterity." So they were looking toward the future. They were looking generations and generations and generations ahead and knowing that they were writing a Constitution for all that period of time, and that circumstances and that the world would change, just as it had changed in their own lives very dramatically. So they knew all about change. . . . And I think that they laid down – sometimes they laid down very specific rules. Sometimes they laid down broad principles. Either way we apply what they say, what they meant to do. So in that sense, we are all originalists.[276]

The result of this is Balkin's "convergence": we may all be originalists in some nominal sense, but it excludes nothing that a progressive constitutionalist might otherwise want to do, and leaves it unclear what originalism stands for or what it excludes. It is only in this contentless sense that "we are all originalists [now]."

The Title VII debacle

A now classic, or infamous, example of this sort of "living originalism" (to use Balkin's phrase) is *Bostock v. Clayton County*.[277] A six-justice majority of the Court held, in an opinion written by the uber-originalist Justice Gorsuch, that the prohibition on "discrimination on the basis of sex" in Title VII of the 1964 Civil Rights Act covers discrimination on the basis of sexual orientation and gender identity.[278] The Court expressly defined its project as originalist – it wrote, and emphasized throughout, that "[t]his Court normally interprets a statute in accord with the ordinary public meaning of its terms at the time of its enactment."[279] The Court found sexual orientation and gender identity to be encompassed with sex discrimination by a but-for comparator argument reminiscent of an analytic philosophy seminar: "If the employer fires the male employee for no reason other than the fact he is attracted to men, the employer discriminates against him for traits or actions it tolerates in his female colleague."[280] This purports to show that "it is impossible to discriminate against a person for being homosexual or transgender without discriminating against that individual based on sex."[281] The fact that no one in 1964 thought that sexual orientation or gender identity discrimination were encompassed within sex discrimination was deemed irrelevant; that is mere expected applications originalism, whereas the semantic principle embodied in the statute, properly understood, turned out to be broader.[282]

The inescapable consequence – the price of entry for anyone who approves of decisions like *Bostock* – is to call "originalist" an outcome that, very possibly, not one of the legislators who enacted the statute, or the voters who elected them, would have thought included within the language they enacted. This is a kind of law without mind,[283] antithetical to the classical conception of the public authority as entrusted and charged with the power and duty of making purposive, reasoned ordinations to promote the common good. *Bostock*-style living originalism severs the enactors' understanding of the operative content of their enactment from an abstract principle that the interpreter attributes to the enactment. Because that procedure is hardly inevitable, hardly required by the very nature of interpretation or anything of that sort, this curious, highly abstract "originalism" is always driven by an implicit normative account.

Let me expand upon this point by distinguishing between two basic lines of critique of the *Bostock* decision. The first critique, made by Justice Kavanaugh in dissent, is that *Bostock* just gets originalism wrong.[284] On this view Justice Gorsuch, purporting to write an originalist opinion, erred on the theory's own terms, because Gorsuch failed to understand that originalism tries to capture the *ordinary* public meaning as of the time of enactment, not the *literal* public meaning.[285] "Discrimination on the basis of sex" may or may not include discrimination on the basis of sexual orientation and gender identity, by a process of logical entailment revealed by the sort of comparison cases and counterfactuals used by analytic philosophers. But that is neither here nor there for the work of judges, whose task is to understand what an ordinary user of language would take words to mean (at least absent some term of art). And there is no doubt, either in 1964 or today, that it is no betrayal of ordinary English to say things like "the company discriminated on the basis of sexual orientation, but not on the basis of sex," or vice versa.

Kavanaugh's conclusion from all this is that Gorsuch simply needs to do originalism right. But one might draw a very different conclusion. If originalism is so difficult that one of its leading champions cannot apply it correctly, one might conclude instead that originalism is simply a dangerously unreliable technology, one that induces fatal rates of human error. It is pragmatically irrelevant that, in some logically possible world, a perfect originalist judge would use the technology properly. "Real originalism has never been tried" is a mockery, not a viable constitutional stance. It is more than a bit ironic that originalists harp on the unreality of Dworkin's ideal construct, "Judge

Hercules" – a figure expressly offered as a philosophical heuristic device, a clarifying thought experiment – while arguing that originalism is a juristic technology that is too complex to be handled correctly by an actually existing Supreme Court largely composed of originalists. In other words, Justice Kavanaugh's critique should be taken to suggest, if it suggests anything, what I have called the pragmatic argument for the illusory character of originalism. It is a technology that is too unstable and unreliable to be applied "correctly" in real cases.

A different critique of *Bostock* appeared in Justice Alito's dissent, and it illustrates the other version of the argument – Dworkin's theoretical point that the choice between expected applications originalism and semantic principles originalism can't be made without appealing to normative principles of political morality. Justice Alito emphasized that on the majority's view, the "original public meaning" is taken to be a meaning that literally no one at the time of enactment thought of and that literally no one would have accepted, had it been put to them – as I have suggested, a counterintuitive construal of a method that calls itself "originalism."[286]

As against this, Justice Gorsuch argued two basic points (putting aside an utterly implausible claim that, in fact, as of the time of enactment, the Court's current holding was not unforeseen).[287] The first point was that

> to refuse enforcement just because . . . the parties before us happened to be unpopular at the time of the law's passage, would not only require us to abandon our role as interpreters of statutes; it would tilt the scales of justice in favor of the strong or popular and neglect the promise that all persons are entitled to the benefit of the law's terms.[288]

Second, Justice Gorsuch argued that the expected applications approach would prove inconsistent with too much settled law. "The employer's position also proves too much. If we applied Title VII's plain text only to applications some (yet-to-be-determined) group expected in 1964, we'd have more than a little law to overturn."[289]

In other words, the first of Gorsuch's two arguments sounds in justification, appealing to a principle of impartial justice and equality before the law; the second sounds in fit, in continuity with past decisions. But those are Dworkinian claims. Here at the heart of *Bostock* is the question whether to define the original public meaning according to expected applications or according to semantic principles. The Court's argument for the latter approach neither does nor could draw upon resources internal to originalism itself; rather it draws upon normative principles of political morality (justification), including the principle of continuity with the past (fit). *Bostock*, like *Seila Law*, like *Chiafolo*, and like so many products of the Roberts Court, is ultimately Dworkinian. In this, one of the most prominent originalist decisions of the Roberts Court, it turns out that originalism is illusory.

Hybrid Views

I conclude with a brief mention of some hybrid views that attempt somehow to combine originalism with elements of classical law. There is a handful of rather similar views in this space.[290] In any of these versions, the basic idea is to combine originalism with an emphasis on the common good.

As a rhetorical posture in what passes for the "marketplace of ideas," this sort of position is straightforwardly attractive. Recall that the classical approach itself includes positive law, in the form of *lex*, or more broadly the *ius civile* promulgated by particular jurisdictions in order to determine and implement background legal principles. The thought naturally arises, then, that one might claim to have it both ways – and appeal to all concerned – by professing adherence to the classical law at the level of overall framework while plugging in originalism, as it were, as the reigning method for interpreting the positive-law part of the classical framework.

The approach fails, however. The combination is unstable in principle. Even if it is rhetorically appealing to paste the phrases "common good" and "originalism" together, the glue will not hold. While as I have argued the classical law includes *positive law* in the sense of the *ius civile*, and indeed puts positive law into a right relationship with law generally, originalist *positivism* is a different approach altogether. The latter, antithetically to the classical law, aims to exclude any consideration of *ius* from the interpretation of *lex* (except insofar as the positive lawmaker itself happens to adopt *ius*), and thus cannot be combined in a stable way with common good constitutional interpretation.

For concreteness, let me focus on a view advanced by Jeff Pojanowski and a co-author, Kevin Walsh, under the label "enduring originalism."[291] This view attempts to, in effect, confine originalism to the space in which the constitutional order is itself subject to determination. It argues a series of second-order propositions: (1) the common good requires that society coordinate on a settled, stable, and adequately just constitutional framework for common life; (2) within the space of determination, where the choice is among reasonably just frameworks, the natural law does not take sides, as it were, on questions like what the precise scope of presidential powers is, or whether judicial review is available for given questions; and finally (3) applying originalism to such questions provides the stability and durability of legal meanings that allow a reasonably just framework to operate over time.[292] Note that this type of view claims to work even if the natural law exists, or despite its existence, because it confines originalism to the space of determination, as to which natural law does not specify anything in particular.

The argument either fails to state a view different than the classical law, or, to the extent it is distinctive, fails on its own terms. As stated it already concedes a key methodological point: originalism cannot be defended on the ground that interpretation "just works that way," or that originalism just is inherent in the enterprise of discerning the meaning of law, or inherent in the rule of law, or anything like that. Instead the argument is that originalism must be justified by higher-order principles of political morality, such as constitutional stability, constraining judicial discretion, promoting democracy, or what have you. This is non-positivist at the level of justificatory method, even if it tries to preserve a kind of positivist originalism at the operative level.

But then it is at best unclear what in this scheme is distinctively originalist, for the classical law already has this two-level structure. If the point of "enduring originalism" is that no well-functioning legal system allows just any official to consider the full range of first-order moral argumentation at every moment, that is a truism. The classical law certainly does not allow that. As we have already seen, the classical law structures and channels consideration of the *ius naturale* and other sources of law by means of an institutional division of authority between lawmakers and law-appliers, by doctrines of deference, by presumptive textualism, and other devices. Whether the discretion at issue is that of judges or of other officials, constraint of interpretive discretion is already built in to the classical law. The end result is the phenomenon of convergence we have discussed. Attempts to combine originalism with non-positivist foundations merely collapse back into the classical law, albeit under the strictly nominal label of "originalism."

Where "enduring originalism" is distinctively originalist in substance, on the other hand, the problems it faces are daunting. The first and perhaps main problem is that proposition (3) above fails: the putative fixation of original meaning by itself cannot guarantee durability. Absent further normative judgment at the point of application, of the very sort the theory is intended to exclude, *fixation of meaning does nothing to prevent the mutable, progressive form of "living originalism"* championed by Balkin and others. To repeat, the crucial question is the one identified by Dworkin: at what level of generality should interpreters read the (fixed) meaning of abstract constitutional texts like "equal protection of the laws" and "due process of law"? Asserting over and over again, at ever-increasing volume, that the meaning must be fixed as of the time of enactment simply does not tell us *what* that meaning is, at what level of generality it should be read, not without additional normative argument.

The so-called living originalists cheerfully deny, with a straight face, that they argue for a "change in meaning" or any such thing; they cheerfully deny that they threaten the enduring character of the constitutional framework. Rather they argue for a particular, but abstract, reading of what that framework supposedly always provided. They read the original and enduring meaning, in other words, at a sufficiently high level of generality so that, *without change of meaning,* it can encompass whatever strange moral novelties later generations have dreamt up. No amount of insistence that meaning must endure over time comes to grips with their argument. Here, the end result is the collapse of originalism, not into the classical tradition, but into standard versions of progressive living constitutionalism.

One might try to fortify Pojanowski's argument against the ever-present possibility of "living originalism" by arguing that meaning should be read at a lower level of generality, according to the specific expectations of the framers and ratifiers, in order to promote durability and stability. But that merely illustrates the core methodological problem, which is that originalism by itself cannot yield any such conclusion about the level of generality; further contestable principles of political morality must be invoked to justify it. And in any event, the choice for a low level of generality is hardly self-evident even on the terms of the theory, for reading constitutional provisions according to specific expectations actually undermines durability and stability on another dimension. As the founding era recedes into the remote past, specific expectations will cover fewer and fewer cases that actually arise, leaving more and more to the unsettled present judgment of new interpreters. For an old written constitution such as ours, rarely amended, the proposal is a nonstarter.

The inability to exclude the restless mutations of "living originalism" merely exemplifies a larger problem, which is that no account of the value of settlement and stability can fully exclude normative judgment at the point of application. Those who apply the law must inevitably, in some domain of cases, have recourse to general background principles of law and to the natural law in order to decide how texts should best be read. Pojanowski, in other words, does not clearly come to grips with the problem identified by Aquinas (and, much later, by modern legal theorists) that the limits of foresight on the part of the lawmaker inevitably give rise to "hard cases," in which the rule the lawmaker prescribed for ordinary cases is ambiguous, or is vague, or otherwise misfires – fails to track the common good – due to unusual circumstances.

In easy cases, where all relevant legal sources point in the same direction and the law's commands neatly track the common good, any version of originalism or positivist interpretation will reach the same result as classical legal interpretation. We are not to imagine that classical interpreters are constantly invoking higher law or claiming that cases are extraordinary. As we have seen, in the great bulk of ordinary cases, they proceed by means of a presumptive textualism (albeit justified on different grounds than modern positivism) that handles the great bulk of ordinary cases. In easy cases, then, there is no difference between originalist and classical interpretation from the standpoint of considerations of legal predictability, certainty, and stability. As Dworkin pointed out, those considerations are themselves directly justifiable as a matter of political morality, and are thus easily welcomed and taken aboard by non-positivist modes of interpretation.[293]

What happens in hard cases like *Riggs v. Palmer*, however? What happens when, due to the limits of foresight, texts are irreducibly ambiguous, conflict with powerful principles and background norms of the legal system (*ius*), or otherwise seem absurd as applied to unusual circumstances, giving rise to a grave question about how the legal sources are to be applied and reconciled? Where the specified determinations are ambiguous or in which the central cases they are intended to address encounter an exceptional situation, the relevant determinations must be interpreted – and in our own legal tradition, historically speaking, have in fact been interpreted – in light of background principles of the *ius naturale* and the *ius gentium*, the ends of rightly ordered law, and the larger ends of temporal government. In such cases, the justification of originalism by reference to certainty and stability loses all force; there is no escape from normative argument, internal to law, to determine what the law provides. When hard cases arise, justifications sounding in legal predictability, certainty, stability, and the like have *already* failed.[294]

Pojanowski's argument implicitly compares clear, settled positive rules with "a sea of competing, unentrenched norms."[295] But this is never the issue in hard cases. There is no longer any question of simply "following the clear text" or "following the original understanding"; the whole question is how exactly the text is to be understood and interpreted in the face of ambiguity, reconciled with other indisputable commitments of the legal system itself, or interpreted in the face of seemingly absurd results, in which surface meaning patently contradicts the common good. This is what the classical lawyers mean when they distinguish "the letter of the statute" from "the statute," a locution that sounds nonsensical to the modern positivist. The classical lawyers mean that the statute as *lex* must be harmonized with the statute as part of a more general body of law (*ius*) oriented to the common good. But *ius* may be just as settled and entrenched as *lex*, albeit in different ways. The dangerous pathology of originalism is that by focusing to excess on one part of the overall framework, enacted *lex*, it distorts the whole. In the end, it is a mere conceptual error (a "nirvana fallacy") to compare putatively "clear" texts with an implausible vision of chaotic, unstructured legal principles.

So far I have said nothing about the basic empirical supposition underlying Pojanowski's argument, one that is by no means obviously sound. Indeed it seems obviously suspect. The idea is that original-ism conduces to stability and durability over time, but there is little reason to think this is true. It is an entirely contingent question whether originalism does or does not, in fact, promote systemic goods of settlement, stability, and coordination; and the evidence from our world hardly suggests that it does. In our world, originalism is quite often practiced as a disruptive method, an essentially Protestant method of hermeneutic that, taken to its logical extreme, invokes *sola scriptura* to unsettle doctrines long established in the law. Now the method need not be taken to that extreme – the fainthearted interpreter may flinch from the logical consequences of originalist premises, or claim that the original understanding itself licenses the doctrine of precedent – but the potential for radicalism creates a kind of threatening overhang for any long-standing body of legal doctrine. (As Chapter 5 will mention, there has been a spate of recent origi-nalist proposals, judicial and academic, to overturn long-standing doctrines of administrative law, with potentially vast disruptive con-sequences.) Originalism's disruptive quality should be unsurprising once we reflect that the original idea of originalism, as it were, was to oppose and unsettle the progressive law made during the Warren and Burger Courts. As with the Protestantism it instantiates, originalism is at bottom a mode of rebellion against an established order and its developing doctrine. This is not, of course, to say that disruption is necessarily bad – it depends on what is being disrupted, and why – but it does make it difficult to defend originalism as a guarantor of stability.

Put another way, "enduring originalism" needs to distinguish two very different questions: (1) whether the common good underwrites operating-level originalism as of 1789 or 1868; (2) whether the common good underwrites operating-level originalism as of 2022. These two situations turn out to be very different because in 2022 it is just true that much or most of our law, as practiced since 1789 or 1868, has been profoundly non-originalist. In the second situation, introducing originalism into a (largely) non-originalist system threatens the very kind of disruption and dis-coordination that the view aims to prevent through originalism.

Finally, while settlement and coordination are important goods, they are hardly the only goods. Second-order considerations are important, but so too are first-order ones. The classical tradition emphasizes that justice is the ultimate aim of law, and that peace and justice are both fundamental aims of law. If the originalist regime supposedly underwritten by the common good yields "stability" of a sort by producing a steady, predictable stream of morally horrid first-order results, or merely fails to prevent such results, then the common good condemns rather than supports originalism. At a minimum there should be some reflective equilibrium between the second-order goods of settlement and durability, on the one hand, and evaluation of the justice of first-order outcomes, on the other. Otherwise the praise of second-order goods threatens to become a kind of sacred fetish, overriding all first-order considerations in the name of a partial and myopic account of what justice requires.

In this sense, Pojanowski faces a typical dilemma, whose structure is familiar from debates over the choice between rule-utilitarianism and act-utilitarianism.[296] The appeal to enduring settlement and stability, their argument runs, would be undermined if interpreters could, at the point of application, ever recur to first-order assessments of whether the particular decision does or does not track the substantive content of the natural law. On the other hand, because the justification for that approach ultimately sounds in natural law, a stream of first-order results inconsistent with the natural law purchases a kind of stability at the price of everything else that natural lawyers are supposed to care about. Why this lexical priority for stability (subject only to some sort of threshold of sufficient or adequate justice) is the right view of what the natural law requires is at best unclear. Put differently, if interpreters are issuing decisions directly contrary to the intrinsic limits of the *ius naturale*, the limits of determination have already been transgressed. As I argue in Chapter 5, that is indeed our situation.

The sting in this dilemma, of course, is that if conversely the "enduring originalism" approach *ever* allows interpreters to consider principles of political morality in hard cases, at the point of application, then the game is up. At that point, one is merely arguing over the precise scope of discretion for interpreters in what is essentially a regime of common good constitutionalism. The theoretical distinctiveness of the originalist view grounded in stability has already been forfeited.

In the end, Pojanowski's worry about "a sea of competing, unentrenched norms" is telling and characteristic. Animating much of originalism, however it is nominally justified, is a single anxiety: the horror of judgment. For the originalist, to cut loose the anchor of text and original understanding inevitably means drifting helplessly amidst a welter of normative arguments, without a common standard.

We have seen that in fact originalism by no means avoids normative judgments; it merely leaves them implicit and unacknowledged. But the fundamental anxiety is also unjustified in itself. For most of the world outside the United States, that anxiety is nearly incomprehensible. The world is full of legal systems influenced by the *ius commune*, few of which practice originalism in anything like the American form, and many of which are demonstrably governed by the rule of law. In those systems, enacted text is taken very seriously precisely because taking text seriously is itself an important contribution to the common good, but judgments based on enduring principles are brought to bear in order to understand what text means. That judgment is not formless or chaotic, but rather structured by traditions, presumptions, institutional division of labor, and jurisprudence, including jurisprudence about the allocation of authority among various actors within the system. Originalism's horror of judgment is deeply parochial.

The main point is clear. The hybrid views that attempt to fuse the common good with originalism, however appealing they may seem at a political and rhetorical level, are intrinsically unstable, because they attempt to combine an essentially positivist approach with the classical approach. The latter respects enacted positive law (in the sense of *lex*), but is not itself positivist in the modern sense. In the classical law, the basis of respect for *lex*, and the manner in which it is translated into interpretive principles, are quite different than anything found in originalist theory properly so called, and the two are ultimately incompatible.

More generally, even apart from the hybrid versions, originalism as such lacks the theoretical resources needed to solve the dilemmas we have examined. The epicycle to which originalists often resort – a sharp distinction between "meaning," which is fixed, and "applications," which are shifting – is a counsel of despair. That distinction is not the remedy for the ills of originalism, but the disease itself; it is the very thing that allows originalism to be turned into, in effect, a form of progressive and very much living constitutionalism. Jurisprudence is ultimately a practical art, the art of doing justice according to law in particular cases. To posit, in a blindly fideistic act, an eternal fixed "meaning" floating above any particular application is not only a case of poor legal theology, but has no cash value in reality. Originalism is not so much wrong as illusory.

Chapter 4

Progressive Constitutionalism and Developing Constitutionalism

If originalism is illusory, what of its main competitor, progressive constitutionalism? The latter approach comes in a number of partially overlapping variants. Sometimes the stress is on the "living tree" of constitutionalism,[297] sometimes – in Anglo-American theory – on the "common-law" aspect of constitutionalism,[298] and sometimes on what the Court calls "the evolving standards of decency that mark the progress of a maturing society."[299]

I have two objectives in this chapter. The first is simply to expound and critique the true nature of legal progressivism, which is rooted in a particular mythology of endless liberation through the continual overcoming of the reactionary past. Animated by this mythology, progressive jurisprudence restlessly defines new targets to be overcome. In so doing it distorts the real nature of law by instrumentalizing it to serve the will of individuals who seek liberation from any and all unchosen constraints. (This is so even when, as a proximate issue of policy, progressivism transfers an issue from the "private" to the "public" sphere. The ultimate objective is always a further liberation of the human capacities.) It thereby uncouples law from reason, the exercise of which is grounded in the natural law and directed toward the common good.

Second, I ask whether common good constitutionalism is or is not progressive, in some sense. If originalism is an illusion, does it not follow that common good constitutionalism must be a species of living constitutionalism?

My answer is no, for we have to draw a distinction. It is true that under common good constitutionalism, the original public meaning of enacted positive texts is not the sole touchstone of constitutionality.

It does not follow, however, that there is no fixed touchstone at all. Originalists constantly posit this false alternative, in which the only choices are original meaning on the one hand or "subjective preferences" and "living constitutionalism" on the other. (On the originalist view, it is inexplicable that the world features any number of nations that do not practice originalism yet are indisputably governed by the rule of law.) Rather, common good constitutionalism holds that enduring, objective principles of just governance inform positive law, the law of nations, and the natural law alike. These principles do not themselves evolve, although their applications may develop, over time, in changing circumstances. To adapt a famous phrase of the Oxford theologian and literatus St. John Henry Newman, the applications of those principles "change in order to remain the same."[300]

So I will say that common good constitutionalism is a kind of *developing constitutionalism*, but not a kind of progressive constitutionalism. Developing constitutionalism celebrates continuity with the enduring principles of the past; it recognizes change in applications only insofar as necessary in order for those principles to unfold in accordance with their true natures and to retain those natures in new environments. Progressive constitutionalism, by contrast, treats legal principles as themselves changing over time in the service of an extrinsic agenda of radical liberation. In so doing, it instrumentalizes the law.

The Liturgy of Progressive Constitutionalism: *Obergefell* and Its Aftermath

In 2015, *Obergefell v. Hodges*[301] announced a constitutional right to same-sex marriage, founded on a constitutional right to "define and express [one's] identity."[302] The Chief Justice, in dissent, complained about the majority's "entirely gratuitous" aspersions against supporters of traditional marriage: "It is one thing for the majority to conclude that the Constitution protects a right to same-sex marriage; it is something else to portray everyone who does not share the majority's 'better informed understanding' as bigoted."[303] In this, the Chief Justice betrayed a deep misunderstanding about what sort of activity he was participating in. He thought that he was participating in a legal decision. In fact, he was participating in a ritual drama – as the villain. The celebration of progressive judicial heroism, and its overcoming of the bigotry of the ages, requires the very aspersions that the Chief Justice thought gratuitous.

The progressive judge instrumentalizes the law in the service of a very particular liberationist narrative, in which "rights" are continually "expanded" to free an ever-larger set of individuals from unchosen obligations and constraints – legal, moral, and traditional, even biological. I have argued elsewhere that progressive constitutionalism is the embodiment, in law, of the "liturgy of liberalism" – the repetitive impulse of liberal political theology to celebrate a sacramental moment of overcoming of the unreason and darkness of the traditional past.[304] I will not repeat those arguments here, but take them as incorporated by reference. For present purposes, what matters is that the legal progressive celebrates the heroism of judges or other officials who overcome the forces of reaction, liberating legal subjects from putatively irrational constraints founded in arbitrary power. This is what gives legal progressivism its restless and aggressive dynamism.

The heroes and canonized saints of legal progressivism – think Ruth Bader Ginsburg – are invariably agents who have *produced* social or political "change," rather than those who have, say, fended off change. Another corollary is that the progressive legal imagination has an ever-receding horizon. Whatever the question, whether race relations, women's rights, gender identity, or what have you, the *bien-pensant* judge should always be able to say, "We have made progress, but there is still much to do." But of course, even after more progress is made, the goal never seems to have come any closer; the real goal is itself the never-ending celebration of the overcoming of unchosen constraints.

Given this, the dynamic character of progressive legalism is structural, not contingent. It constantly, and at an ever-increasing tempo, disrupts traditions and views that have constituted the very foundations of our law, condemning them as rooted in "animus." Consider the Obama administration's relentless attempt to force the Little Sisters of the Poor to either fund abortifacient contraceptives or, at least, to take action to pass the responsibility elsewhere.[305] The very point of the administration's conduct, on my view, was not (or not only) to force one smallish order of nuns to provide contraceptives – indeed, the very fact that the administration offered a "voluntary" opt-out underscores that the real objective lay elsewhere. Rather, the objective was ceremonial – to force the nuns to *acknowledge publicly* the progressive state's just authority even in matters of religion, the authority to require *either* provision *or* the exercise of an opt-out, as the state saw fit. The main point was to stage a public, sacramental celebration of the justice of progress and of the overcoming of reactionary opposition.

Another example involves *Obergefell* itself. One puzzle is why such a judicial decision was necessary at all, when the tide of politics was running in favor of same-sex marriage anyway. Simple nonintervention, by means of any of the standard techniques available to the majority justices, would very plausibly have attained the same policy ends with far less political conflict. As far as instrumental political rationality went, all that was necessary was to do nothing.

But a conspicuous conflict with the settled *mores* of millennia was, of course, the point. On the progressive view, it was right and just to have same-sex marriage not merely embodied in law, but declared a requirement of fundamental justice, coupled with a conspicuous defeat of the forces of reaction. *Obergefell*'s radical and public dismissal of a legal restriction that prevailed in Western law for millennia, stamping it as unreasoned prejudice and animus, was no accident. The dynamic commitments of legal progressivism are illuminated and measured precisely where, and because, it departs from the inherited constraints of our law.

Instrumentalized Law

I mentioned that the progressive legalist instrumentalizes the law in the service of the relentlessly liberationist project. What exactly does that mean? On the classical view, law is an ordinance of reason for the common good. To instrumentalize the law is to use it as a tool for extrinsic ends that warp its true nature. As Aquinas observed, a law that is out of step with natural justice (procedural or substantive) does not simply become no-law, as though it had never been created; rather, it results in a perverted caricature of law.[306]

Progressives and originalists instrumentalize law in different ways. Originalists, as positivists, treat law as simply will, not reason – the uncommanded will of the sovereign, or (in the more modern, softer version) norms created by officials authorized to do so by a conventional rule of recognition, a convention ultimately resting on nothing other than social acceptance – a softer, more diffuse form of collective will. Progressives also treat law as an instrument of the will rather than the reason, but in a different way, as a means to liberate the individual will from all unchosen constraints. Under either approach, law is treated as "a means to an end,"[307] not in the sense that it is directed purposively to the common good – law rightly understood is internally and intrinsically ordered to the end of the real common good of the community – but in the sense that the inner integrity of the law is twisted for extrinsic, unrelated purposes.

Progressivism thus treats the law as an instrument that must be bent toward the realization of ever-more radical forms of individual liberation and social egalitarianism. This is not to say, of course, that progressivism does not turn enthusiastically to state coercion, but it does so always in the name of the liberation of the individual from the unreasoning forces of tradition, authority, and even natural biology. "Though American conservatives often speak of the Progressive movement as a corruption of liberalism, it is a natural, even correct outgrowth of the liberal achievement in a democratic context to be concerned with identifying and expanding the *conditions* of liberty (health, security, etc.) – and this expansion was precisely what the Progressives attempted to bring about."[308]

Developing Constitutionalism

Under developing constitutionalism, the fundamental background principles of the constitutional order, derived from the natural law and the law of nations and then incorporated (by determination) into the positive law, remain constant over time. Interpreters develop those principles in changing circumstances, unfolding their logic, but the principles themselves are not understood to be subject to the interpreters' sovereign will. Common good constitutionalism thus recognizes the phenomenon of development of doctrine, but not for progressive, liberationist, and disruptive ends. Rather the purpose is to preserve the rational principles of the constitutional order as the circumstances of the political, social, and economic environment change. In this sense, the aim of developing constitutionalism is fundamentally "conservative" under one familiar use of that polysemous term. In another sense, however, it is not conservative at all in the current American sense, because it does not merely urge caution and a slow pace of change. Instead it posits that law has a real nature, an objective integrity that transcends the particulars of any given constitutional order.

To distinguish developing constitutionalism from progressive constitutionalism, one needs an account of which developments are genuine and which are corrupt. This chapter aims to sketch and apply such an account. I outline and then apply to real cases Newman's famous "notes" or indicia that sort genuine developments from corruptions.[309] The latter are evolutions in which the relevant principle is *itself* taken to change – a form of modernism, the continual overcoming of benighted tradition that powers progressive constitutional law.

I begin by emphasizing the positive, offering two models of developing constitutionalism consistent with the common good. The first is Justice Sutherland's famous opinion in *Village of Euclid, Ohio v. Ambler Realty Co.*,[310] notorious to libertarians, which upheld a municipal zoning scheme as against claims that it infringed upon property rights. *Euclid* demonstrates that non-originalist constitutionalism need not be progressive; there is a third way, the way of the classical legal tradition. The second positive model is a contribution to the *ius gentium*, an international consensus declaration in favor of pro-life principles signed in October 2020.[311] The declaration underscores that the development of international human rights principles need not take on standard progressive content, under which abortion is one of the holiest sacraments. I then turn to an anti-model. Armed with Newman's "notes" of false or corrupt development, I return to the Court's decision in *Obergefell v. Hodges*, which declared a constitutional right of same-sex marriage, as a prime example of progressive sacramental constitutionalism. Taken together, the positive and negative models are meant to argue in support of a constitutionalism that is both flexible and traditionalist – very much in the spirit of the classical law.

Newman and the Development of Doctrine

To explain the categories of legitimate and corrupt development, I will draw upon the famous treatment of the development of doctrine by St. John Henry Newman – a treatment that immediately concerned theological doctrine, but that expressly addressed doctrine from many domains of human life, and drew on a wide range of examples. For Newman, development was the process by which enduring principles, themselves unchanging, could find fresh applications in changing circumstances, and by so doing could unfold their real natures.

Newman articulated seven "notes" of genuine development, as opposed to corruption: (1) "preservation of type," which in his language means unity of external expression; (2) "continuity of principles"; (3) "power of assimilation"; (4) "logical sequence"; (5) "anticipation of its future"; (6) "conservative action"; and (7) "chronic vigor."[312] I will not parse through these individually, because their essential aim and thrust is clear enough. Newman identifies markers or indicators that the later doctrine is essentially continuous with the earlier one and grows out of it, rather than representing a break with the past that mutilates or fundamentally transforms the core and essence of the doctrine. A valid development, then, merely amplifies a legal principle's internal plan of growth or changes its accidental expression under new circumstances. "To borrow Newman's analogy: An acorn that somehow changed into a walnut would be a mutation. But an acorn that never developed into an oak would be lifeless."[313]

Although progressive constitutionalists sometimes adopt this metaphor of the "living tree" for themselves, in practice they mean something very different by it, such that the fundamental constitutional principles of the past are themselves seen to have been benighted, and therefore must be overcome. For Newman, those principles are to be tended and developed into full growth. From this standpoint, progressive constitutionalism is not a relative or neighbor of developing constitutionalism. Instead the two are in fact opposites, antonyms. Progressive constitutionalism (as exemplified by *Obergefell*) is akin to modernism in theology, which urges evolution of principles themselves rather than faithful applications of them in different circumstances that present themselves over time.[314] For Newman, by contrast, the essential aim of the theory of legitimate development is, in a sense, profoundly conservative. It is to ensure that "old principles reappear under new forms" such that "[a doctrine] changes with them in order to remain the same." As circumstances change restlessly over time, principles must develop – in Newman's sense – precisely in order to retain their enduring, inherent shape.

A Model Opinion

Let us now turn to real cases and see how they fare in light of Newman's schema. In a 1926 case that is well known to American law students, *Village of Euclid v. Ambler Realty Co.*,[315] Justice Sutherland wrote for the Court to uphold a zoning scheme in Ohio. Drawing upon a deferential version of the police power framework, Sutherland announced that "if the validity of the legislative classification for zoning purposes be fairly debatable, the legislative judgment must be allowed to control."[316] Implicitly drawing upon the ideas of determination and deference within a margin of appreciation, Sutherland added

it may thereby happen that not only offensive or dangerous industries will be excluded, but those which are neither offensive nor dangerous will share the same fate. But this is no more than what happens in respect of many practice-forbidding laws which this Court has upheld, although drawn in general terms so as to include individual cases that may turn out to be innocuous in themselves. ... The inclusion of a reasonable margin to insure effective enforcement, will not put upon a law, otherwise valid, the stamp of invalidity. ... In the light of these considerations, we are not prepared to say that the end in view was not sufficient to justify the general rule of the ordinance, although some industries of an innocent character might fall within the proscribed class. It cannot be said that the ordinance in this respect "passes the bounds of reason and assumes the character of a merely arbitrary fiat."[317]

Euclid thus illustrates the classical framework of deferential judicial review under an arbitrariness standard. It also illustrates the status of property rights within a larger framework ordered to the common good. In that view, property rights – although recognized as an important component of human dignity and development – nonetheless have a secondary status, both in the sense that they are the product of civil determination, and in the sense that the public authority may and should regulate them in the interests of the common good.

For my purposes here, however, the critical issue lies elsewhere: Sutherland's further argument that under an evolving conception of constitutionalism, the legal authority of the state might *expand* over time, through the application of constant principles to changing circumstances:

Regulations the wisdom, necessity and validity of which, as applied to existing conditions, are so apparent that they are now uniformly sustained, a century ago, or even half a century ago, probably would have been rejected as arbitrary and oppressive. Such regulations are sustained, under the complex conditions of our day, for reasons analogous to those which justify traffic regulations, which, before the advent of automobiles and rapid transit street railways, would have been condemned as fatally arbitrary and unreasonable. And in this there is no inconsistency, for, *while the meaning of constitutional guaranties never varies, the scope of their application must expand or contract to meet the new and different conditions which are constantly coming within the field of their operation.* In a changing world, it is impossible that it should be otherwise.[318]

This is, in effect, a non-originalist, developmental justification for the administrative state put in the framework of common good constitutionalism and grounded in the Due Process Clause. Background principles of the classical constitutional order establish the legitimate authority of the state to specify rights within reasonable bounds and to arbitrate among competing rights when they conflict. Those principles do not change, but their application changes as the economy and society change and develop over time, and legal doctrine develops accordingly. Greater complexity and interdependence imply greater scope for the guiding hand of public authority.

Sutherland here shows that, contrary to a widespread recent assumption, *the unfolding development of doctrine over time need not be a libertarian project*, one that increases individual autonomy in ever-more elaborate and insistent ways. Progressive living constitutionalism assumes, usually implicitly, an individualist theory of rights in which autonomy expands relentlessly; the progressive often assumes, without any basis whatsoever, that the unfolding path of the law will always go in a progressive direction. (In the limiting case, becoming aware of the problem, the progressive may attempt to mandate a no-backsliding principle[319] as a matter of constitutional law.)[320] Conversely, originalists often implicitly assume the same, although they find that process objectionable – except as to property rights and economic rights.

Euclid shows that both views are incorrect by contradicting their common assumption that developing constitutionalism is a one-way ratchet in favor of "expanding liberty," understood in opposition to communal aims. Rather, doctrinal development over time is perfectly consistent with the law becoming ever more oriented to the common good, understood as itself *including* the good of individuals and their liberties. As economic and social relations become increasingly interdependent, it becomes ever more obvious that no rights are truly "individual" and that one person's exercise of rights invariably affects others and society generally. Applying unchanging principles to new circumstances, the law allows increasing scope for regulatory determinations that shape, constrain, and adjust rights to order them to the common good. In a more recent case, the Court reached a similar conclusion while interpreting the requirement that governmental takings of property be for a "public use," under the so-called "takings" clause of the Fifth Amendment (and by incorporation the

Fourteenth Amendment):[321] "our jurisprudence has recognized that the needs of society . . . have evolved over time in response to changed circumstances. . . . [O]ur public use jurisprudence has wisely eschewed rigid formulas and intrusive scrutiny in favor of affording legislatures broad latitude in determining what public needs justify the use of the takings power."[322] This is determination in the service of developing constitutionalism, a model of how judicial review should work.

Furthermore, as I will discuss in a later section on rights, the correct way to think about this unfolding of public authority over time is *not* that the individual's rights are "overridden" by collective interests. It is that rights are always already grounded in and justified by what is due to each person and to the community. Adjusting them in light of the common good is to unfold their true nature and to identify their scope and limits, not to compromise or overpower them.

There is thus no reason why we may not transpose *Euclid*'s insight from property rights to so-called personal rights. (Of course, on certain conceptions of rights, property rights just are personal rights, and conversely, on certain conceptions, the basic justification for personal rights just is "self-ownership." If so, the point I want to make is even easier.) The common-law entitlements often used to define personal "rights" and "liberties," not merely property rights, are themselves ordinances created by the public authority as determinations of background principles of *ius naturale* and *ius gentium*. Those determinations legitimately aim to order rights to the common good, setting the boundaries of rights and adjusting apparent conflicts among rights to that end. This is emphatically not to affirm a utilitarian doctrine that such rights can be overridden on the basis of aggregate utility. Intrinsic evils are intrinsic evils and no government may command them. Instead, the point is that the common good of family, city, nation, and even of the international order is itself the good of individuals, and that rights must be ordered accordingly.

What might be an example of a *Euclid* for civil liberties? I will mention only one important possibility to suggest how this sort of argument might run. Our free speech law, largely a product of the Holmesian skepticism and Millian libertarianism that underpins the "marketplace of ideas," is in roughly the same obsolete condition as the nineteenth-century vision of property rights to which Sutherland adverted in *Euclid*; it must be updated in light of changing circumstances. We have learned primarily from experience, and secondarily from work in economics, social psychology, and other social sciences, how radically imperfect is the marketplace of ideas.[323] That marketplace displays a pervasive and increasing complexity and interdependence of the sort that, in *Euclid*, justified an expanding scope for regulation of property relationships. Indeed, it has become increasingly impossible to even disentangle the concept of a marketplace of ideas from property relationships in the first place.

If this broad claim is true – and I will make it more specific in the next chapter, with examples from current free speech law – the consequence is that the market for ideas should no more be seen as presumptively immune from authoritative guidance than is any market for goods. Of course the public authority too may err, but as in *Euclid*, the ordinary response to that possibility is judicial review for arbitrariness. Or, as thinkers as diverse as J. F. Stephen[324] and Ronald Coase[325] observed, we do not ordinarily take the possibility of error on the part of the magistrate as adequate reason for conclusively disabling the authority of the magistrate altogether in the government of ordinary business affairs, and there is no systematic reason to treat the market for ideas differently. In a world of increasing interdependence, in which the speech acts of each may indirectly affect the speech environment of all, *Euclid* suggests (as we have seen) that "[s]uch regulations [should be] sustained, under the complex conditions of our day, for reasons analogous to those which justify traffic regulations, which, before the advent of automobiles and rapid transit street railways, would have been condemned as fatally arbitrary and unreasonable."[326] A developing constitution oriented to the common good may well become *less* libertarian over time, not out of hostility to rights, but due to the insight that rights themselves are based on and justified by what is due to each as members of a political community, and are thus to be ordered to the common good.

Human Rights Without Progressivism: A Model Declaration

Common good constitutionalism is, of course, not merely the province of judges; it is the proper governing approach for all public officials. Let me now turn to a second positive model of development without progressivism, a constitutional project (broadly defined) outside the courts and on the international plane. A stock enemy for legal conservatives, especially in the United States, is the international human rights project broadly understood, whether embodied in international institutions in the strict sense, in supranational bodies like the European Court of Human Rights, or in national legislation like the United Kingdom's Human Rights Act of 1998. Despite the heavily Catholic origins of this tradition,[327] which indeed had important socially conservative features, the perception among legal conservatives is that the human rights project has been hijacked.

There is no doubt that such a perception has a great deal of basis in fact,[328] although the picture is not uncomplicated. Consider that the United States is in global perspective a radical libertarian and libertine outlier with respect to various legal rights, such as abortion rights after the first trimester and the judicially declared right of same-sex marriage. By contrast, the European human rights equilibrium (for example) tends to restrict abortion to the first trimester unless weighty reasons are involved. (I do not defend that equilibrium either; I merely note that it is less libertarian than the regime that has prevailed in the United States since the 1970s.)[329] So too the European Court of Human Rights has repeatedly rejected claims for a convention right of same-sex marriage,[330] and has upheld the right of states to make public displays of religious tradition like crucifixes in school classrooms.[331]

That said, it is true that the international human rights community does feature an interlocking network of nongovernmental organizations, bureaucrats, legal academics, and policy-makers who relentlessly push an easily identified agenda of progressive desiderata, prominently featuring expansive abortion rights, sexual orientation and gender identity rights, and similar progressive programs. Thus it is understandable for social conservatives to equate the international sphere with progressivism.

But there is nothing inevitable about this state of affairs. There is no reason why states that do not subscribe to the standard agenda cannot form alternative models of international human rights discourse, contributing to the *ius gentium* by declaring, honoring, and eventually enforcing nonprogressive principles. As a proof-of-concept, let me point to the "Geneva Consensus Declaration on Promoting Women's Health and Strengthening the Family," an international instrument sponsored by Brazil, Hungary, Indonesia, and the United States, and signed to date by thirty-odd nations representing more than 1.6 billion people.[332] The Declaration establishes "four pillars," four principles to which the subscribing nations adhere: "(1) better health for women, (2) the preservation of human life, (3) strengthening of family as the foundational unit of society, and (4) protecting every nation's national sovereignty in global politics."[333] The second, third, and fourth principles are antithetical to the programmatic commitments of international progressives. Although not immediately couched in the idiom of "rights," those principles point to a vision of *human rights without progressivism* – a vision that sounds oxymoronic only if one labors under the mistaken assumption that the only possible conception of rights is the progressive conception. In the next chapter, I will argue for a classical conception of the foundation of rights in the common good that is fully capable of supporting an international human rights movement without progressivism.

To be sure, such a movement will inevitably contain different emphases and empower different actors than does the progressive human rights regime. Consider that the signatories to the Geneva Consensus Declaration, while representing roughly a fifth of the world's population, contain none of the North European and Nordic countries that, on the progressive conception, are typically taken as the gold standard for human rights. The new human rights internationalism will be a movement of the global south and east, including very large nations like Brazil and Indonesia that, broadly speaking, take a more traditionalist view of social questions. One may debate whether this is good or bad, but there is no doubt that it is perfectly possible to have a developing program of international human rights without progressivism.

An Anti-Model

Having offered two positive models, I conclude with an anti-model, an example of progressive constitutionalism that cannot be defended on Newman's conception of the development of doctrine. I return to *Obergefell v. Hodges*,[334] in which the Supreme Court declared a constitutional right of same-sex marriage, under a confusing mix of due process and equal protection theories. *Obergefell* is what progressive constitutionalism looks like when it has become detached from the objective legal and moral order that underpins classical legal theory and the common good.

The core of marriage

As a doctrinal matter, the *Obergefell* majority attempted to portray its holding as a development from earlier caselaw that had established a "right to marriage" in various circumstances.[335] *Loving v. Virginia*[336] involved an interracial couple who were criminally prosecuted for marrying in the District of Columbia and for cohabiting in Virginia;[337] *Zablocki v. Redhail*[338] involved a man who was prohibited from marrying "in Wisconsin or elsewhere" for failure to pay child-support obligations;[339] and *Turner v. Safely*[340] involved prison inmates barred from marrying without permission.[341] How might one think about such cases within the framework of common good constitutionalism? Is *Obergefell* a valid development from them?

Even the *Obergefell* majority acknowledged that in global and historical perspective, marriage has for millennia been defined as the union of male and female for the purpose of procreation.[342] For the majority this was at best simply an inert fact, at worst a lamentable pattern of bigotry to be ignored once its own more enlightened appreciation of justice or "injustice"[343] arrived on the scene. In fact, however, it is powerful evidence of the *ius gentium* and *ius naturale*. Marriage is not (merely) a civil convention, a mere corporate form created by the civil authority to allocate some package of legal benefits. It is a natural and moral and legal reality simultaneously,[344] a form itself constituted by the natural law in general terms as the permanent union of man and woman under the general *telos* or indwelling aims of unity and procreation (whether or not the particular couple is contingently capable of procreating).

Against this background, the role of the civil authority is determination – to specify the natural-law concept within reasonable bounds for purposes of civil law, by making concrete the accidents of the institution, the surrounding network of specific rules that put flesh on the bones of the general concept given by the natural law. A civil specification that distorts the essence of the natural institution would be unreasonable and arbitrary, from the standpoint of common good constitutionalism. On this account, the predecessor cases to *Obergefell* were all correctly decided. They invalidated legislative or administrative action that tacked on arbitrary and artificial criteria that were extrinsic to marriage properly understood, and were thus unreasonable in just the way the classical law condemns. In all three, the civil authority had confused the core and essence of the natural institution with its accidents, attempting to cripple or mutilate the institution by grafting onto it naturally irrelevant or arbitrary accidents – for example, by defining marriage not to include marriage between differing races. As the Chief Justice argued in dissent, "[n]one of the laws at issue in those cases purported to change the core definition of marriage as the union of a man and a woman. . . . Removing racial barriers to marriage therefore did not change what a marriage was any more than integrating schools changed what a school was."[345]

The very same logic, however, shows that *Obergefell* should have come out the other way. For the civil authority to specify in law that marriage can only be the union of a man and a woman fits the *telos* of the institution and thus determines through the civil law what the natural law prescribes in any event.[346] The Court purported to discern, under new circumstances, what justice had always required with respect to marriage, but in fact it warped the core nature of the institution by forcibly removing one of its built-in structural features. The union of man and woman in marriage is not (merely) some mechanism for satisfying individual desires and preferences for lifelong companionship, although doing so is an important byproduct of the marital state. Rather, the *telos* of the institution is oriented toward the common good through reproduction, the *sine qua non* of a continuous political community and of a flourishing, fully human polity.

Justice Alito, to his credit, observed that "[the majority's] understanding of marriage, which focuses almost entirely on the happiness of persons who choose to marry, is shared by many people today, but it is not the traditional one. For millennia, marriage was inextricably linked to the one thing that only an opposite-sex couple can do: procreate."[347] To treat that feature of marriage as dispensable was no development in the sense of unfolding of an enduring principle, but rather an attempt to break a traditional and natural legal institution by sheer force of will in the service of a liberationist agenda. In that ultimate valorization of will at the expense of the natural reason, *Obergefell* in particular and progressive constitutionalism in general are in deep kinship with originalist positivism.

Chapter 5

Applications

I turn now to some further applications, in the areas of the administrative state, subsidiarity and federalism, and rights, including the areas of free speech, due process, and access to the courts. The applications have been chosen on two grounds, thematic and substantive. Thematically, I chose applications with a view to range, showing that there is no part of public law that is off limits to the classical perspective, and also with a view to illustrating one or more of the themes laid out in earlier chapters: the role of *ius*, instead of or in addition to *lex*; the developing (but not progressive) character of constitutional doctrine over time; the broad scope for public authorities to secure the goods identified by the *ragion di stato*; the importance of determinations; the deferential role of judges; and the orientation of rights and law generally to the common good.

Substantively, the aim is to begin to show how the classical legal tradition can be adapted to provide the goods of peace, justice, and abundance – including their updated cognates, health, safety, security, and a right relationship to the natural environment – under the conditions of a large and complex modern polity and economy. I have no ambition to write a comprehensive treatise, as the Introduction explained, but instead merely offer some suggestive illustrations to begin a project that will work itself out over time. In terms of first-order substantive applications, Section C discusses the classical theory of rights and questions of free speech, including pornography and political speech; takings law (constitutional property rights) and environmental law; and standing law, involving rights of access to courts. These applications should be read in conjunction with others I have provided in previous chapters, such as the discussions of economic regulation, zoning regulation, international human rights law, and nontraditional marriage. Together, these applications make a start on an enormous enterprise of bringing the classical law back into contact with modern problems.

That said, first-order applications are merely part of the story. A crucial point is that under modern conditions, the contribution of classical legal theory to the promotion of peace, justice, and abundance can also be indirect, shaping the methods, procedures, and institutions by which government supplies common goods. One occasionally encounters a silly misconception that classical legalism is entirely substantive. The slightest acquaintance with the classical legal tradition, from which many of the procedures used in modern legal systems derive, should refute this mistake. The common good is, above all, a structure of justification. So long as methods, procedures, and institutions are justified with reference to the common good, rather than to other ends, they are perfectly respectable in classical terms, although they will of course still have to be assessed for prudential value.

Thus the chapter begins, not with rights, but with the administrative state (Section A) and the internal allocation of authority across and within government and civil society, including the crucial principles of subsidiarity and solidarity (Section B). Today, in all developed nations, the administrative state assumes an ever-more central place in the making, implementation, and even interpretation of law. Any theory of law that does not take account of it in some way is, merely for that reason, grievously defective.

In particular, the administrative state is today the main locus and vehicle for the provision of the goods of peace, justice, and abundance central to the classical theory. The administrative state is where those goods are translated and adapted into modern forms such as health, safety, a clean environment under intelligent stewardship, and economic security. Under contemporary conditions of extreme economic and social complexity, bureaucracy properly and intelligently deployed is an engine of unsurpassed power for promoting the common good. Again, this is not a matter of conceptual necessity; bureaucracy may either be ordered to the common good, or not be, and non-bureaucratic forms of government can be and have been ordered to the common good. But it is an interpretation of how, under the conditions that describe our present, the determination of the constitutional order has worked itself out over time, especially but not only in the United States, the case I know best.

A. The Administrative State: The Living Voice of the Law

In this section I examine the crucial role of general legal principles – the closest modern Anglo-American legal theory has come to recognizing *ius* – in the administrative state. I also examine deference to agencies, perhaps the most controversial component of modern administrative law, and argue that it can be firmly grounded in the classical idea of *determinatio*. The choice of these two subtopics is no accident. Because I suggest that the administrative state can, when rightly ordered, provide a modern translation of the classical triptych of goods (peace, justice, and abundance adapted to include health, safety, and security), I will not even attempt to specify desirable first-order policies; to do so would be a category error, a misunderstanding of the role of the common good in legal theory. There will be no discussion here of highway policy, of the limits of free trade, or of the social cost of carbon. Orienting the relevant policies to the common good is a matter for political authorities, subject to appropriate judicial review; legal theorists as such can say little about the first-order merits. Rather, I will aim to show that, in different ways, both progressivism and originalist-positivism misunderstand the fundamentals of the administrative state. Both neglect the central role of long-standing *ius*, general legal principles, in orienting the administrative state to the common good.

To understand the modern administrative state, we must first look to the remote past. In the very first book of the *Digest* of Justinian, the great jurist Papinian lists the sources of the *ius civile*, the civil law of Rome, as "statutes, plebiscites, decrees of the Senate, imperial decrees, or authoritative juristic statements" – and then immediately adds that "praetorian law is that which the praetors have introduced in aid or supplementation or correction of the *ius civile*."[348] Just as the *ius civile* is, in part, a determination or specification within reasoned boundaries of the more general principles of the natural law, so too the annual edicts of the urban praetors – high magistrates of Rome, just beneath the consuls, with jurisdiction over suits between citizens – added specification to or adjusted the contours of the *ius civile* as necessary. Even more detailed specification could be added through the application of the edict to facts in particular cases by the praetor's own court, and by administrative orders called interdicts, which in some respects did much the same work as modern administrative regulation. Interdicts "protected all kinds of public and private interests that the praetor thought were in need of protection. There were interdicts to protect the use of public roads, navigation on public rivers, the good condition of sewers, and public places against damage from construction – but also private possessions, servitudes, inheritances, and more."[349]

Overall, the function of the praetor was both to adjudicate lawsuits and to determine important questions of administrative policy within the bounds of the *ius civile*, adjusting it to particular situations and changing circumstances. Each praetor's edict was in force only for the praetor's own term, but each successive officeholder tended to adapt the edict of his predecessor as a baseline, making adjustments at the margin. The result was a system in which, as the jurist Marcian put it, the edicts of the praetors were "the living voice of the *ius civile.*"[350]

Although there can of course be no straight mapping of this system onto our own, very different one, there is an imperfect but useful analogy here to the functions of the great executive departments, tribunals, and independent administrative agencies of our constitutional order, as it has developed over time. These bodies act under the authority of great, often very general statutes and executive orders that are, in many cases, quite old and need to be fleshed out, supplemented, and adapted to changing conditions over time. Administrative agency heads use edicts to set broad policy outlines within the contours of the positive law, and those policies are then further specified and applied to particular cases by administrative adjudicators and, ultimately, the courts. The whole process is one of successive, iterated determinations of the general into the particular, and of the adaptation and adjustment to changing circumstances of broad positive instruments. In this sense, administrative agencies have come to occupy the position once held by common-law courts;[351] agencies make and interpret law in a system featuring, by and large, broadly deferential judicial review.[352] Agencies are the living voice of our law.

In this system what, if anything, ensures that agencies act for the common good? Nothing; asking for certainty is to ask more than any system of government can give. Administrative agencies will always make blunders and even engage in localized abuses – just as did common-law courts in their heyday. Nonetheless, there is much to be said about how law can help agencies act to fashion reasoned ordinances that conduce to the common good. I argue that our current body of administrative law, itself a central component of our largely unwritten constitutional order, is not structured around positive textual rules or *ad hoc* administrative commands, although both of those things do continue to play important roles. Rather our administrative law is built around juridical principles that are part of the larger domain of political morality,[353] yet retain their distinctive character as legal morality – in just the way Dworkin characterized all of law toward the end of his career.[354] These principles are not necessarily traceable to or rooted in positive enacted texts such as the Administrative Procedure Act of 1946.[355] Instead they are principles of broader legality and natural procedural justice that are, nonetheless, indisputably part of our law.

Our administrative "law," then, arguably amounts to law as *ius*, not merely as written positive *lex*. In this sense, what Ulpian said in majestic terms – that "the law [*ius*] is the art of goodness and fairness, and of that art, we jurists are deservedly called the priests"[356] – is emphatically true of our administrative law, even or especially today. There is no inconsistency between seeing administrative law, administrative lawyers, and judges in this way and in seeing the system as one that is broadly deferential to our praetors and other magistrates. After all, broad deference to administrative determinations is itself a juridical principle, rooted in political morality, that can serve the common good.

Rules, commands, or principles?

It is well to begin with some background, both historical and theoretical. Since the expansion of the administrative state in the Progressive Era,[357] legal theory has asked how the increasing complexity and interdependence of economy, society, and administrative institutions would affect jurisprudence. I will trace out a central thread of this debate by examining the views of Roscoe Pound, Carl Schmitt, and Ronald Dworkin on the forms that law takes in the administrative state. During his progressive phase, before he did a notorious about-face and became a vehement opponent of the administrative state,[358] Pound argued that the increasing complexity of the state would result in the widespread replacement of general rules in favor of *ad hoc* commands *and* that this was a good thing. Schmitt and others, such as Friedrich Hayek, agreed with Pound's basic prediction but took the opposite normative view of it. Schmitt feared that the proliferation of rapid-fire, *ad hoc* administrative commands would drive out genuine jurisprudence based on legal principles, in the classical tradition.

Dworkin, however, suggested that both sides of the debate (with Pound on one side, and Schmitt and Hayek on the other) were mistaken about their joint prediction. In Dworkin's view, under conditions of increasing social and economic complexity, law would come to rely *more*, not less, on jurisprudential principles, as opposed to positive sources such as either general rules or *ad hoc* commands. I will argue that Dworkin's basic view has been vindicated – after a fashion, anyway. The scale, complexity, and rapidity of lawmaking in the modern state grew to such a point that neither general rules nor *ad hoc* commands could keep up. Rather, actors in the system, particularly judges, turned to general principles of lawmaking to maintain a supervisory role for legality. Administrative law, particularly the jurisprudence of judicial review of administrative action, turns out to be pervaded by principles of what used to be called "general" law, unwritten jurisprudence.[359] Today's administrative law, then, is *ius* at least as much as it is *lex*.

Many of the principles that pervade administrative law are process-oriented, and thus aimed not at policing the substance of agency decisions but rather at ensuring that the administrative state operates through and by means of orderly lawmaking and rational decision-making.[360] In important cases, these principles seemingly stem from intuitions about natural procedural justice and float free of any enacted source of law; a number predate the enactment of the Administrative Procedure Act. In other cases, they are vaguely attributed to open-ended constitutional texts like "due process of law." Whatever the details, administrative law has not come to be dominated by *ad hoc* agency commands, as Pound and other, later theorists of the Progressive Era anticipated. Rather today's administrative law features a thick ecology of legal principles that jostle, compete, and develop over time.

Pound and the death of rules

In a famous address on "The Growth of Administrative Justice" given in 1923 and published a year later,[361] Pound, in his early incarnation as a leading advocate for progressive legal reform, argued that the classical jurisprudence of the nineteenth century was increasingly obsolete. For Pound, the centerpiece of classical jurisprudence was the general rule, most characteristically generated by the common law. The classical legalists had supposed that the political virtues of legality – equality before the law, restraint of arbitrary decision-making, and legal clarity and certainty – would be guaranteed by the generality and formality of rules.

Pound subverted this view by arguing that in the increasingly complex and integrated social and economic environment of the administrative state, the opposite was true: general common-law rules created debilitating uncertainty, arbitrariness, and unfairness. (In these respects, Pound was adapting for the American case a set of arguments that Jeremy Bentham had made about the English common law in the mid-nineteenth century.)[362] General rules did not necessarily decide concrete cases, and to find out how or whether the general rules applied to a particular case, one would have to speculate on the later decisions – perhaps years later – of the generalist judges who sat in common-law courts. The proliferating complexity of the underlying behavior and transactions made these effects of uncertainty, arbitrariness, and unfairness increasingly severe. For Pound, the consequences were debilitating, not least for business itself:

> Especially in the complicated economic organization of today the law cannot say to the business man, well, you guess; you employ a lawyer by the year to give you the best guess that he can, and then as the result of litigation we will tell you five years afterwards whether your guess as to the conduct of your business was the correct one or not.[363]

The consequence, to his mind, was that all parties, emphatically including regulated parties, would actually be better off on the dimensions of legal predictability and certainty by shifting to a regime of specific administrative orders, issued *ex ante*, before or at the moment of the relevant transaction, and tailored to their concrete circumstances. And in fact, administrative institutions were already supplying these new forms:

> We are in a busy, crowded world, and when we do anything today we must specialize. . . . We cannot waste our time and substance on the mere incidents of our life . . . We try to tell men in advance what they may do and what they may not, as far as possible; and our administrative commissions are nothing but traffic officers, as it were, with signals to tell us when to cross and when not to cross, and where to cross.[364]

On this vision, the future of the law lay in a regime of increasingly specific positivism: in the limit, every industry and indeed every firm would act under the specific superintendence of bureaucracies clarifying their legal obligations at every important step. Needless to say, for legal traditionalists, this was a horrifying vision, and one which would eventually come to be considered horrifying by Pound himself as well.

Schmitt and the tyranny of commands

Pound's basic prediction, and his later negative evaluation of the results, were shared by a number of theorists, American, English, and continental. Prominent among these were Lord Hewart, whose book *The New Despotism* was published in 1929,[365] and, somewhat later, Friedrich Hayek, author of *The Road to Serfdom* in 1944.[366] I will focus here, however, on what is in my view the most interesting version of this critique, by the German legal theorist Carl Schmitt, writing in the same year as Hayek.

In an article entitled "The Plight of European Jurisprudence,"[367] Schmitt expressed his fears that genuine jurisprudence was in the process of being eliminated by the development of "motorized" law-making in the administrative state – delegated rulemaking and *ad hoc* orders. Genuine jurisprudence, which Schmitt associated with the *ius commune*, was a matter of legal principles being advanced, contested, argued, and elaborated over time by a community of jurisprudents. These were neither technicians of law nor primary practitioners of other disciplines, neither compilers of regulations nor philosophers, but lawyers in the tradition of the Roman jurists and civilian glossators, custodians of legal principles and doctrines understood as embodiments of justice. In this vision, the threat from the acceleration of lawmaking in the administrative state is that delegations of rulemaking power to agencies and proliferating *ad hoc* commands will progressively eliminate any scope for the autonomy of legal principles and their jurisprudential elaboration. As Schmitt put it:

> [T]he compulsion for legal regulations to accommodate the tempo of changing conditions was irresistible. . . . Law became a means of planning . . . by an authorized agency but not publicly announced and often only sent to those immediately concerned. . . . These developments have created a critical situation for jurisprudence, which cannot enter into a race with the motorized methods of decrees and directives. It cannot keep up. Rather, it must become aware of the fact that it has become the last refuge of law. It must remember its own task and seek to safeguard the unity and consistency of law, which is being lost in the frenzy of legal impositions.[368]

The alternative that Schmitt proposed in response to this perceived crisis, namely, a turn to the nationalist and historicist customary-law vision of Carl Friedrich von Savigny, is of little relevance for our purposes here. What is of interest is that Schmitt went beyond early Pound not only by evaluating the proliferation of administrative commands as a threat, but also by going beyond the former's central dichotomy between general rules and *ad hoc* orders to include legal principles as a crucial jurisprudential category of interest. For Schmitt, the main threat of the administrative state is that it will crowd out a true jurisprudence of principle. As Ronald Dworkin's work would later show, however, Schmitt's conclusion is hardly obvious.

Dworkin and principles
Despite their varied normative views of the matter, the foregoing theorists shared a broad consensus, albeit with differences of detail, on the basic prediction that the growth of the administrative state would produce a long-term shift away from general legal rules to *ad hoc* commands. A very different view of the predictive question came from Ronald Dworkin.[369]

Dworkin took aim at the legal positivism of Jeremy Bentham and American derivatives, such as Justice Holmes and his successors. On Dworkin's view, positivism – at least in its earlier, vital form, before it degenerated into a mere thesis of analytic philosophy – was intended by its champions to bring democratic accountability and transparency, clarity, certainty, and predictability to the law, in place of the (putative) obscurity, legalistic elitism, and arbitrariness of principle-ridden common-law rulemaking. The basic positivist hope was to simplify the law and make it more predictable and democratically intelligible. For Dworkin, however, this view was already obsolete by Bentham's time;[370] the functions of the state were already sufficiently ambitious to make simple appeals for clarity, certainty, and democratic law-creation implausible, especially in "hard cases" where statutes and constitutional provisions were conflicting, ambiguous, or silent. Certainly, by the era of Holmes and other political positivists, the increasing complexity of the state and its law made nonsense of the simple picture of a transmission belt from legislative majorities through statutes to courts, promoting accountability, transparency, and certainty. Agencies were increasingly interposed between legislatures and courts, and this critical increment of complexity raised a myriad of questions about the scope of administrative power, the rationality of its exercise, and the power of judicial review.

What consequences would flow from the infeasibility of simple positivism in a changing environment? In an illuminating passage, Dworkin argued that the result would be an increasing reliance on a jurisprudence of legal principles on the part of legislators and judges – precisely the sort of jurisprudence whose abolition Schmitt feared:

> Changes in society's expectations of law and judges were well under way, however, even in the 1930s when [leading positivist judges] wrote, and with accelerating velocity in the decades that followed, that made positivism's general conception of legality steadily more implausible and self-defeating. Elaborate statutory schemes became increasingly important sources of law, but these schemes were not – could not be – detailed codes. They were more and more constructed of general statements of principle and policy that needed to be elaborated in concrete administrative and judicial decisions; if judges had continued to say that law stopped where explicit sovereign discretion ran out, they would have had constantly to declare . . . that legality was either irrelevant to or compromised in their judgments.[371]

In a similar vein, Dworkin wrote:

> The thesis that a community's law consists only of the explicit commands of legislative bodies seems natural and convenient when explicit legislative codes can purport to supply all the law that a community needs. When technological change and commercial innovation outdistance the supply of positive law, however – as they increasingly did in the years following the Second World War – judges and other legal officials must turn to more general principles of strategy and fairness to adapt and develop law in response. It then seems artificial and pointless to deny that these principles, too, figure in determining what law requires.[372]

Let me offer an interpretation of these points. At least since the first real flowering of the administrative state in the years around World War I, judges have wondered and worried about how the administrative state might be kept broadly within the bounds of law.[373] In the nightmare vision common to Hewart, Hayek, and Schmitt, "motorized law" in the form of delegated rulemaking and *ad hoc* commands would displace legal reason with executive fiat. Although judges could enforce clear statutory limits, under positivist theory they were supposed to exercise "discretion" when statutes were ambiguous or silent, and in the administrative state that discretion would in effect be transferred to agencies. But given circumstances of increasing complexity, a regime of *de novo* interpretation and discretion and of judge-made general rules of common law could not keep up either, for all the reasons given by Pound. The dilemma seemed insoluble. Dworkin's insight, however, was that lawmakers and judges could and would preserve a role for legality by other means. Rather than pursue the increasingly futile attempt to formulate first-order, content-laden rules, lawmakers and judges would turn to codes based on abstract, general jurisprudential principles, cast at a higher level of generality.

The triumph of principle
By and large, Dworkin's view has turned out to be correct. Recall Dworkin's suggestion that the growing importance of "general statements of principle" would occur, in part, through "statutory schemes" that would subsequently be "elaborated in concrete administrative and judicial decisions." There is a central statute, indeed a super-statute, that bears out Dworkin's view by embodying general statements of high principle: the Administrative Procedure Act (APA). And likewise, there is an evolving body of doctrine and principle, centering on judicial review of administrative action, that fits his account perfectly. I will begin with a few general points about the APA and then offer specific examples.

The later Pound, after his about-face, advocated stridently for legal constraints on the administrative state.[374] The final product that emerged from the push-and-pull of ideological conflict and legislative compromise in the years 1941–46 is in many respects the opposite of the younger Pound's prediction for the future of administrative law. The centerpiece of the APA is neither general rules nor *ad hoc* commands. As to the former, the very definition of "rule" is "an agency statement of general *or particular* applicability and future effect";[375] the latter, denominated "orders," are permissible under an indefinite range of circumstances but are at least presumptively subject to judicial review, which would defeat Pound's traffic-control rationale for agency commands. Rather the APA, especially in its provisions for judicial review and the grounds of judicial review, is best seen as a charter of general principles. Administrative action must not be "arbitrary" and "capricious";[376] agencies may make rules without public process so long as "the agency for good cause finds" that compliance would be "impracticable, unnecessary, or contrary to the public interest";[377] and so on. Our great charter of administrative procedure is full of generally stated principles whose interpretation inherently requires judgments of political morality (including, of course, the principle of role morality that underpins deference) and whose application is situational.[378] The APA is the modern equivalent of the "natural law codes" of the Napoleonic era,[379] codes built around general principles.

The view of the APA as being, in critical respects, a charter of relatively abstract principles is not inconsistent with the critical point – famously made by Justice Jackson in *Wong Yang Sung v. McGrath*[380] and then picked up by Jackson's clerk, William Rehnquist, in the *Vermont Yankee*[381] decision – that the APA is a grand compromise, a treaty of peace. What Jackson actually said was that "[t]he Act . . . represents a long period of study and strife; it settles long-continued and hard-fought contentions, and enacts a formula upon which opposing social and political forces have come to rest. It contains *many compromises and generalities* and, no doubt, some ambiguities."[382] This makes the essential point: treaties and constitutions often contain general principles precisely *because* they are products of compromise. One sometimes encounters the strange assumption that contested compromises necessarily yield documents filled with specific provisions. That is possible, but it is also extremely common that parties who have ongoing first-order disagreements, but good second-order reasons for maintaining a long-run relationship, will agree to disagree by enacting general concepts of justice on which they agree, while leaving for the future fights about specific conceptions of those principles.

In truth the APA is a bit of a hodgepodge. While it contains rather specific instructions about certain elements of administrative procedures, in key sections it falls back on high-level concepts that command widespread agreement. These concepts, however, admit of competing conceptions, with the effect that the adoption of the concepts does not in and of itself conclude future questions. Rather the concepts provide a framework for interpretation, arguments, and dueling principles – in short, for administrative jurisprudence. The very complexity and contestation that is endemic to the administrative state produces compromise on abstract principles, which must then be "elaborated in concrete administrative and judicial decisions," as Dworkin put it.

In an administrative law setting, as elsewhere, the basic Dworkinian enterprise of law as integrity[383] is to combine "fit" and "justification." It deploys arguments that fit past legal decisions and that justify those decisions in light of arguments about which conceptions of arbitrariness are most attractive on grounds of political morality, attempting to bring those conceptions into coherence with the wider body of law. Administrative law has just this character. I will provide three brief examples.

Arbitrary and capricious review

A fundamental precept of the APA is that the exercise of administrative discretion should not be "arbitrary." But of course, the whole problem in concrete cases is uncertainty as to what counts as arbitrariness, since the concept admits of many possible conceptions. This is all grist for the Dworkinian mill. The body of caselaw that the Court has generated under the heading of "arbitrary and capricious" review is only tenuously connected to the positive source of law that gave rise to it. As such, the former is best seen as a rich mix of arguments about the best conceptions of rationality and legality, with subsidiary principles worked out as interpretations of those conceptions.

Is it "arbitrary and capricious" to fail to consider reasonable alternatives and explain why the agency rejected them in favor of the
course it chose? The Court has said yes.[384] When an agency changes
its policy, however, must it show that the new policy is better than the
old? Generally speaking, the answer is no, with certain exceptions.[385]
(The obvious tension between those two principles is itself merely
grist for further argument.) If the only rationale an agency offers
is transparently pretextual, is that valid? No.[386] All these questions
implicate fundamental issues of rationality and political morality,
including institutional morality. The result is some of the most
normatively and theoretically saturated jurisprudence to be found
anywhere in public law.

Administrative procedure

The triumph of principle is even more apparent in the law of administrative procedure. That body of law is full of principles that courts
state confidently and use routinely, but whose source in positive law
is often unclear; at any rate, these principles function independently
of any positive-law source. Consider a few examples: (1) agencies must
follow their own rules;[387] (2) a court can evaluate an agency action
only on the grounds that the agency advanced in the administrative
proceedings;[388] (3) the president may not dictate agency decisions
in formal adjudication.[389] All of these ultimately stem from caselaw
predating the Administrative Procedure Act, and in that caselaw there
is little or no effort to deduce the principles from enacted legal texts;
rather the principles are seen either as being already part of the fabric
of the law, or as having been extrapolated from and inherent in the
nature of courts, the presidency, agencies, and their relationship.[390] In
all three cases, although it is possible to argue that the principles are
justified by the implicit premises of the APA or by due process, somehow understood, courts spend almost no time worrying about those
textual foundations. Rather they announce and apply the principles
in common-law fashion.

The omnipresence and importance of these principles in judicial
review of agency action is plausibly a consequence of the increasing

complexity of the administrative state. Under these conditions, as we have seen, judges have looked for ways to maintain the role of legality. (In Dworkin's words, "if judges had continued to say that law stopped where explicit sovereign decision ran out, they would have had constantly to declare . . . that legality was either irrelevant to or compromised in their judgments.")[391] One way to maintain legality was to proceduralize administrative law – to allow sweeping delegations of authority to administrative agencies, as courts did both before and (especially) after 1935, but to condition agency discretion on procedural regularity.[392] The unwritten procedural principles I have mentioned come into prominence in the critical period between World War I and the enactment of the APA in 1946 and represent an important aspect of the judicial response to the relevant challenge.

Reviewability and fundamental principles

One main thread of the reviewability doctrine has wrestled with the "committed to agency discretion by law" exception to the presumption of reviewability for agency action.[393] And the main thread of interpretation of that provision has focused on the "no law to apply" test.[394] That test attempts to tie reviewability to a discrete question of positive law: is there a statute (or constitutional provision, but I will ignore that possibility) that supplies standards against which to examine the agency action? If there is no such statute, if the law has "run out," then the agency has unreviewable discretion – or so the idea goes.

The "no law to apply" test exemplifies the sort of positivist framework – (1) rules plus (2) zones of unreviewable "discretion," once rules run out – that Dworkin argued is inadequate, given the complexity of the administrative state, because it would fail to preserve an adequate role for legality. Hence, in Dworkin's view, we should observe principles filling the gap. And in reality that is what we do see; reviewability doctrine, in practice, goes well beyond the "no law to apply" test. As commentators have noted,[395] courts can always ask whether the agency's exercise of discretion is arbitrary and capricious. As Justice Scalia famously observed, there is always at least one fundamental constraint of legal principle to apply, namely that the agency must act with regard for public rather than private purposes.[396] So the "no law to apply" test does not obviously capture how reviewability does or should work. What we see instead, as Justice Scalia also argued, is

> "the 'common law' of judicial review of agency action" – a body of jurisprudence that had marked out, with more or less precision, certain issues and certain areas that were beyond the range of judicial review. That jurisprudence included principles ranging from the "political question" doctrine, to sovereign immunity (including doctrines determining when a suit against an officer would be deemed to be a suit against the sovereign), to official immunity, to prudential limitations upon the courts' equitable powers, to what can be described no more precisely than a traditional respect for the functions of the other branches. . . . All this law, shaped over the course of centuries and still developing in its application to new contexts, cannot possibly be contained within the phrase "no law to apply."[397]

Needless to say, this "body of jurisprudence" is a set of "principles," as Dworkin predicted, that arise because of the great complexity of the administrative state. The variety of situations in which reviewability questions arise, and of institutions with respect to which such questions arise, is so great that no single, simple test can capture the relevant considerations.[398] The result is a complicated, evolving body of doctrine infused with principled arguments over political morality and the role morality of institutions – precisely the sort of jurisprudence that Schmitt feared would be lost in the administrative state.[399]

Overall, then, the development of the rich body of administrative law is entirely compatible with Dworkin's prediction that the increasing complexity and scale of the modern state in the Progressive Era would result in greater reliance on legal principles, not less. In the nature of the case, of course, it is difficult to show cause and effect in such matters; the questions are too diffuse, the scale of the problems too large, and the timescale too long. There are simply too many moving parts. At a minimum, however, it does seem clear that the crowding-out of legal principles feared by Schmitt has not occurred and that the dominance of *ad hoc* administrative commands anticipated by Pound (and also feared by Schmitt) has not come to pass.

Perhaps surprisingly, administrative law, especially the judicial review of administrative action, has become, if not a "forum of principle," at least a battlefield of competing principles. In light of this development, one might argue that the fundamental demand Schmitt made upon jurisprudence – that "[i]t must remember its own task and seek to safeguard the unity and consistency of law, which is being lost in the frenzy of legal impositions"[400] – has been accomplished within administrative law, by the development of a jurisprudence of principles. Such principles are *ius*, in all but name. Agencies are in this sense the living voice of our positive law, and the administrative law that surrounds and structures them is best understood to be as much *ius* as *lex*.

Deference and determination

So far I have said little about what remains arguably the most controversial topic in administrative law: the question of deference. In earlier chapters I connected deference in constitutional cases to the classical idea of determination, and I will pursue that theme here in the administrative context. *Determinatio* is an excellent lens for thinking about *Chevron* deference, *Auer* deference, and other such structures even *within* the positive law, as well as the relationship between positive administrative law and natural law.

There are two distinct points here. One is strictly analogical: *determinatio* describes not only the relationship between natural law and positive law, but also the relationship between higher and lower levels of positive law, such as statute on the one hand and administrative regulation or adjudication on the other. On this account, agency action often determines, gives concrete form to, general principles laid out in statutes or agency legislative rules (which are binding unless and until changed through valid rulemaking procedure). This is close, theoretically, to the point that executive action is a "completion power" that carries general legislative commands into execution.[401]

Agencies may even make rationally arbitrary choices within the scope of the broad boundaries of the general statutory or regulatory principle.[402]

This account also has implications for the scope of judicial review. Precisely because agency action often takes the form of determination of general statutory principles, agencies are often in the position of architects carrying out a commission whose broad goals have been set by Congress. Judges should thus afford agencies leeway to carry out the task of the architect. They should allow agencies to specify policy within the bounds and for the purposes of the overall statutory task, even when the agency, choosing between alternative ways of making the statute concrete, cannot offer reasons for *preferring* one specification to another. Remarkably, the Supreme Court more or less endorsed exactly this picture by holding, in *FCC v. Fox Television Stations, Inc.*[403] in 2009, that an agency charged with giving specificity to a general statutory limit on "indecent" broadcasting could change its policy without adducing reasons to show that its new policy was *better* than the old.[404] Barring issues of reliance interests or a change of specific factual findings, an agency charged with giving form to a broad, general, or ambiguous statutory authority is entitled simply to show that its (change of) policy amounts to a valid specification. Deference flows from determination.

The other way of cashing out *determinatio* is somewhat more ambitious. So far we have been discussing cases in which agency action makes more concrete higher sources of binding positive law, such as a statute or the agency's own prior binding legislative rule. Perhaps agency rules and adjudications can also, sometimes, be seen as ways in which agencies themselves supply specifying content directly to the natural law, rather than through the medium of some earlier act of positive lawmaking. Agencies, that is, could be taken to have the authority to invoke general principles of the natural law as starting points for their own actions (always assuming they otherwise have legal authority to take action in the relevant procedural format, such as authority to make rules or to adjudicate).

Two obvious doctrinal contexts come to mind. First, subject to minimum legal requirements in statutes and the Constitution, agencies typically have broad discretion to make procedural rules for their own rulemaking and adjudication (whether at the level of administrative law judges or of the agency itself). Agencies may thus draw upon principles of natural law in order to supply general principles for formulating procedures and for interpreting their statutory and constitutional obligations. Even where, for example, background requirements of constitutional due process in adjudication do not require a hearing before taking away a government benefit, nothing prevents an agency from affording one anyway as a determination of the natural procedural presumption in favor of hearings. Helmholz explains that such a presumption was deeply embedded in the *ius commune:* "Justice required that every person affected by litigation be cited and heard by an impartial judge. The ability to speak in defense of one's own person and property was a right that could not be denied to any person consistently with the law of nature."[405] The natural-law presumption could be overcome by a sufficient showing that the common good required it, but it would be a perfectly valid starting point for the agency's reasoning, one to which courts should defer. (I have argued at length elsewhere that a deferential framework should apply to constitutional due process cases.)[406]

A second doctrinal context involves agency consideration of the "relevant factors" under arbitrariness review, as laid out in the seminal *Overton Park* decision.[407] It has always been slightly mysterious where, exactly, the relevant factors come from, putting aside factors whose consideration Congress has either mandated or barred. The basic principle is that discretionary factors must be logically relevant to the agency's decision, leaving open the question of their source.[408] Under the conception of determination laid out here, general principles of natural law, perhaps cast as principles of equity or "fairness," should be straightforwardly eligible as "relevant factors." An example might be *EPA v. EME Homer City Generation, L.P.*,[409] a complex air regulation case in which statutes left open what principle EPA should choose to allocate responsibility for interstate air pollution among states. The Court observed that the principle EPA chose was both efficient and "equitable . . . because, by imposing uniform cost thresholds on regulated States, EPA's rule subjects to stricter regulation those States that have done relatively less in the past to control their pollution."[410] EPA here drew upon a natural principle of justice, that responsibility should at least presumptively lie where fault lies, to make concrete a general statutory command.

The connection between deference and determination extends to other contexts within and without administrative law. Thayerian deference in constitutional judicial review, for example, is easily susceptible of a similar analysis.[411] Without belaboring the point further, I will simply observe that dim echoes or professional memories of *determinatio* in the *ius commune* may well form part of the deep background matrix of legal principles out of which modern deference doctrines arose.

B. Subsidiarity and Solidarity: "A Giant's Strength"

I turn now to the complex of problems surrounding subsidiarity, solidarity, and, in the case of the United States, federalism. Here, I argue for a view about the relationship between public authority and subsidiarity, a view that I will base upon a well-known epigram from Shakespeare's *Measure for Measure*: Isabella's famous exclamation "O, it is excellent / To have a giant's strength, but it is tyrannous / To use it like a giant."[412] In context, this is a complaint about the risks of abuse of power, yielding tyranny in the limiting case, and I will not ignore that context; I will offer some ideas about how to address those risks. But I will take both halves of the statement seriously, the excellence of the giant's strength as well as the risk of tyranny, and will treat Isabella's Principle as a kind of *complexio oppositorum* – a combination of opposites that must be held in constructive tension with each other.

I will begin by suggesting that the giant's full strength is released in a state of exception – when, under unusual circumstances, the malfunctioning of subsidiary institutions means that the common good requires extraordinary intervention by the highest level of public authority in the juridical order, for the purpose of helping those subsidiary institutions function correctly in an overall scheme that conduces to the common good. I emphasize here that subsidiarity in this sense is fundamentally a *positive*, empowering principle, one that confers affirmative powers on the highest governing authority and yet also imposes positive duties to come to the aid of – provide *subsidium* to – jurisdictions, institutions, societies, and corporations[413] that are failing to carry out their work in an overall social scheme that serves the common good.

Subsequently, I turn from the giant's strength to the second half of the maxim: the prudence and restraint with which that strength should be exercised. The very principles that grant positive authority in exceptional circumstances to the highest public authority in the juridical order also limit the scope and purposes of the exercise of that authority. I suggest ways of institutionalizing those limits and purposes though procedural mechanisms and canons of statutory and constitutional interpretation.

Subsidiarity as a state of exception

I begin with the following claim: the right lens for understanding subsidiarity is the state of exception.[414] The state of exception does not imply unbounded power for the public authority; far from it. Rather it both empowers and constrains. It gives the public authority at the highest level of the system extraordinary power to do what is necessary for the common good, the strength of a giant, yet it also restrains and limits that power by the very rationale for conferring it in the first place:

> *Various circumstances may make it advisable that the State step in to supply certain functions.* One may think, for example, of situations in which it is necessary for the State itself to stimulate the economy because it is impossible for civil society to support initiatives on its own. One may also envision the reality of serious social imbalance or injustice where only the intervention of the public authority can create conditions of greater equality, justice and peace. In light of the principle of subsidiarity, however, this institutional substitution must not continue any longer than is absolutely necessary,

since justification for such intervention is found only in the *exceptional nature* of the situation.[415]

To understand this basic conception of subsidiarity, we need to start from the beginning. The core original meaning of *subsidium* is the military reserve that stands ready to enter battle if the front line faces a crisis.[416] The reserve, and whoever commands it, is thus subject to both a power and a duty: to intervene when necessary, but not to intervene when unnecessary. The latter may be just as dangerous to the common good as the former, as when, for example it undermines the coherence and activity of the fighting units on the front line. The whole point of the reserve is that it is committed only at the crisis of the battle, if ever.

In this sense, subsidiarity implies a positive power and a correlative positive duty for the highest public authority in the jurisdiction, triggered by an exceptional situation: the authority is both enabled and duty-bound to intervene when other competences cannot carry out their functions in an overall scheme oriented to the common good. Put differently, the logic is one of safeguarding, of extraordinary power and responsibility to preserve, protect, and restore the proper functioning and competences of subsidiary jurisdictions and authorities. The idea is to restore a previously functioning normative order of subsidiarity,[417] in which subsidiary jurisdictions and corporations are aided so that they might function as they normatively should and normally do.

All this is in contrast to the libertarian sense of "subsidiarity" that is most often heard: that of a negative limitation, according to which the public authority should not intervene if a given function is more appropriately carried out at a lower level. This view is not invalid; it is a corollary of the positive sense, a statement of the limitations inherent in the positive grant of power for certain purposes and under certain conditions. But the corollary should not be mistaken for the main theorem. On the view I have stated, subsidiarity is fundamentally positive, in two senses: it supplies the highest public authority with positive power to act in certain extraordinary circumstances, and it enjoins that authority with a positive duty to act where those circumstances obtain. In the words of the canonical treatment by Johannes Messner, subsidiarity should be understood as creating a public authority with sufficient strength to provide aid at need:

> The principle of subsidiarity function, however, certainly does not signify a weak state standing without authority face to face with a pluralistic society. On the contrary, the more strongly the character of society develops in its federative and corporative branches, both regional and occupational, in conjunction with a plurality of free associations based on economic group interests, the more clearly does the common good principle call for a state with strong authority which will enable it, in a *pluralistic* society with diversified competencies and interests, to carry out its essential functions: namely, to care for the common good and the general interest.[418]

This connection between positive subsidiary, strong authority, and the state of exception is recognized throughout the sources. First, they emphasize, in the words of the *Compendium*, that "the justification for [any] such intervention" by the public authority at the highest level of the political order "is found only in the *exceptional* nature of the situation."[419] And right from the beginning of the tradition, it has been laid down that "[t]he clearest requirement for [state] intervention . . . is where it is necessary for 'peace and good order.'"[420] This principle of necessity as a justification for restoring order is in effect a statement of exceptional authority. Messner, typically, gives the most rigorous and forthright statement of this idea:

> Where the will to moral responsibility in a society shrinks, the range of validity of the subsidiarity principle contracts and the common good function [of the state] expands to the extent that the moral will to responsibility in society fails. In such cases, even dictatorship may be compatible with the principle of subsidiarity.[421]

This sounds alarming, of course, but we should understand that Messner with his massive classical erudition is certainly best understood as speaking not at all of the modern strongman or junta, but rather within the tradition of the carefully cabined Roman model of dictatorship – a fundamentally legal and constitutional authority, limited by term, granted for a certain purpose, and authorized by the Senate.[422] Messner's picture is the restorative and, in a sense, fundamentally conservative one we have mentioned; the purpose of the extraordinary authority called into being by the state of exception is to heal and promote the ordinary and healthy functioning of the subsidiary institutions.

The excellence of the giant's strength, so interpreted, means that at the highest level of the polity, whether it is a single nation-state, a federation, or an empire, there should exist a public authority with the jurisdiction to act, under exceptional circumstances where the operation of subsidiary institutions fails, so as to promote the common good throughout the polity – overriding if necessary the views of any subordinate jurisdiction (subject, however, to enhanced procedural conditions – a topic I take up shortly). Perhaps surprisingly, this highest authority itself follows from the principle of subsidiarity rightly understood, as a positive principle that, at its core, addresses exceptional situations.

State sovereignty?

Let me now briefly address the claim that, in the American context, the sovereignty of the states sets absolute limits on this exceptional jurisdiction of the highest authority, the federal government. This view is pernicious. The so-called sovereignty of the states is best understood as a constitutional principle of respect and comity that the highest authority should take into account, out of prudent respect for legal justice and small-c constitutional arrangements. But like other constitutional principles, it has dimensions of both scope and weight, and is subject to reasonable determination by public authority ordering it to the common good. Within those boundaries, it should not be understood as a hard constitutional limit on the acts of the highest authority.

As a frame for this discussion, let me recur to an older debate in the American constitutional law of so-called "federalism," a debate initiated by a 1994 article by Edward Rubin and Malcolm Feeley.[423] Rubin and Feeley argued that there was a chronic disconnect between, on the one hand, the concept of state sovereignty, and, on the other, the values supposedly promoted or protected by Our Federalism: participation in governance, inter-jurisdictional competition, experimentalism, and citizen choice. Those values could be, and in many polities are, promoted by *decentralization without sovereignty*. Decentralized structures of governance such as departments or other administrative regions can experiment, compete, and encourage political participation and local community, even without affording sovereignty to the subordinate jurisdictional components.[424]

Indeed, American states as such are poorly situated to promote the relevant values. Participation in governance is most meaningful on the scale of the town or at most city, but governance at the scale of a state like California or Texas is not meaningfully different, from the individual's perspective, than continent-wide governance. Likewise, there is no meaningful local community at the level of New York State. The values attributed to federalism are, in many cases, really values of subsidiarity and civil society: they are benefits of local or city government, of professional groups and trade associations, and of other civil society corporations, rather than of the curious, clunky, very large political mid-range entities, hovering uneasily between nations and cities, that are the states of the United States.[425] Rubin and Feeley thus concluded, in a deliberate provocation, that federalism in the sense of state sovereignty should be understood as a kind of "neurosis."[426]

The responses were many and furious. One of the main lines of reply was that Rubin and Feeley had overlooked the *precommitment value* of state sovereignty.[427] On this view, state sovereignty functions as an institutional barrier to overweening national power, a barrier that should not be removed just whenever the national authority thinks it has good reason to do so. Unbounded authority to reallocate functions or even alter jurisdictional boundaries to promote federalism values, if lodged in the highest public authority – here, Congress and the president acting together by statute to make reasonable determinations of state and national power – would be too fluid, allowing ill-considered departures from the constitutional scheme in the heat of the political moment.

This debate did not attend to subsidiarity, for these were the days before American constitutional theorists regularly drank from the fountains of comparative constitutional theory and Catholic social thought. This actually helps us to isolate the contribution that the proper theory of subsidiarity can make. Against the background of the debate as I have recounted it, the status of subsidiarity as a principle of exception shows the limits of the precommitment rejoinder to Rubin and Feeley. Those who design a written constitution at a given time act under severe limits of foresight and information and cannot possibly anticipate all future contingencies. This means that rules protecting rigid spheres of state sovereignty or enacting rigid limits on federal power will inevitably clash with exceptional circumstances whose intrinsic logic requires positive federal action to promote and protect genuine subsidiarity.

Indeed, maintaining this sort of flexibility is wise. In the face of uncertainty about the future, excessive constitutional constraint can be as dangerous as insufficient constitutional constraint. The Constitution, emphatically including the vertical distribution between and among subsidiary jurisdictions and the highest-level authority, should be a loose-fitting garment that leaves room for flexibility and adjustment over time as circumstances change. The alternative is not some fantasy of perfect legality, but rather an overly brittle framework that cracks because it cannot bend.

Prudence, subsidiarity, and solidarity

So far I have identified subsidiarity as a positive principle of exception, a principle that calls into being special positive powers and positive duties to act when subsidiary jurisdictions and corporations need assistance to carry out their own functions in an overall scheme that conduces to the common good. Conversely, however, the very logic that brings this power into being also limits it; the highest public authority should not intervene when doing so is unnecessary to help, or would affirmatively hamper, subordinate bodies in the execution of their functions. Although it is excellent to have a giant's strength, it is tyrannous to use it like a giant. The issue is, as so often, one of regnative prudence.

How is this regnative prudence to be institutionalized, however? I have suggested that hard institutional precommitments misconceive the core logic of subsidiarity, which comes into play precisely when unanticipated and exceptional breakdowns in the ordinary functioning of subsidiary jurisdictions and corporations occur. What is necessary, therefore, is some way of making regnative prudence concrete in lived institutions without turning to law for a rigid precommitment that will not and indeed should not be observed anyway, when a crisis of subsidiarity becomes sufficiently grave. In considering how to navigate through this dilemma, I will very briefly sketch some intermediate solutions: procedural principles and canons of judicial interpretation for statutes and constitutional instruments. The aim of these devices is to put flesh on the commitment to subsidiarity, while not straitjacketing the public authority in a state of exception.

Procedural principles
As I have suggested, one approach is to draw upon legislative procedure[428] and administrative law[429] to embody principles of the constitutional order as process norms without making them hard precommitments. The mechanism here is to put such principles on the view-screen of decision-makers, to place the principles on the agenda for consideration, without forcing those decision-makers to adhere to any particular rules (or to a court's interpretation of those rules). In turn, this sort of approach comes in softer and harder versions. In the softest version, decision-makers are merely asked to certify that they have considered a certain principle; in a harder version, they may be asked to give reasons for rejecting its application or overriding it, reasons that might be evaluated for rationality by a court after the fact.

How could this work, exactly? I will offer some examples from the American setting, just for the purpose of illustrating the ideas. In the setting of legislation, one possibility is to have standing second-order rules within legislative houses, whether created by joint legislation or by the separate houses themselves, that would require legislators to certify that they have considered principles of subsidiarity when enacting new laws. In an administrative-law setting, agencies might be required – either directly by statute, or indirectly by interpretation of the Administrative Procedure Act's prohibition of decision-making that is arbitrary and capricious or otherwise not according to law[430] – to explain why they are overriding ("pre-empting") state law, even where Congress has expressly given them authority to do so.

An example from existing law is the Unfunded Mandates Reform Act of 1995 (UMRA),[431] which addresses the problem of mandatory requirements in national law that apply burdensome duties to states and localities and Native American tribes, yet are not funded by the national government. The Act

> requires congressional committees to specify, quantify, and describe any federal mandates that the proposed bill would impose on state, local, and tribal governments and to identify those that are unfunded by the federal government. The UMRA also allows legislators to raise a point of order during floor deliberation in order to focus debate on any unfunded mandate and to require a recorded vote to waive the objection.[432]

The Act does not ultimately prohibit such mandates; rather it uses internal legislative procedure to cause decision-makers to consider whether the mandates should be enacted.[433]

Statutory and constitutional interpretation
How might this conception of subsidiarity as exceptional authority in the service of the common good work at the level of statutory and constitutional interpretation? The approach I have suggested yields a strong canon of interpretation, to be applied unless contradicted by clear and specific language to the contrary: statutes and consti-tutional provisions should be interpreted to allow the highest public authority in the polity to exercise prudential judgment about whether an exceptional situation exists, such that subsidiary institutions have in some way failed and the positive powers and duties of subsidiarity

have been triggered. Let me briefly mention two concrete cases to illustrate.

The first is a case of statutory interpretation involving the Affordable Care Act ("Obamacare"), *King v. Burwell*.[434] Simplifying to an absurd degree, the question was whether the statutory provision for a "health exchange established by a State" could allow a federally established health exchange to step in and confer the same benefits when a given state failed to establish a health exchange.[435] The majority held that it could, citing a mélange of textual and other considerations;[436] the dissenters objected that the plain language of the statute barred federally established health exchanges.[437] In my view, the core principle that majority needed was the strong principle of subsidiarity I have articulated. Under that principle, absent a more specific prohibition from Congress, it is entirely in accordance with the positive power and duty of subsidiarity for the federal government to step into the shoes of a state that has failed in its own subsidiary functions.

For a constitutional example, consider *Gonzalez v. Raich*,[438] which posed the question whether the national government could use its commerce powers to ban the cultivation and possession of so-called "medical marijuana" in California. The state had allowed "medical" use in defiance of existing federal criminal prohibitions and despite a federal interest in controlling the illegal interstate market in marijuana, which would be heavily affected by California's action.[439] This was not a case in which subsidiarity required the decision to be made at the lowest possible level of government; rather it was a case in which a subordinate jurisdiction had attempted to arrogate to itself, in effect, the power to change national policy concerning a highly controversial drug. That was in itself a failure of subsidiarity, rightly understood. Sensibly, a majority held, in an opinion by Justice John Paul Stevens (with Justice Scalia concurring in the judgment), that the prohibition fell comfortably within the federal government's constitutional authority.[440] This was to treat national constitutional power in the right way, based on Marshall's opinion in *McCulloch*: as a loose-fitting garment that leaves room for the constitutional order to grow and develop over time, while maintaining its fundamental principles.[441]

On this approach, the principles sought to be protected by the discourse of "state sovereignty" are not ignored or belittled. Subsidiary political jurisdictions, like subsidiary corporations of all types, have legitimate roles in an overall scheme for the promotion of the common good, and in that sense they are owed a duty of justice by the highest public authority not to be unnecessarily disrupted in the performance of those roles. This is the core of truth in the usual libertarian and state-sovereignty construal of subsidiarity. But the very statement of this truth suggests it cannot be embodied rigidly in a written code, for it is impossible to say in advance when exceptional circumstances will arise, such that the public authority has both a positive right and a positive duty to bring aid that corrects the malfunctions of the subsidiary bodies. Rather that truth should be embodied in the prudential judgment of the public authority, as a principle of comity and of respect for the constitutional place of subsidiary jurisdictions. I have suggested some ways to institutionalize this middle way, which gives the highest public authority the strength of a giant when necessary, but also aims to temper the exercise of that strength with prudence and self-restraint.

C. Rights and the Common Good

For liberal constitutional theory, emphatically including both its right wing (originalism) and its left wing (progressivism), rights are central to the project of ever-increasing autonomy. Liberal constitutional theory thus caricatures non-liberal approaches to constitutional theory as "authoritarian," by which is meant non-liberal approaches are incapable of recognizing or respecting rights. But this is false. Classical legal theory emphatically has a conception of rights – just not a liberal conception. To elucidate this by example, in what follows I will apply the classical conception both negatively and positively.

Negatively, I illustrate the classical conception with a pair of the Court's most execrable and also revealing decisions. One is *United States v. Alvarez*,[442] which partially invalidated the Stolen Valor Act,[443] a statute making it a crime to falsely claim to have received (*inter alia*) the Congressional Medal of Honor. Another example is *Ashcroft v.*

Free Speech Coalition,[444] in which the Court invalidated an attempt to prohibit "virtual" child pornography. *Ashcroft* and *Alvarez* are decisions that only a Court ideologically oblivious to the common good could have issued. Positively, I suggest some rights supported by common good constitutionalism that are ignored or underdeveloped by liberal accounts of rights. One example involves rights to promote environmental goods through law – including through litigation. I will argue that the current doctrine of "standing" must be seriously restricted insofar as it bars such suits, and more broadly that "standing" should be reshaped precisely to encourage plaintiffs representing the public interest rather than litigating private grievances.

I will sketch all this with a very light hand, and deliberately so. The aim is not to offer a comprehensive analysis of issue after issue, but merely to illustrate the processes of thought that result when a common good framework is brought into contact with recent legal questions. Excellent work by other scholars has already begun to examine how rights oriented to the common good look.[445] Once we have the basic conception framed correctly, the rest of the picture can be filled in over time.

The classical view of rights

There is an important sense in which the allocation of right is the foundation of the *ius commune*.[446] It is certainly true that rights could be held either by individuals or by groups and be asserted by them. The crucial distinction, however, between the classical and modern conceptions involves the question of the *justification* of rights. Even where rights may be held and asserted by individuals, such rights may be justified in strictly individualist terms or instead in terms of the common good, which is also the good of individuals, their highest good. An example from modern American free speech law would involve the difference between autonomy-based justifications for speech rights, which focus on protecting the free expression of individual views and preferences, and political justifications for speech rights, which focus on speech as a contribution to the common political processes of a community.

The latter sort of justification for rights is the ordinary case for the classical account of law.[447] On the classical conception, rights are *iura* (the plural of *ius*) because *ius* is justice – affording to each what is due to each. Crucially, what is due to each, on the classical view, is itself determined by the common good, right from the ground up. Here the contrast with liberal theory is critical. It is not true, of course, that liberal theory takes no account of collective interests. But it takes account of them (1) aggregatively, as a summation of individual interests ("the greatest good of the greatest number") and (2) as an override to rights justified in individualist terms, as when liberal jurisprudence talks of a "public order" override to rights determined elsewhere. On the classical conception, by contrast, the common good enters into the very definition of rights themselves, from the beginning. There is no question of "overriding" rights for the common good. Rather it is a question of tailoring the scope of rights to the common good because that is the justification that already animates those rights, at every stage.

The contrast emerges clearly when we consider the doctrinal formulas that govern adjudication of rights in both current American law and European human rights law. In American law, the courts say – roughly speaking, but in a typical formulation – that individual rights can be trumped or overridden when there is a "compelling governmental interest" and the government can show that the law at issue is the "least restrictive alternative."[448] The implicit premise of this framework is that the interests of "government" as representative of the political collective, on the one hand, and the rights of individuals, on the other, are opposed and must be balanced against each other. It is, implicitly but unmistakably, a utilitarian and aggregative conception of rights. I believe, subject to correction, that a similar point can be made about the proportionality test that is broadly characteristic of European constitutional and human rights law, under which, roughly speaking, a right can be overridden when but only when the government acts in accordance with law, for a legitimate public or democratic aim, and in the least intrusive manner necessary, without imposing gratuitous or disproportionate harm on individuals.[449] Here too, talk of "balancing" collective and individual interests already betrays a departure from the classical conception.

Rights, properly understood, are always ordered to the common good and that common good is itself the highest individual interest. The issue is not balancing or override by extrinsic considerations, but internal specification and determination of the right's proper ends and, therefore, its proper boundaries or limits. Deference to the political authority within reasonable limits – the "margin of appreciation" of human rights law – is built into this conception from the start, rather than tacked on as a controversial addition.

Free speech

The classical conception helps to explain and lends coherence to the account of rights that was familiar to the Constitution's framers. I will begin with the freedom of speech, which provides a clean illustration both of the classical conception and of the pragmatic importance of the shift in perspective on rights I am advocating.

Let us return to the work by Jud Campbell I mentioned earlier on founding-era conceptions of natural rights to free speech. Campbell's work shows that "for most of American history, the governing paradigm of expressive freedom was one of limited toleration, protecting speech within socially defined boundaries. And the modern embrace of content and viewpoint neutrality . . . occurred only in the 1960s as the Supreme Court merged earlier strands of rights jurisprudence in novel ways."[450] In other words, although the natural rights tradition is sometimes treated as an empty vessel for modern libertarian views, that is an anachronism. In fact the classical conception, even in its natural right variant, had a different legal structure than the highly libertarian free speech law that emerged after World War II. The classical conception recognized rights as defeasible by legislation that ordered or limited speech to the common good.

> [N]atural rights at the Founding scarcely resembled our modern notion of rights as determinate legal constraints on governmental authority. Rather, Americans typically viewed natural rights as aspects of natural liberty that governments should help *protect*

against private interference (through tort law, property law, and so forth) and that governments themselves could *restrain* only to promote the public good and only so long as the people or their representatives consented. And assessing the public good – generally understood as the welfare of the entire society – was almost entirely a legislative task, leaving very little room for judicial involvement. Natural rights thus powerfully shaped the way that the Founders thought about the purposes and structure of government, but they were not legal "trumps" in the way that we often talk about rights today.[451]

In a sense, moreover, it is inaccurate to say that rights were "defeasible" in the classical structure. Rather more accurate would be to say that rights were *determinable.* That is, rights (as *ius*) are intrinsically ordered to the common good, but the common good is not given in a fixed, identical form for all polities at all times; instead it subsumes a range of general principles we have discussed under the heading of *ragion di stato*,[452] principles that as always have dimensions of scope and weight, and that may in some cases conflict with one another. The common good, then, is itself subject to public *determinatio* or concretization, as are the rights that flow from the common good.

Because of the basic structure of determination, judges would defer to the legislative specification within broad boundaries of reasonableness – the familiar structure of judicial review that we have already seen in earlier chapters. Judges, in this framework, ask whether the public *determinatio* has transgressed the broad boundaries of reason and become "arbitrary" – a word frequently invoked in the caselaw. The closest analogue in modern law is probably to (forgiving versions of) arbitrariness review under the Administrative Procedure Act, which focuses not on placing substantive limits on the scope of government action, but on ensuring that government action is adequately reasoned in light of the interests at stake. In a very loose sense, under the classical structure, all constitutional law is like modern administrative law.

In light of all this, there is no doubt that the structure of free speech protection will be less libertarian under common good constitutionalism than under the law that has been propagated by federal courts since the 1960s. That body of law is, in global perspective, an outlier; it is extreme, in part because of its radical emphasis on autonomy. Let me now give some examples from the modern caselaw and show how they would come out differently under common good constitutionalism. The answer in each case is that government would have much broader regulatory authority. (This is not to say, of course, that the classical approach to rights always and necessarily has this character. Rather it justifies rights differently. We will shortly see some cases in which it recognizes rights that the individualist approach rejects.)

Stolen valor

One of the most egregiously misguided decisions in the United States Reports is the so-called "stolen valor case," *United States v. Alvarez*.[453] A federal statute made it a crime to falsely represent oneself as having been awarded a defined range of public honors. The defendant falsely claimed to have received the Congressional Medal of Honor – the Nation's highest decoration for valor.[454] The plurality opinion, by Justice Anthony Kennedy, framed the question as whether the government could prohibit false statements of fact which the government took to be socially harmful, and then condemned that asserted power as obviously overbroad, portraying the government as aiming to create an Orwellian Ministry of Truth.[455]

In fact the question at hand was much narrower: whether the government could prohibit false statements that threaten to destroy a public and common good, the military honors system, that is itself inherently reputational, inherently based on speech by people about other people. The plurality acknowledged, as it had to, that "[w]here false claims are made to effect a fraud or secure moneys or other valuable considerations, say offers of employment, it is well established that the Government may restrict speech without affronting the First Amendment."[456] But if that is so, if the government may act to maintain the public integrity of market transactions, why may it not act to maintain the public integrity of something higher and more central to the *res publica*, the integrity of military honors? The Court's unexplained privilege for governmental protection of the commercial marketplace relative to the protection of public honors is bizarre, almost a parody of bourgeois constitutionalism. What is clear is that it is just as much a vision of the common good as that underlying the challenged law, merely an implausible and unappealing vision.

In a fallback argument, the plurality suggested that the Stolen Valor Act was not necessary to achieve the government's objectives, mainly because private, decentralized "counterspeech" by individuals could suffice to shame those who falsely represented themselves as holders of public honors.[457] A moment's reflection suggests that the Court here effectively forced the privatization of the enforcement function needed to uphold the integrity of the honors system. Private individuals would bear the burden first of detecting the fraud, and then the probably greater burden of speaking out against it, all while subject to the usual free-riding pathologies of the Tragedy of the Commons,[458] such that each would have an incentive to let others take the lead in confronting the false claimant. Public institutions exist in part to address exactly this sort of problem and to help achieve the result that each would prefer for all, absent the problem of collective action. To say that "the freedom of speech" requires decentralized private enforcement of the military honors system is akin to saying that the constitutional prohibition on unreasonable searches and seizures requires decentralized, vigilante efforts to enforce the criminal laws. Only a Court systematically oblivious to the common good – or, more accurately, in the grip of an implausibly libertarian vision of the common good as promoted solely by decentralized individual action, even with respect to the public system of military honors – could imagine such a restriction.

Obscenity

An equally egregious case is *Ashcroft v. Free Speech Coalition*,[459] in which the Court, again through Justice Anthony Kennedy, invalidated as "overbroad" a federal law that barred the creation of virtual child pornography – that is, child pornography created with computer imagery or with adult actors posing as children.[460] The law, Kennedy wrote – in words that ought to be infamous – "prohibits speech that records no crime and creates no victims by its production."[461] This is John Stuart Mill's harm principle[462] taken to its logical endpoint, and the endpoint is a grotesque place for the law to be, a grotesque parody of the common good of a community. The victim is both, and simultaneously, the person watching and the whole polity. Child pornography tears at the very fabric of natural human order in ways that cannot be accounted for in a narrow calculus of immediate harms in production or use. Even as to the immediate individual consumer of virtual child pornography, it is grotesque that a polity that engages in paternalistic regulation of addictive drugs, of automotive safety (seatbelt laws), and of motorcycle safety (helmet laws) and a dozen other subjects should not do so for depictions of child pornography. Whatever sort of decision this is, it is hardly oriented toward a tenable account of the common good. Whatever the outer boundaries of rational determination of the right of free expression, the law at issue fell comfortably within those bounds and thus comfortably within the government's authority.

The point generalizes beyond virtual child pornography to pornography generally. However our current law of obscenity and protected sexual speech should be described, it is not an originalist body of law. It is, at bottom, a product of the free speech revolution of the 1960s and 1970s, which perhaps not coincidentally occurred roughly simultaneously with the sexual revolution. From the classical perspective, one of the core tasks of political authority is to protect the health, safety, and morals of the public from those who would degrade them, in several senses. It is not just a matter of ensuring individual consent (the liberal theory of rights, founded in autonomy), but of ensuring a public environment that is not overrun by material damaging to the moral well-being of the political community. Public prohibition of pornography is a form of environmentalism for morals, and should be left to the reasonable determination of public authorities on the same terms, and under the same deferential limits, as the other issues we have discussed. Certainly an authentic originalism, as opposed to an originalism that is merely a cover for a libertarian account of political well-being, would so hold. On the other hand, as I have argued throughout, there is in a sense no such thing as authentic originalism; the inescapable need to import some theory or other of political well-being to make originalism operative is precisely what makes it an illusory approach to constitutional interpretation.

A note on blasphemy

Earlier, I mentioned an important discovery – in a law student note – that blasphemy prosecutions were consistently upheld against free speech challenges, and other challenges, during the founding era and well beyond, throughout the nineteenth century and indeed into the twentieth:

> Until well into the twentieth century, American law recognized blasphemy as proscribable speech. The blackletter rule was clear. Constitutional liberty entailed a right to articulate views on religion, but not a right to commit blasphemy – the offense of "maliciously reviling God," which encompassed "profane ridicule of Christ." The English common law had punished blasphemy as a crime, while excluding "disputes between learned men upon particular controverted points" from the scope of criminal blasphemy. Looking to this precedent, nineteenth-century American appellate courts consistently upheld proscriptions on blasphemy, drawing a line between punishable blasphemy and protected religious speech. At the close of the nineteenth century, the U.S. Supreme Court still assumed that the First Amendment did not "permit the publication of ... blasphemous ... articles." And in 1921 the Maine Supreme Court affirmed a blasphemy conviction under the state's First Amendment analogue. Even on the eve of American entry into World War II, the Tenth Circuit upheld an anti-blasphemy ordinance against a facial First Amendment challenge. Only in the postwar period did the doctrine promulgated by appellate courts begin to shift.[463]

This history is important on several grounds. It is further evidence that the shift away from the classical worldview happened quite recently, in historical perspective. As with obscenity law, the reigning approach to free speech law is essentially an innovation of the era after World War II. Relatedly, the history of blasphemy in our law poses a grievous challenge for originalism and its libertarian allies. That history underscores that whatever the founding era meant by the "Blessings of Liberty," the program of modern liberal legal theory was not it. Nor can it really be otherwise. Every polity proclaims and enforces truths that cannot be questioned, at least at certain times or places or in certain ways; it is idle to pretend otherwise. Our own certainly does. The point here is not to urge the reinstatement of blasphemy laws in their classical form, but rather to illustrate the fundamental challenge that the history poses for originalism, insofar as originalists pretend that the enforcement of public morals and of public piety is foreign to our constitutional order.

Environmental rights

I now turn to a different topic, environmentalism, in part for its intrinsic importance to a developing conception of *ragion di stato*, and in part to illustrate that a revived classical conception of rights does not always cut in one direction, recognizing a narrower set of rights. On the contrary, in this domain a classical conception supports a broadening of rights to proceed in court, in order to allow individuals to act on behalf of the *res publica* to promote environmental concerns.

As to the first point, environmental justice in anything like its modern form does not appear in classical catalogues of the principles of the *ragion di stato*. But it is not hard to see how environmental justice follows by a genuine development of the tradition, preserving its principles while adapting their application to changing circumstances. Since the sixteenth century, human knowledge of the environment has substantially increased and circumstances have objectively changed. And a right relationship to the environment is almost a defining example of a genuinely common good,[464] one that is shared by all without diminution while being a good for each taken individually, and arguably a precondition for the enjoyment of any other goods.

As to the second point, our environmental law largely developed in the same period in which classical law was being abandoned and forgotten. Our environmental law is thus pervaded by premises, particularly individualist premises about the nature and scope of rights, that are inconsistent with common good constitutionalism. In important respects, that law could be reformed to embody rights ordered to the common good. Two illustrations follow.

Standing and the "injury in fact" test

In important cases, such as *Lujan v. Defenders of Wildlife*,[465] the Court has denied standing to environmental plaintiffs who were deemed unable to show "injury in fact."[466] The point of the test is, in important part, individuation; it is to assess whether the plaintiff has suffered a distinctive and individual harm, rather than a "generalized grievance," a general undifferentiated harm to the public at large. But general common harm is, of course, precisely the sort of harm in which common good constitutionalism is especially interested. From the common good perspective, the "injury in fact" test has things precisely backward. Tongue only somewhat in cheek, one might say that the better standing test should be whether the plaintiff can show some sort of connection between the complaint and the common good; the aim should precisely be to exclude suits for strictly private individual benefit.

The standard argument here, made by Justice Scalia in *Lujan* and elsewhere, has been twofold: allowing such suits would undermine the restriction of the judicial power under Article III to "cases and controversies,"[467] and also the separation of executive and judicial powers, by making the courts "virtual continuing monitors of the wisdom and soundness of Executive action."[468] The former objection has always begged the question; the very issue to be decided is whether individual injury in fact is necessary to create a "case or controversy." On an older view, all that is necessary is a cause of action created by statute or other valid source of law.[469]

As for the latter objection, it sounds principally in Article II of the Constitution,[470] rather than Article III, and it has always been slightly unclear why it is a *standing* problem as opposed to a merits argument for the constitutional invalidity of the provisions authorizing the court to set aside executive action at the behest of the relevant plaintiff. That said, the objection seems strained even on its own terms. The plaintiff's claim will always be a legal claim, not a bare claim that the judgment of the relevant executive body is simply unsound – unless that unsoundness rises to the level of arbitrariness, which is itself relevant under the law (both the positive administrative law of the Administrative Procedure Act and the natural law, which uses arbitrariness as the measure of the limits of valid determination). None of this is to deny that the executive should be afforded proper deference on the merits, within the broad boundaries of the executive's determination of the legislature's determinations. The point is that such deference is itself sufficient to accommodate any relevant Article II concerns.

The caselaw, however, is not entirely insensitive to the legitimate scope of determination by the public authority. In concurrence in *Lujan*, Justice Kennedy argued that Congress could itself articulate injuries that would serve as the predicate for injury in fact,[471] and later cases have confirmed this principle.[472] The availability of determination reduces the operative difference between conceiving lawsuits as public actions ordered to the common good and basing standing on private, individual injury in fact – although it does not eliminate the important symbolic resonances of the difference in the legal conceptions themselves.

Two straightforward corollaries of the view I have advanced are the validity of state lawsuits to enforce environmental laws, and of *qui tam* actions for the same purpose. As to the former, in *Massachusetts v. EPA*,[473] states sued the EPA to force it to take jurisdiction over climate change issues.[474] The Court's analysis was awkward, because it was obliged by extant doctrine to fold the states' claims into a framework geared to individual injuries, while also gesturing toward older precedent that recognized the sovereign rights of states to sue as *parens patriae* to represent the common good of their citizens.[475] The latter should count as, in itself, a fully sufficient basis for state standing, regardless of injury to the state's proprietary interests in its own right. At a minimum, the language of individual injury is misplaced, a kind of category mistake, as to a governing entity charged with stewardship of the good of the community and its environment – a point I return to shortly.

As to *qui tam* actions, where the legislature (or the executive exercising delegated power) creates rights of action that enlist the individual claimant as a "private attorney general" acting in the public interest, that decision should be strongly presumed to amount to a valid *determinatio* of the right to proceed into court and raise any claims that the public and its governing authority could lodge. There is no convincing reason that the governing authority may not charge members of the general public with executing public functions as "private attorneys general." Absent patent arbitrariness, "standing" should create no further constitutional barrier to the right to sue. And indeed the Court, with some wobbling, has ultimately been hospitable to *qui tam* actions, although only by awkwardly holding them to satisfy the restrictive conception of individual "injury in fact" – the theory being that the *qui tam* claimant has an interest as the assignee of a claim.[476] The better and more straightforward ground would be that the public authority may entrust others with particular duties at need and reward them, as it sees fit, for undertaking those duties.

Of course the standing principles I have mentioned here sweep beyond the environmental cases in which they are perhaps most insistently present, and which almost definitionally implicate the common good. The logic of the view here is that the Court went fundamentally wrong in the 1970s when, dredging up some scattered caselaw from the past, it began to reject otherwise valid suits by interpreting Article III to bar "generalized grievances" that are "common to all members of the public."[477] It is quite perverse to deny standing because the claimant seeks to represent the common good of all citizens; that is precisely the sort of claim that should be given priority, not disavowed. The timing here is no accident; the period after World War II, especially during and after the 1960s, was when our law began to deviate from classical principles into ever-more stringent forms of liberal individualism.

Put differently, modern standing doctrine is premised on an assumption directly denied by common good constitutionalism: that an injury is *either* individual *or* common. As we have seen, however, the classical conception holds that the common good is also the good of individuals, and conversely that injury to the common good is itself an individual harm. Standing doctrine created since the 1970s, then, is distinctively liberal doctrine that is out of step with the classical approach.

Here and elsewhere, as I have been at pains to emphasize, the view flowing from common good constitutionalism is not some import of strange foreign legal principles or traditions into the good ol' common-law system. Quite the opposite. Until roughly the 1970s, the "injury in fact" test in its current signification was no part of our law. Rather the only test of standing was whether the claimant had a cause of action and a "legal right" or "legal interest" sufficient to ground the suit. As an interpretation of Article III, that view was long-standing, equally consistent with the language, and compatible with the common good, insofar as it allowed legislatures to specify and determine rights to use in accordance with the public interest, treating individual claimants as delegates and representatives of the common good.

The "public trust" doctrine and the stewardship principle

On the merits, common good constitutionalism supports an expansive version of the "public trust" doctrine. This is a family of ideas with different formulations, but in one way or another they all give the state both the right and duty of stewardship over crucial environmental resources for the benefit of the public – the original example being tidelands and navigable waterways. The underlying principle, however, extends much more broadly. The *Institutes of Justinian* held that air, running water, the sea, and the seashore were common resources open to all by natural law.[478] By a straightforward development of doctrine, the environment and climate generally should be seen in the same way.

The consequence would be a high-level principle of public law, both constitutional and administrative: a broadly strengthened authority of government to act as steward of the public trust. This stewardship principle would be taken to be both a small-c constitutional principle and a canon of interpretation; it would be expressly taken to support interpretations of constitutional and statutory texts, and of judge-made doctrines, that promote the public trust. At a constitutional level, the "public use" requirement for public "takings" of property rights under the Fifth and Fourteenth Amendments should be interpreted broadly,[479] in a manner consistent with the recognition that action to protect the environment is ordered to the common good, that property rights are also ordered to the common good, and (hence) that public stewardship is itself in the interests of the property claimants, their own highest good.

Perhaps even more importantly, the principle would be taken as foundational to the administrative state. In the American executive branch, very much along these lines, a recent Presidential Memorandum expressly made "environmental stewardship" an important determinant of agency regulatory priorities, directing the head of the Office of Management and Budget to "provide concrete suggestions on how the regulatory review process can promote public health and safety, economic growth, social welfare, racial justice, *environmental stewardship*, human dignity, equity, and *the interests of future generations*."[480] The courts ought to recognize the broad principle of public trust and environmental stewardship as a "relevant factor" in any administrative law case where they are asked to review agency action for arbitrariness, unless clear and specific statutes state otherwise, and should construe substantive agency authority broadly under organic statutes.

For present purposes, there is no need to accumulate further examples. It is clear enough that a reorientation of public law to the common good would have major consequences in many areas. Throughout the previous examples, however, the discussion has aimed to emphasize that judges and other officials cannot help acting on one or another conception of the common good, and in fact that they have always done so. In that sense, common good constitutionalism offers a far better interpretive account of our developing constitutional order than do the accounts of the critics.

Conclusion

As I hope the preceding discussion has made clear, a revival of common good constitutionalism will require a break with the immediate past – partly at the level of actual law, as in the case of our absurdly hypertrophied free speech jurisprudence and our misdirected standing jurisprudence, and partly at the level of theory, which has so far lost its bearings that it fails to see the powerful elements of classical jurisprudence that implicitly structure our law even today. What does such a break entail, and how might it occur? Let me offer some concluding remarks addressed both to (what economists call) the demand side of the problem – what is to be done? – and to the supply side – what reason is there to think that those who can act will do so?

Here a typical error often arises. It is easy to interpret the problem of "what is to be done?" solely or mainly in pragmatic terms. But the main thing that is to be done, first and foremost, is to think clearly. The speculative reason must guide the practical reason. We have first to understand the law as it really is; only then can we understand where we have abandoned the law as it really is, and how to recover it. And thinking clearly is the principal contribution that a work of scholarship might conceivably be able to make, perhaps the only contribution. So a book of this sort will have done its job if I can make clear that the classical law has the right account of the real nature and structure of law, and then discuss where, and how, we have departed from the classical law.

Referring to law as it really is means, in my view, recapturing Ulpian's description of law as the art of goodness and fairness. It is a positivist misconception to think that "how the law really is" stands to one side, that "political morality" stands to another, and our task is to decide how they relate. The aspiration for justice is built into law from the ground up and from the start. This does not mean, it should go without saying, that justice and law are identical. Although law is a department of political morality, it is a distinctive department of political morality in which distinctive considerations are brought to bear, among them a division of institutional roles, as I have argued throughout.

Once we begin to think clearly, it is apparent that somewhere along the way we have rejected our own magnificent legal heritage – partly without understanding that we were doing so, in an ill-considered fit of rebellion. There is no one definite point at which the classical heritage of our law was officially rejected. It has been a process, not a moment, and the result has by no means been a thoroughgoing erasure, as I have emphasized throughout. Certainly throughout the nineteenth century judges frequently, easily, and openly drew upon the categories of the classical tradition. Sometime around World War I positivism became a major force in American law, and by the time legal theory was reconsolidated after World War II, the *ius commune* had been reduced to something like a set of echoes within the prevailing Legal Process framework. Consider the quasi-teleology and purposivism of much Legal Process theorizing, which, however, lacked the underlying intellectual structures of the *ius commune* needed to provide underpinnings for those features.

Whatever happened, whenever it happened, and for whatever reasons, the current situation is clear enough. And an odd situation it is, rife with strange tensions and contradictions. The law has officially disavowed its own classical heritage but in practice draws upon and develops it, all while afflicted by a strange amnesia, a near-total lack of self-awareness that it is doing so. Even the administrative state, or especially the administrative state, which on some erroneous views is the least classical part of our operative constitutional order, is shot through with principles of *ius* that structure and channel its legality on behalf of the common good. Their protests notwithstanding, the two major schools of judging constantly encourage judges to "legislate morality"; they constantly underwrite judicial action on implicit conceptions of the good for persons subject to the law. And all the while, they officially maintain a commitment to different types of positivism: originalism (at least in the currently prominent version) on the theory that law can be identified strictly by reference to conventions giving legal force to past acts of sovereign will, and progressivism on the theory that the aim of the legal instrumentalist should be to liberate human will from all unchosen, objective constraints, first and foremost the master constraint that is law's real, unchanging nature.

To be sure, the classical law and in particular the natural law was only ever driven underground. Its existence could be officially denied or said to be irrelevant, but it could never be eradicated from the judicial mind. Despite a series of decisions making resolute efforts to deny the basic and inescapable authority of government to legislate morality, it has remained clear to all but the radical ideologues of liberty that every decision of authority is based on some conception or other of the common good. In a number of cases, what happened is simply that the justices would draw upon principles of natural justice without labeling them as such. Consider the Delphic statement, right at the beginning of the Court's opinion in *Bowen v. Georgetown University Hospital*[481] in 1988, that "retroactivity is not favored in the law"[482] – a statement not attributed to any positive source of constitutional law, if only because there was no source that, as conventionally interpreted in 1988 or today, could have supported that very general statement. In this sense, a revival and development of the classical law already have a great deal of material to work with even in the period after the 1960s. Yet it is true that important sectors of our law would today be very different if the classical law had been consistently applied as a self-conscious approach, as it was from the founding era throughout the nineteenth century.

The consequence of all this is that something has to give. In order to revive and renew the classical tradition in and for American public law – which is also, I suggest, to arrive at the best constructive interpretation of most of our current constitutional order – one must break with the immediate past. The last few chapters of a long chain novel have to be partly ripped up, partly reinterpreted in drastic terms.

What, if anything, justifies ripping up substantial segments of the recent development of our law? What of the claims of fit? The basic answer is that there has *already* been a serious tear in the fabric of our law; the chain novel has already been mutilated in part. Both progressives and (reacting to them) originalists, imagining themselves mortal enemies, cut themselves off from the classical heritage of our law, constructed imagined pasts, and invented traditions that projected their own premises backward in time, erasing the classical law for present purposes. No matter what we do today, the pattern of our law will already have been torn in a fundamental way. The only question now is how best to repair it.

This is a macro-level claim about our legal practice. A micro-level analogy from within that practice may be helpful. On a smaller scale, courts have often faced a similar type of doctrinal situation. In this sort of sequence, caselaw falls into three periods. In the first period, the courts develop a long-standing, rich line of precedent up until a certain point. Then, in the second period, the court issues a sudden, perhaps ill-considered decision breaking with that long-standing line of precedent, thereby effecting a rip in the legal fabric. Later still, in the third period, the court faces a kind of dilemma of fidelity, of integrity. There is no way to keep faith with all the precedents, assuming they are fundamentally at odds with one another; one has to choose.

Faced with this situation, the Supreme Court has sometimes chosen to overturn the precedents from the second period and return to the older, long-standing rule, especially when the new approach was an abrupt innovation, poorly reasoned, unstable, or incoherent. Consider *Solorio v. United States*,[483] in which the Court overruled a precedent from about twenty years earlier which had held that a military tribunal could only try a service member if the offense had a "service connection."[484] That overruled precedent had itself departed from a venerable contrary rule. The Court observed in *Solorio* that the decision to be overruled had "doubtful foundations," took a "novel" approach that produced "confusion," and must "bow to the lessons of experience and the force of better reasoning."[485] The previous chapters have suggested that all those features, on a larger scale, are true of the odd path of public law since the early to middle part of the twentieth century, when our law began, in a curious and clearly novel way, to become confused about its own nature, based on interpretive views with exceedingly dubious foundations.

Broadly speaking, it is not as though in recent decades our courts have consistently taken any course, even a bad course. Rather, I suggest, they have oscillated incoherently between progressivism and originalism, while implicitly pursuing a distorted program of incorporating political morality of a sort into the law, even as they occasionally deny doing so, even to themselves. The situation is untenable, intellectually and pragmatically. The best way forward is to look backward for inspiration. A revival and adaptation of the classical law, translated into today's circumstances, is the only way to restore the integrity of our law and of our legal traditions.

So much for what is to be done. What of the supply side? In what feasible scenario might the classical legal tradition be revived, either in the United States or elsewhere? Who might have both the desire and willingness to do so? Here too, I think it is a kind of category error for scholars to worry overmuch about such things with respect to the accounts they themselves offer. If we have a true account of law, what the great and the mighty make of it is up to them, and is mostly determined by the vagaries of history and politics rather than by anything a book may say. Furthermore, originalism and progressivism between them currently have a strong, if weakening, grip on legal institutions. Each buttresses the other in a kind of symbiosis of rivalry, exploiting the other as its necessary hate-object and fundraising target. In the short run, the dual-headed regime of progressivism and originalism will continue, with each claiming to be the other's nemesis, while in fact propping each other up.

Nonetheless, there are reasons for optimism about the longer run. The intellectual foundations of the joint regime are being steadily undermined, and conflicts between the two reigning modalities are becoming sharper by the day. It is ever more clear that each approach, despite its protestations, necessarily embodies some substantive account of the good life for a political community. The pretense of neutrality toward the good, on which each approach relies in different ways, no longer fools very many. As the conflict between the two sharpens, an opportunity for the revival of the classical law arises, for when thieves fall out, honest men come into their own. Power is not enough to maintain a legal regime whose ideological pretensions are discredited, at least not indefinitely.

If it is true that the classical tradition captures the real nature of law, then our institutions have, for about two generations now, been acting on false theories of law, moderated and tempered only by the fact that their practice has been somewhat better than their theory. Because law is ultimately a practical science – because the speculative reason ultimately aims to guide the practical reason to a just conclusion – acting on false theories that contradict law's real nature has bad consequences in the real world, just as basing treatments on false medical theories might do. The obvious errors of originalist decisions like *Bostock*, the disruption they have spread, and the obvious cynicism and instrumentalism of progressive jurisprudence, have combined to create a vague but real sense of dissatisfaction with the reigning alternatives among younger lawyers. Roughly simultaneously, an overpowering wave of scholarship, cited in earlier chapters, has discredited key originalist claims. One is about the genesis of the administrative state, a claim that turns out to rest on an invented libertarian tradition. (The administrative state did not originate with Woodrow Wilson, and it did not somehow shatter or betray fundamental constitutional constraints.) The other is about the founders' own views of the proper approach to constitutional interpretation. No amount of fundraising by the Federalist Society can get well-read law students and younger legal academics to unsee that the founders were nothing like Robert Bork. They were in fact classical lawyers and natural lawyers.

Let us imagine, even if only as a thought experiment, that lawyers in Europe, the New World, and beyond were right when, for almost two millennia, they thought of law as the art of justice ("goodness and fairness"), and thought that the right conception of justice looked to the common good of the community, not merely to individual autonomy and preference satisfaction. If so, then a legal order in which the originalist party denies that law is the art of justice at all, and the progressive party denies that justice transcends the satisfaction of the individual will, rubs against the grain of reality. Sooner or later, on this view, law's real nature will reassert its claims.

Notes

1 There were of course second-order debates about how local law, *ius proprium*, and the *ius civile* or civic law related to the *ius commune* generally and to the natural law (*ius naturale*) and law of nations (*ius gentium*). By and large, the impulse of the jurists was to harmonize sources through interpretation wherever possible, rather than force the issue of which body of law had priority in a particular jurisdiction.

2 *See generally* Charles Donahue, Jr., *Ius Commune, Canon Law, and Common Law in England*, 66 TUL. L. REV. 1745 (1992) ("In the realm of basic principles, organizing ideas, techniques of argumentation, and habits of thought, the parallels are sufficiently great that one might want to call the common law simply a variant, admittedly an eccentric variant, of the multitude of legal systems that ultimately derive from the *ius commune*"); Richard Helmholz, *Magna Carta and the Ius Commune*, 66 U. CHI. L. REV. 297 (1999); RICHARD H. HELMHOLZ, NATURAL LAW IN COURT: A HISTORY OF LEGAL THEORY IN PRACTICE (2015) (hereafter "Helmholz, Natural Law"); Patrick J. Smith, *Sir John Fortescue and the Ius Commune*, https://iusetiustitium.com/sir-john-fortescue-and-the-ius-commune ("The influence of the *ius commune* on Bracton and Glanvill is well known and well documented. But it's worth observing that this influence continued well after the foundation of the English legal tradition and it constitutes, therefore, an important part of the concrete order underpinning modern American law"). Overall, the following judgment seems entirely sound:

> [B]oth English and continental law formed part of the very same legal tradition. Their specific technologies or solutions

might have varied to some degree or the other, but they shared a common genealogy that bound them together more strongly than that which drew them apart. ... English common law and continental civil law formed part of a single European tradition from which they both drew as well as contributed.

Tamar Herzog, European Law and the Myths of a Separate English Legal System 22–23 (2018) (hereafter "Herzog, Myths"). *See also* Tamar Herzog, A Short History of European Law: The Last Two and a Half Millennia 167–82 (2018) (hereafter "Herzog, European Law"). As I discuss below, a corollary of all this is that constitutional lawyers can easily go wrong by assuming that references to the "common law" in the founding era exclude the *ius commune*. In fact the *ius commune* was itself part of the common law, broadly understood.

3 *See* Dig. 1.1 (Ulpian, *Institutes* 2) (A. Watson, trans., 2009). *See also* Thomas Aquinas, Summa Theologica, pt. I-II, q. 90 art. 4 (Fathers of the English Dominican Province, trans., Christian Classics reprt. 1981). For a modern account of legislation as reasoned governance, see Richard Ekins, *Legislation as Reasoned Action*, in Gregoire Weber et al., Legislated Rights: Securing Human Rights Through Legislation (2018).

4 For an early and classic explication of a somewhat similar point, *see generally* H. Jefferson Powell, *The Original Understanding of Original Intent*, 98 Harv. L. Rev. 885 (1984). For more recent sources, see note 241 below, and especially the excellent distillation in Jonathan Gienapp, *Written Constitutionalism, Past and Present*, 39 Law and History Review 321, 324 (2021):

Originalists' understanding of constitutional writtenness ... is anachronistic, a species of modern constitutional thinking that they unwittingly and uncritically impose on the eighteenth century. Founding-Era constitutionalists by and large were not positivists. They tended to think that much of law was "out there" – like the principles of mathematics or natural philosophy – awaiting discovery through reason and observation. No doubt plenty of law was made by human beings, and understanding how different kinds of law interacted and fit together posed vitally important questions. But it was impossible to understand law – and most of all fundamental law, of which constitutions, as the highest municipal authority, were a central part – without understanding its non-positivist dimensions. To a degree that cannot be ignored, those who made the United States Constitution presupposed this conception of law and its attendant understanding of constitutional content. . . . If we are interested in understanding the original Constitution – the one that eighteenth-century actors made, recognized, and debated – then we must see their work from the non-positivist perspective that once predominated and that informed their choices. Only then can we begin to make sense of the written constitution that they presented to the world. If we choose to interpret the Constitution from any other perspective, then we choose to interpret something other than the original Constitution. Whatever merits that other Constitution might boast, it will not be original – and thus will not be the Constitution that originalists claim to be recovering and the only one that can be said to possess original meaning.

5 *See generally, e.g.,* Henry M. Hart & Albert M. Sacks, The Legal Process: Basic Problems in the Making and Application of Law (1958).
6 *Cf.* Lawrence Lessig, *Fidelity in Translation*, 71 Texas Law Review 1165 (1993).
7 Aquinas, note 3 above, at pt. I-II, q. 90 art. 4.
8 So, for example, I have no stake in, and need take no position on, the nth-decimal debates between and among positivists and Dworkin exegetes. Although I draw on Dworkin's work for certain (limited) purposes, I spend no time rehashing his debates with H.L.A. Hart, Joseph Raz, or Hart's and Raz's epigones. This is partly because the purposes for which I draw on Dworkin do not require doing so; partly because I believe that Dworkin's

major critiques of Hart, THE CONCEPT OF LAW (1994), are essentially correct (and were later in effect conceded, not rebutted, by Hart); and, most importantly, because I prosecute Dworkin's core points about the non-positivist practice and phenomenology of judging and legal practice inductively, through the accumulation of examples within my areas of expertise, rather than through abstract jurisprudential argument.

9   *See* RONALD DWORKIN, LAW'S EMPIRE 228–38 (1986).

10 In Chapter 2 I rely heavily on important treatments of the classical and natural law in America by Richard Helmholz, William Novak, Stuart Banner, and others cited there. Other essential treatments of the natural law, and its relationship to the classical law generally, include JOHANNES MESSNER, SOCIAL ETHICS: NATURAL LAW IN THE WESTERN WORLD (rev. ed. 1965); HEINRICH A. ROMMEN, THE NATURAL LAW: A STUDY IN LEGAL AND SOCIAL HISTORY AND PHILOSOPHY (Russell Hittinger, ed., Liberty Fund ed. 1998); ALEXANDER PASSERIN D'ENTREVES, NATURAL LAW: AN INTRODUCTION TO LEGAL PHILOSOPHY (Routledge ed. 2017); HADLEY ARKES, BEYOND THE CONSTITUTION (reissued Princeton University Press 2021); Brian McCall, THE ARCHITECTURE OF LAW: REBUILDING LAW IN THE CLASSICAL TRADITION (University of Notre Dame Press 2018); and especially the illuminating treatment in JAVIER HERVADA, CRITICAL INTRODUCTION TO NATURAL RIGHT (2d ed. 2020). *See also* the brief but magisterial overview by Wolfgang Waldstein, *The Significance of Roman Law for the Development of European Law*, https://iu setiustitium.com/the-significance-of-roman-law-for-the-develop ment-of-european-law.

11 Because my main reliance on Dworkin is for his critiques of positivism and originalism, it is immaterial for my purposes whether, or in what sense, Dworkin is best understood as a natural lawyer, or whether his interpretivism really is a third way, different than both the classical law and positivism. (For an excellent overview of the issues, *see* PETAR POPOVIC, THE GOODNESS OF RIGHTS AND THE JURIDICAL DOMAIN OF THE GOOD, chapter 5 (2021).) As far as the critique of positivism goes, Dworkin and the classical law stand on common ground. Dworkin himself

noted wryly that rejecting the fundamental claim of positivism, namely that law can (only) be identified without reference to political morality (except, on some inclusive views, insofar as the positive law itself incorporates moral standards), put him in alliance with the classical law: "[If] any theory which makes the content of law sometimes depend on the correct answer to some moral question is a natural law theory, then I am guilty of natural law." Ronald Dworkin, *"Natural" Law Revisited*, 34 UNIVERSITY OF FLORIDA LAW REVIEW 165 (1982). In the same methodological space, compatible with the classical law even if not expressly written from within the classical tradition, see the illuminating account of fundamental and general constitutional principles in N.W. BARBER, THE PRINCIPLES OF CONSTITUTIONALISM (2018).

12 *See generally* Ronald Dworkin, *Hard Cases*, 88 HARV. L. REV. 1057 (1975) (describing the role of principles in judging close cases, a role that is not reducible to mere political policy preferences).

13 *See* DWORKIN, LAW'S EMPIRE, note 9 above, at 4–11.

14 [If contemporary judges think that their concrete convictions were in conflict with their abstract ones, because they did not reach the correct conclusions about the effect of their own principles, then the judges have a choice to make. It is unhelpful to tell them to follow the framers' legal intentions. They need to know which legal intentions – at how general a level of abstraction and why. So Bork and others who support the original understanding thesis must supply an independent normative theory – a particular political conception of constitutional democracy to answer that need. That normative theory must justify not only a general attitude of deference, but also what I shall call an interpretive schema: a particular account of how different levels of the framers' convictions and expectations contribute to concrete judicial decisions.

Ronald Dworkin, *Bork's Jurisprudence*, 57 U. CHI. L. REV. 657, 664 (1990) (reviewing ROBERT H. BORK, THE TEMPTING OF AMERICA: THE POLITICAL SEDUCTION OF THE LAW (1990)).

15 Ronald Dworkin, *The Moral Reading of the Constitution*, N.Y. REV. BOOKS, Mar. 21, 1996, at 46, https://www.nybooks.com/articles/1996/03/21/the-moral-reading-of-the-constitution. I will take my argument as having been carried, in substance, to the extent that originalists try to take such moral readings on board by having recourse to what some call "inclusive positivism," and what Dworkin called "Pickwickian Positivism." See RONALD DWORKIN, JUSTICE IN ROBES 188 (2006). "Inclusive positivism . . . is only an attempt to keep the name 'positivism' for a conception of law and legal practice that is entirely alien to positivism." Ibid. The same is true of versions of "inclusive originalism" that attempt to preserve the name while surrendering all the content to the classical legal tradition. I discuss this issue of convergence between nominal originalism on the one hand and the classical legal tradition on the other in Chapter 3.

16 See Dworkin, Law's Empire, note 9 above, at 239.

17 Another way of putting this point is that I have no need for Dworkin's distinction between principles and "policies," which many have criticized as arbitrary and unmotivated. As Dworkin conceived it, the distinction seems to assume a typical liberal opposition between "individual rights" and "collective interests," imagining the latter as aggregated social utility that may or may not "override" individual rights. See Popovic, note 11 above, at 164–67. On the conception I urge here, by contrast, the common good is itself a constitutional principle, the highest constitutional principle, just as the common good is itself the highest interest of individuals. As we will see, the common good (or one of its variants, such as *salus populi*) was frequently cited by classical lawyers in America as a fundamental constitutional principle authorizing broad action by public authorities on behalf of the public welfare.

18 *See, e.g.,* JOHN PAUL II, ENCYCLICAL LETTER *CENTESIMUS ANNUS*: ON THE HUNDREDTH ANNIVERSARY OF *RERUM NOVARUM*, art. 10, 15 (1991); PONTIFICAL COUNCIL FOR JUSTICE AND PEACE, COMPENDIUM OF THE SOCIAL DOCTRINE OF THE CATHOLIC CHURCH ¶¶ 192–96, 185–88 (2004) (hereafter "Compendium"). Within the project,

there are of course many further problems to be worked out about the relationships among these principles. As merely one example, see the discussion of the relationship between solidarity and subsidiarity, and their connections to the scope of political authority (nation or empire?), in Richard Ekins, *The State and Its People,* AM. J. JURIS. (2021) (reviewing Barber, Principles of Constitutionalism, note 11 above).

19 *See generally* LON L. FULLER, THE MORALITY OF LAW (rev. ed. 1969). In what follows, an awkward issue of exposition – although not a problem of theory – is that positivism need not involve a written text, merely a conventionally recognized rule of law (which might, for example, be an unwritten custom). For concreteness, I will focus on written *lex* as the paradigm of a positive enactment of the civil law, but all of my points can apply with equal force to a customary rule. This also allows me to engage the Supreme Court's recent pronouncement, a very confident pronouncement indeed, that "only the written word is the law." See note 32 below.

20 *See* Aquinas, note 3 above, at pt. II-II, q. 50 art. 1. For the connections between prudence and natural law, *see generally* FERENC HORCHER, PRUDENTIA IURIS: TOWARDS A PRAGMATIC THEORY OF NATURAL LAW (2000).

21 For an excellent overview of that many-faceted debate, *see generally* Aileen Kavanaugh, *Recasting the Political Constitution: From Rivals to Relationships,* 30 KING'S L. J. 43 (2019).

22 See the clearheaded comments by Professor Conor Casey of the University of Liverpool in a video lecture for the Oxford/ Blackfriars Common Good Series, https://youtu.be/MpZCKrp E5gw.

23 *See* Adrian Vermeule, *Liberalism and the Invisible Hand,* 3 AM. AFFAIRS 149 (2019); Adrian Vermeule, *Echoes of the Ius Commune,* 66 AM. J. JURIS. (2021) (reviewing Barber, Principles of Constitutionalism, note 11 above).

24 As I explain at length in ADRIAN VERMEULE, LAW'S ABNEGATION: FROM LAW'S EMPIRE TO THE ADMINISTRATIVE STATE (2016).

25 *See generally* CASS R. SUNSTEIN & ADRIAN VERMEULE, LAW AND LEVIATHAN: REDEEMING THE ADMINISTRATIVE STATE (2020).

26 Chevron, U.S.A., Inc. v. Nat. Res. Def. Council, Inc., 467 U.S. 837, 842–43 (1984).

27 Adrian Vermeule, *Rationally Arbitrary Decisions in Administrative Law*, 44 J. LEGAL STUD. S475 (2015).

28 *See generally* John Dewey, *Liberty and Social Control, in* 11 JOHN DEWEY: THE LATER WORKS, 1925–1953 360 (Jo Ann Boydston, ed., 1987); Robert L. Hale, *Coercion and Distribution in a Supposedly Non-Coercive State*, 38 POL. SCI. Q. 470 (1923).

29 *See* BERNARD WILLIAMS, ETHICS AND THE LIMITS OF PHILOSOPHY 108–10 (1985).

30 For an argument reaching the same conclusion from different premises, *see* Jordan L. Perkins, *On the Necessity of a "Common Good": Or, Against Originalism*, https://www.jordanlperkins.com/post/on-the-necessity-of-a-common-good-or-against-originalism.

31 Hawaii Housing Authority v. Midkiff, 467 U.S. 229, 240–41 (1984).

32 *See* Bostock v. Clayton Cty., Ga., 140 S. Ct. 1731, – (2020) ("Only the written word is the law . . . This Court normally interprets a statute in accord with the ordinary public meaning of its terms at the time of its enactment"). To be sure, there are endless, variant definitions of originalism, the sign of an unstable research program. In an older version, the watchword was "original intent"; in newer versions, "original law" or "original methods" originalism; and so on. The differences among these sub-conceptions do not make any difference to the points I will make. Hence I will speak (like the Court in Bostock) of original public meaning originalism, which emphasizes the supposed "fixation" of original meaning at the time of enactment. As discussed in Chapter 3, there is much less to fixation than meets the eye.

33 Ibid.

34 Rafael de Arízaga, *Notes on the Ius Commune Part I: The Hydra of Legal Positivism*, IUS & IUSTITIUM (Feb. 23, 2021), https://iuse tiustitium.com/notes-on-the-ius-commune-part-i-the-hydra-of-le gal-positivism. At the level of scholarly justifications, the leading theoretical defenses of originalism today are explicitly positivist. *See, e.g.,* William Baude, *Is Originalism Our Law?*, 115 COLUM.

L. Rev. 2349, 2353 (2015); Stephen E. Sachs, *Originalism as a Theory of Legal Change*, 38 Harv. J. Law & Pub. Poly. 817 (2015). However, there have always also been normative, non-positivist justifications for originalism, sounding in principles of political morality. Perhaps the most famous of these is an early argument of Antonin Scalia's that originalism appropriately constrains judicial discretion. *See* Antonin Scalia, *Originalism: The Lesser Evil*, 57 U. Cinn. L. Rev. 849 (1989). As discussed in note 15 above, in Chapter 3, and elsewhere, such justifications either fail on their own terms or, where successful, merely replicate the constraining and structuring devices of the classical law, which are themselves justified by reference to the common good. Those devices by no means allow any judge or other official to consult the full range of first-order moral considerations whenever the judge wants to. In other words, the reigning positivist version of originalism is the version that gives it *distinctive* content, and hence it is the version on which I will focus, although other versions are addressed at various points throughout. See, in particular, the discussion of hybrid versions of originalism in Chapter 3.

35 Here and elsewhere, some of the relevant text is incorporated into a forthcoming work co-authored with Professor Conor Casey in the Harvard Journal of Law & Public Policy, tentatively entitled "Myths of Common Good Constitutionalism."

36 *See generally* Stephen E. Sachs, *Finding Law*, 107 Calif. L Rev. 527 (2019).

37 *See* Janneke Gerards, General Principles of the European Convention on Human Rights 160–97 (2019).

38 R.H. Helmholz, *What Explains the Disappearance of Natural Law?* Syndicate (Mar. 17, 2021) (responding as part of a symposium about Andrew Forsyth, Common Law and Natural Law in America: From the Puritans to the Legal Realists (2019)), https://syndicate.network/symposia/theology/common-law-and-natural-law-in-america.

39 Ibid.

40 198 U.S. 45, 65–74 (1905) (Harlan, J., dissenting).

41 22 N.E. 188 (N.Y. 1889).

42 299 U.S. 304 (1936).

43 140 S.Ct. 1731 (2020).

44 42 U.S.C. § 2000e-2.

45 140 S.Ct. 2183 (2020).

46 576 U.S. 644 (2015).

47 Village of Euclid, Ohio v. Ambler Realty Co., 272 U.S. 365 (1926).

48 Annex to the Letter Dated 2 December 2020 from the Permanent Representative of the United States of America to the United Nations Addressed to the Secretary-General: Geneva Consensus Declaration on Promoting Women's Health and Strengthening the Family, U.N. Doc. A/75/626 (Dec. 2, 2020), https://docu ments-dds-ny.un.org/doc/UNDOC/GEN/N20/344/30/PDF/N20 34430.pdf?OpenElement.

49 See Dworkin, Law's Empire, note 9 above.

50 Examples are too numerous to mention, but compare the titles of these two: Garrett Epps, *Common-Good Constitutionalism Is an Idea as Dangerous as They Come*, THE ATLANTIC (Apr. 3, 2020), https://www.theatlantic.com/ideas/archive/2020/04/common-go od-constitutionalism-dangerous-idea/609385; Randy E. Barnett, *Common-Good Constitutionalism Reveals the Dangers of Any Non-Originalist Approach to the Constitution*, THE ATLANTIC (Apr. 3, 2020), https://www.theatlantic.com/ideas/archive/2020/04/dan gers-any-non-originalist-approach-constitution/609382.

51 A recent spate of excellent work includes Conor Casey, *"Common Good Constitutionalism" and the New Debate Over Constitutional Interpretation in the United States*, (2021) 4 PUBLIC LAW 765–87; Timon Cline, *Common Good Constitutionalism and Vaccine Mandates*, APPALACHIAN LAW JOURNAL (forthcoming 2021); Stéphane Sérafin, Kerry Sun, & Xavier Foccroulle Menard, *The Common Good and Legal Interpretation: A Response to Leonid Sirota and Mark Mancini*, 30 CONST. F. 39 (2021); RACHAEL WALSH, PROPERTY RIGHTS AND SOCIAL JUSTICE: PROGRESSIVE PROPERTY IN ACTION (2021). *See also* the entries in the symposium on common-good constitutionalism hosted by *Ius & Iustitium* in September 2021 (https://iusetiustitium.com/symposium-se

curing-the-common-good) and the excellent video lecture series hosted by the Common Good Project, a joint initiative of the Oxford Law Faculty and Blackfriars Hall, YOUTUBE, https://you tube.com/channel/UCq25IwskSdpq7FNZWSThrVA.

52 CHARLES L. BLACK, JR., STRUCTURE AND RELATIONSHIP IN CONSTITUTIONAL LAW (1969).

53 DIG. 2.14.38 (Papinian, *Questions* 2) (A. Watson, trans., 2009).

54 Compare the thin and mistaken conception of the common good in JOHN RAWLS, A THEORY OF JUSTICE 219 (rev. ed. 1999) ("the common good I think of as certain general conditions that are in an appropriate sense *equally to everyone's advantage*") (emphasis added).

55 ARISTOTLE, 3 POLITICS 1279a–b, 77–78 (C.D.C. Reeve, trans., Hackett ed. 1998).

56 NICCOLÒ MACHIAVELLI, FLORENTINE HISTORIES (Laura F. Bannfield & Harvey C. Mansfield, Jr., trans., Princeton University Press 1988) (1532).

57 BARTOLUS OF SAXOFERRATO, ON THE GOVERNMENT OF A CITY 3 (Jonathan Robinson, trans., 2012) (online publication) (*c.*1330), http://individual.utoronto.ca/jwrobinson/translations/bartolus _de-regimine-ciuitatis.pdf.

58 John Goyette, *On the Transcendence of the Political Common Good* 13 NAT'L CATHOLIC BIOETHICS QUARTERLY 133, 137 (2013).

59 *See generally* CHARLES DE KONINCK, *The Primacy of the Common Good against the Personalists: The Principle of the New Order*, in 2 THE WRITINGS OF CHARLES DE KONINCK (Ralph McInerny, ed., trans., 2016) (1943).

60 WALTER FARRELL, O.P., THE NATURAL LAW ACCORDING TO AQUINAS AND SUÁREZ 13 (Cajetan Cuddy, O.P., ed., Cluny Media ed. 2019) (1930); *see also* Steven A. Long, *Understanding the Common Good*, 16 NOVA ET VETERA, 1135 (2018).

61 DIG. 1.1.10 (Ulpian, *Rules* 1) (A. Watson, trans., 2009).

62 Although some have supposed there is a tension or even inconsistency between these components of the common good – for example, a tension between focusing on the structural

preconditions of justice and focusing on the legitimate ends of government – I can see no such tension; the two formulations just address different and compatible aspects or phases of the same problem. For an account in a similar spirit, *see generally* George Duke, *The Distinctive Common Good*, 78 Rev. Politics 227 (2016).

63 *See generally* Giovanni Botero, The Reason of State (Robert Bireley, S.J., ed., trans., Cambridge University Press 2017) (1589); Robert Bireley, S.J., The Counter-Reformation Prince: Anti-Machiavellianism or Catholic Statecraft in Early Modern Europe (1990).

64 *See* Botero, note 63 above, at 71.71.

65 *See, e.g.,* British North America Act 1867, 30 & 31 Vict. ch. 6 § 91; Irish Free State Constitution of 1922, art. 12: "The sole and exclusive power of making laws for the peace, order and good government of the Irish Free State . . . is vested in [the legislature]."

66 For historical overviews, see John Henry Hackett, The Concept of Public Order (1959); Gladden Pappin, *From the Common Good to Public Order and Back* (unpublished manuscript) (on file with author).

67 European Convention on Human Rights art. 9, Nov. 4, 1950, 213 U.N.T.S. 221.

68 *See, e.g.,* Mass. Const. preamble ("all shall be governed by certain laws for the common good") and art. IV (providing authority for state legislators to make laws "as they shall judge to be for the good and welfare of this commonwealth"); Alaska Const. art. VII (legislature may "provide for public welfare"). See also Jacobson v. Massachusetts, 197 U.S. 11, 26–27 (1905) (upholding mandatory vaccination for smallpox against due process challenge): "There are manifold restraints to which every person is necessarily subject for the common good. . . . In the constitution of Massachusetts adopted in 1780, it was laid down as a fundamental principle of the social compact that the whole people covenants with each citizen, and each citizen with the whole people, that all shall be governed by certain laws for 'the common good'.

... The good and welfare of the Commonwealth, of which the legislature is primarily the judge, is the basis on which the police power rests in Massachusetts."

69 123 U.S. 623, 668 (1887).

70 61 Mass. 53 (1851).

71 Ibid. at 86. For the connection between the *sic utere tuo* version of the maxim and Ulpian's precepts, see Elmer E. Smead, *Sic Utere Tuo Ut Alienum Non Laedas: A Basis of the State Police Power*, 21 CORNELL L. REV. 276, 279 (1936).

72 94 U.S. 113 (1877).

73 Ibid. at 124–25 (quoting Thurlow v. Massachusetts, 46 U.S. (5 How.) 504, 583 (1847)).

74 76 U.S. 41 (1870).

75 17 U.S. (4 Wheat.) 316 (1819).

76 WILLIAM J. NOVAK, THE PEOPLE'S WELFARE: LAW AND REGULATIONS IN NINETEENTH-CENTURY AMERICA 243 (1996).

77 See, e.g., United States v. Lopez, 514 U.S. 549, 551 (1995) (invalidating the Gun-Free School Zones Act).

78 McCulloch v. Maryland at 415.

79 320 U.S. 591 (1944).

80 Ibid. at 601 (emphasis added; internal citation omitted).

81 See United States v. Lopez, 514 U.S. 549 (1995) (holding that a federal prohibition on firearms in school zones was unconstitutional); United States v. Morrison, 529 U.S. 598 (2000) (holding that a portion of the Violence Against Women Act of 1994 was unconstitutional).

82 Nat'l Fed'n of Indep. Bus. v. Sebelius, 567 U.S. 519, 563–74 (2012) (upholding the relevant portion of the law as an exercise of Congress' taxing power).

83 47 U.S.C. § 303.

84 5 U.S.C. § 553(b)(3)(B).

85 Adrian Vermeule, *Liturgy of Liberalism*, FIRST THINGS (Jan. 2017), https://www.firstthings.com/article/2017/01/liturgy-of-liberalism.

86 See generally LOUIS VEUILLOT, THE LIBERAL ILLUSION (George Barry O'Toole, trans., National Catholic Welfare Conference 1939).

87 I address this issue at length in Adrian Vermeule, The Constitution of Risk (2013).

88 *See* Aquinas, note 3 above, pt. I-II, q. 95, art. 1.

89 See Edmund Waldstein, O. Cist., *Contrasting Concepts of Freedom*, https://thejosias.com/2016/11/11/contrasting-concepts -of-freedom.

90 In this respect, the framers and ratifiers were men of their time: "the common good" and "public utility" were dominant concepts in European, and especially British, political thought in the seventeenth and eighteenth centuries. Although there were bitter debates about what those concepts entailed and who would define the common good, the concept itself was common ground. *See generally* Peter N. Miller, Defining the Common Good: Empire, Religion and Philosophy in Eighteenth-Century Britain (1994).

91 U.S. Const. art. I, § 8, cl. 1.

92 *See, e.g., General Welfare Clause*, The Tenth Amendment Ctr., https://tenthamendmentcenter.com/general-welfare-clause.

93 297 U.S. 1 (1936).

94 Ibid. at 64 ("The true construction undoubtedly is that the only thing granted is the power to tax for the purpose of providing funds for payment of the nation's debts and making provision for the general welfare").

95 Ibid. (quoting 1 Joseph Story, Commentaries on the Constitution of the United States § 907 (5th ed. 1891)).

96 17 U.S. (4 Wheat.) 316, 424–25 (1819).

97 Ibid. at 415.

98 *See generally, e.g.,* Leo XIII, Encyclical Letter *Libertas praestan- tissimum*: On the Nature of Human Liberty, ¶ 5 (1888), reprinted in Church and State in the Modern Age: A Documentary History, 283 (J.F. Maclear, ed., 1995).

99 Ronald Dworkin, *The Secular Papacy*, in Judges in Contemporary Democracy: An International Conversation 164 (Stephen Breyer & Robert Badinter, eds., 2004).

100 *See, e.g.,* United States v. Curtiss-Wright Export Corp., 299 U.S. 304, 318 (1936) ("[t]he investment of the federal government

with the powers of external sovereignty did not depend on affirmative grants of the Constitution" but on the fact that they are "inherently inseparable from the conception of nationality").

101 *See Bagehot on the "Dignified" and "Efficient" Parts of the Constitution*, THE CAKE OF CUSTOM, http://cakeofcustom.blogspot .com/2011/06/bagehot-on-dignified-and-efficient.html.

102 *See generally* JOSEPH M. DE MAISTRE, ESSAY ON THE GENERATIVE PRINCIPLE OF POLITICAL CONSTITUTIONS AND OF OTHER HUMAN INSTITUTIONS (1814), reprinted in CONSERVATISM: AN ANTHOLOGY OF SOCIAL AND POLITICAL THOUGHT FROM DAVID HUME TO THE PRESENT (Jerry Z. Muller, ed., 1995).

103 Although I touch on the other subjects later, I say nothing here about the Court's due process jurisprudence on abortion rights. As of the present writing, the Court has agreed to hear a straight-forward challenge to the viability framework established in Roe v. Wade, 410 U.S. 113 (1973). *See* Dobbs v. Jackson Women's Health Organization (No. 19-1392) (Certiorari granted May 17, 2021). With the current jurisprudence under a cloud of uncertainty, I will leave the issue for future work. Suffice it to say I believe there is a straightforward argument, not on originalist grounds, that due process, equal protection, and other constitutional provisions should be best read in conjunction to grant unborn children a positive or affirmative right to life that states must respect in their criminal and civil law. This view is not a mere rejection of Roe v. Wade, but the affirmation of the opposite right, and would be binding throughout the nation.

104 Planned Parenthood of Southeastern Pa. v. Casey, 505 U.S. 833, 851 (1992).

105 Cohen v. California, 403 U.S. 15, 25 (1971).

106 *See generally* Vermeule, note 24 above; ADRIAN VERMEULE & ERIC POSNER, THE EXECUTIVE UNBOUND: AFTER THE MADISONIAN REPUBLIC (2010).

107 *See* Jacobson v. Massachusetts, 197 U.S. 11, 37–38 (1905). *Cf.* Recent Case, *In Re Abbott: Fifth Circuit Upholds Abortion Restrictions During Covid-19 Pandemic*, 134 HARV. L. REV. 1228 (2021).

108 Helmholz, Natural Law, note 2 above, at 69–75.
109 G. Inst. 1.158 (F. de Zulueta, trans., 1946).
110 Helmholz, Natural Law, note 2 above, at 37, 46–53, 73–75.
111 Thomas Aquinas, *Summa Theologica*, pt. I-II, q. 95, art. 2, *in* Aquinas, Political Writings, 130 (R.W. Dyson, ed., trans., 2002) (emphasis added).
112 Ibid. at 131.
113 Vermeule, *Rationally Arbitrary Decisions,* note 27 above.
114 *See* Aquinas, note 111 above, at pt. II-II, q. 57, art. 1, ad. 2, 159–60.
115 John Finnis, *Natural Law Theories*, Stan. Encyclopedia Phil. (June 3, 2020), https://plato.stanford.edu/entries/natural-law-th eories (emphasis added).
116 The result would be, in Aquinas' view, a kind of mixed government with important representative elements. See Aquinas, note 111 above, at IIaIIae 105, q1, 54:

> Hence the best ordering of government in any city or kingdom is achieved when one man is chosen to preside over all according to virtue; when he has under him others who govern according to virtue; and when such government nonetheless belongs to all, both because all are eligible for election to it and because it is elected by all. Such a "polity" is the best form of government inasmuch as it is a benign mixture of kingship, because there is one man who presides; of aristocracy, because it is the rule of several according to virtue; and of democracy, that is, popular power, because the rulers can be elected from the people and it belongs to the people to elect the rulers.

> This is obviously a large topic, on which it is an open question whether Aquinas' views were wholly consistent over time. Compare Aquinas, note 111 above, 5ff. The point is that such judgments are, as Aquinas shows, ultimately prudential and contingent, not inherent in the nature of law. Thanks to Conor Casey for helpful conversations on these points.

117 Karl Popper, The Open Society & Its Enemies, 115 (Princeton University Press 2013) (1945).
118 Ibid. at 338.
119 Ibid. at 118.
120 Judith Shklar, *The Liberalism of Fear*, in Political Thought and Political Thinkers 3, 9 (Stanley Hoffmann, ed., 1998).
121 Adrian Vermeule, *Optimal Abuse of Power*, 109 Nw. U. L. Rev. 673 (2015).
122 Ibid. at 677–83.
123 See Dewey, note 28 above; Hale, note 28 above.
124 198 U.S. 45 (1905).
125 22 N.E. 188 (N.Y. 1889).
126 299 U.S. 304 (1936).
127 1 William Blackstone, Commentaries *122.
128 G. Inst. 1.8. ("All our law is about persons, things, or actions"). Gaius' actual scheme is slightly different – its four books address persons, things, intestate succession and obligations, and forms of action – but the family resemblance is obvious.
129 See the well-known passage in the Introduction on the Study of Law:

> Far be it from me to derogate from the study of the civil law, considered (apart from any binding authority) as a collection of written reason. No man is more thoroughly persuaded of the general excellence of its rules, and the usual equity of its decisions, nor is better convinced of its use as well as ornament to the scholar, the divine, the statesman, and even the common lawyer. But we must not carry our veneration so far as to sacrifice our Alfred and Edward to the manes of Theodosius and Justinian; we must not prefer the edict of the prætor, or the rescript of the Roman emperor, to our own immemorial customs, or the sanctions of an English parliament; unless we can also prefer the despotic monarchy of Rome and Byzantium, for whose meridians the former were calculated, to the free constitution of Britain, which the latter are adapted to perpetuate.

Without detracting, therefore, from the real merits which abound
in the imperial law, I hope I may have leave to assert, that if an
Englishman must be ignorant of either the one or the other, he
had better be a stranger to the Roman than the English institutions. (1 WILLIAM BLACKSTONE, COMMENTARIES, *5)

130 3 Cai. R. 175 (N.Y. Sup. Ct. 1805).

131 Ibid. at 176; *cf.* J. INST. 2.1.13 (J.B. Moyle, trans., 5th ed. 1915)
    (adopting the opinion that "[the beast] does not belong to you
    till you have actually caught it").

132 Yves Casertano, *Justinian Goes Fox Hunting*, IUS & IUSTITIUM
    (May 26, 2021), https://iusetiustitium.com/justinian-goes-fox
    -hunting. In Swift v. Tyson, 41 U.S. (16 Pet.) 1 (1842), the deci-
    sion officially (whether or not practically) discredited by the pos-
    itivist revolution led by Justice Holmes around World War I,
    Justice Story put it this way:

> The law respecting negotiable instruments may be truly
> declared in the language of Cicero, adopted by Lord Mansfield
> in Luke *v.* Lyde, 2 Burr. R. 883, 887, to be in a great measure
> not the law of a single country only, but of the commercial
> world. Non erit alia lex Romae, alia Athenis, alia nunc, alia
> posthac, sed et apud omnes gentes, et omni tempore una
> eademque lex obtinebit [There will not be one law in Rome,
> another in Athens, one now, another in the future, but both
> among all nations and at every time one and the same law will
> obtain].

Ibid. at 19, quoting CICERO, DE RE PUBLICA 3.22.33.

133 Novak, note 76 above, at 32–34. For a nuanced view, emphasiz-
    ing that the founders did not speak with one voice, that there
    are liberal elements in Blackstone's legal theory, and that the era
    was already in transition from a classical conception of law and
    rights to a modern liberal conception, *see* Edmund Waldstein,
    O. Cist., *Hard Liberalism, Soft Liberalism, and the American
    Founding*, https://thejosias.com/2018/04/11/hard-liberalism-soft
    -liberalism-and-the-american-founding. I do not disagree with

this, so long as we do not read it too broadly; it does not entail (and Waldstein certainly does not intend to say) that anything like modern positivism is to be discerned in the founding era or for a long time afterwards.

134 *See* 1 COLLECTED WORKS OF JAMES WILSON, 500, 526, 549 (Kermit L. Hall & Mark David Hall, eds., 2007) (beginnings of chapters in law lectures titled "Of the Law of Nature," "Of the Law of Nations," "Of Municipal Law.").

135 Helmholz, note 2 above.

136 *See generally* Novak, note 76 above. A caution about Novak's presentation (ultimately a semantic issue only) is that he sometimes distinguishes the "common law" from the "natural law." *See, e.g.,* ibid. at 38. And he rightly observes that founding-era commentators often described themselves as advancing views of the common good and public welfare founded in the common law. Ibid. at 38–39. But as we have seen, the Anglo-American common law was itself deeply influenced by the *ius commune*, including the *ius naturale*. Modern students of law, characteristically, tend to think of the common law as a particular institutional mechanism – roughly, decision by judge-made precedent – whereas in the founding era, the common law referred more broadly to a concrete order, a living tradition that emphatically included municipal civil or positive law, natural law, and the law of nations.

137 STUART BANNER, THE DECLINE OF NATURAL LAW: HOW AMERICAN LAWYERS ONCE USED NATURAL LAW AND WHY THEY STOPPED (2021). Throughout, Banner dates the decline of the natural law paradigm to the late nineteenth and early twentieth centuries — well after the ratification of the Reconstruction Amendments.

138 Gienapp, note 4 above, at 324.

139 Herzog, Myths, note 2 above.

140 RELATIONS BETWEEN THE *IUS COMMUNE* AND ENGLISH LAW (R.H. Helmholz & Vito Piergiovanni, eds., 2009).

141 Herzog, Myths, note 2 above, at 22.

142 Helmholz, Natural Law, note 2 above, at 175.

143 Jud Campbell, *Natural Rights and the First Amendment*, 127 YALE
     L. J. 246, 276 (2017) (emphasis in original).
144 Helmholz, Natural Law, note 2 above, at 176–77.
145 Banner, note 137 above, at 12.
146 JOHN HART ELY, DEMOCRACY AND DISTRUST: A THEORY OF JUDICIAL
     REVIEW 48–49 (1980).
147 3 U.S. (3 Dall.) 386 (1798). See Helmholz, Natural Law, note 2
     above, at 233–34:

> For immediate purposes of tracing the role played by the law
> of nature in early American court practice – our main task –
> too much should not be read into the language Justice Iredell
> used in the case. The majority opinion did not rule out use
> of natural law in other contexts than that of determining the
> constitutional validity of legislative action [such as statutory
> interpretation]. That had never been its major role in English
> or European court practice . . . and nothing in Iredell's opin-
> ion precluded reference to it outside the sphere of constitu-
> tional adjudication. The holding in *Calder v. Bull* left that
> possibility open. American lawyers and judges subsequently
> seized the opportunity, even in cases taken before the U.S.
> Supreme Court. [Moreover,] [t]he widely held opinion that the
> written Constitution was "not declaratory of any new law, but
> confirmed . . . ancient rights and principles" even left the door
> open for occasional consideration of natural law principles in
> constitutional interpretation.

148 Helmholz, Natural Law, note 2 above, at 155.
149 *See generally, e.g.,* Edward S. Corwin, *Debt of American
     Constitutional Law to Natural Law Concepts*, 25 NOTRE DAME.
     LAW. 258 (1950).
150 Helmholz, Natural Law, note 2 above, at 142.
151 198 U.S. at 64.
152 94 U.S. 113 (1876).
153 123 U.S. 623 (1887).
154 169 U.S. 366 (1898).

155 197 U.S. 11 (1905).

156 *See* In re Abbott, 954 F.3d 772 (5th Cir. 2020), *cert. granted, judgment vacated sub nom.* Planned Parenthood Ctr. for Choice v. Abbott, 141 S. Ct. 1261 (2021).

157 *See generally* Jerry L. Mashaw, Creating the Administrative Constitution: The Lost One Hundred Years of American Administrative Law (2012); Novak, note 76 above.

158 Novak, note 76 above, at 13.

159 *Munn*, 94 U.S. at 124; *Mugler*, 123 U.S. at 663; *Holden*, 169 U.S. at 392; *Jacobson*, 197 U.S. at 26.

160 The influence of the classical law was hardly confined to economic due process, of course, as the sources cited at the beginning of the chapter show. For an important example from the same period in another strand of the due process caselaw, *see* Hurtado v. California, 110 U.S. 516, 531 (1884) (interpreting "due process of law" in light of, among other sources, "that code which survived the Roman Empire as the foundation of modern civilization in Europe, and which has given us that fundamental maxim of distributive justice *suum cuique tribuere*").

161 David Currie, The Constitution in the Supreme Court: The First Hundred Years, 1789–1888 375–77 (paperback 1992).

162 17 U.S. (4 Wheat.) 316, 421 (1819) ("Let the end be legitimate, let it be within the scope of the constitution, and all means which are appropriate, which are plainly adapted to that end, which are not prohibited, but consist with the letter and spirit of the constitution, are constitutional").

163 123 U.S. at 662–63 (emphasis added).

164 *See* Nevada v. Hall, 440 U.S. 410, 433 (1979) (Rehnquist, J., dissenting) ("The tacit postulates yielded by [the implicit ordering of relationships within the federal system] are as much engrained in the fabric of the document as its express provisions, because without them the Constitution is denied force and often meaning"), *overruled by* Franchise Tax Bd. of California v. Hyatt, 139 S.Ct. 1485 (2019).

165 Campbell, note 143 above, at 276.

166 1 William Blackstone, Commentaries *55.

167　198 U.S. at 52.

168　Ibid. at 57.

169　Patterson v. Bark Eudora, 190 U.S. 169 (1903).

170　Booth v. Illinois, 184 U.S. 425 (1902).

171　Otis v. Parker, 187 U.S. 606 (1903).

172　*Lochner*, 198 U.S. at 59.

173　Ibid. at 67 (quoting *Jacobson*, 197 U.S. at 26).

174　*Lochner*, 198 U.S. at 72 (Harlan, J., dissenting).

175　*Lochner*, 198 U.S. at 62–63; for a defense of this interpretation, *see generally* HOWARD GILLAM, THE CONSTITUTION BESIEGED: THE RISE & DEMISE OF LOCHNER ERA POLICE POWERS JURISPRUDENCE (1995).

176　DAVID CURRIE, THE CONSTITUTION IN THE SUPREME COURT: THE SECOND CENTURY, 1888–1986 48–49 (paperback 1994).

177　*Lochner*, 198 U.S. at 76 (Holmes, J., dissenting).

178　Dworkin, note 15 above, at 181–83.

179　Southern Pac. Co. v. Jensen, 244 U.S. 205, 222 (1917) (Holmes, J., dissenting).

180　*See generally* CARL SCHMITT, ROMAN CATHOLICISM AND POLITICAL FORM (G.L. Ulmen, trans., Praeger 1996).

181　Garrett Epps, *Common-Good Constitutionalism Is an Idea as Dangerous as They Come*, THE ATLANTIC (Apr. 3, 2020), https://www.theatlantic.com/ideas/archive/2020/04/common-good-constitutionalism-dangerous-idea/609385; Randy E. Barnett, *Common-Good Constitutionalism Reveals the Dangers of Any Non-Originalist Approach to the Constitution*, THE ATLANTIC (Apr. 3, 2020), https://www.theatlantic.com/ideas/archive/2020/04/dangers-any-non-originalist-approach-constitution/609382.

182　HENRY M. HART & ALBERT M. SACKS, THE LEGAL PROCESS: BASIC PROBLEMS IN THE MAKING AND APPLICATION OF LAW 101 (1958).

183　Ibid. at 1–2.

184　*See generally* Vermeule, note 24 above.

185　*See* Dworkin, note 15 above; Holberg Prize, *Holdberg Prize Symposium 2007: Law and Political Morality*, YOUTUBE (June 4, 2012), https://www.youtube.com/watch?v=D8D5aIOHRNI.

186　For critique of this notion, *see* Vermeule, *Liberalism and the*

Invisible Hand, note 23 above; Claudio Lombardi, *The Illusion of a "Marketplace of Ideas" and the Right to Truth*, 3 AM. AFFAIRS 198 (2019).

187 Ricardo Calleja, *Imperare aude! Dare to Command! (Part I)*, Ius & IUSTITIUM (Oct. 20, 2020), https://iusetiustitium.com/impera re-aude-dare-to-command.

188 2 Kings 22:2 (Vulgate).

189 22 N.E. 188 (N.Y. 1889).

190 Or, in a less important variant, "dynamism." ANTONIN SCALIA, A MATTER OF INTERPRETATION 18–22 (new ed. 2018) (defining the options as following text, legislative intent, or a third "dynamic" approach promoted by William Eskridge); WILLIAM N. ESKRIDGE, JR., DYNAMIC STATUTORY INTERPRETATION (1994).

191 Scalia, note 190 above, at 38–39.

192 Bostock v. Clayton Cty., Georgia, 140 S. Ct. 1731, 1737 (2020).

193 Dworkin, note 15 above, at 26–33, 211ff.

194 This is the version of textualism I have defended elsewhere. See ADRIAN VERMEULE, JUDGING UNDER UNCERTAINTY: AN INSTITUTIONAL THEORY OF LEGAL INTERPRETATION (2006).

195 Aquinas, note 3 above, at pt. I-II, q. 95, art. 1, ad. 2.

196 Frederick Schauer, *Do Cases Make Bad Law?*, 73 U. CHI. L. REV. 883 (2006).

197 *Cf.* FREDERICK SCHAUER, PLAYING BY THE RULES: A PHILOSOPHICAL EXAMINATION OF RULE-BASED DECISION-MAKING IN LAW AND LIFE, 167–206 (1993) (explaining his theory of "presumptive positivism").

198 Aquinas, note 3 above, at pt. II-I, q. 96, art. 6.

199 For the methodological underpinnings of this sort of approach, *see generally*, Vermeule, note 194 above.

200 Anthony Giambrone, *Scalia v. Aquinas: Lessons from the Saint for the Late, Great Justice*, AMERICA: THE JESUIT REVIEW (Mar. 2016), https://www.americamagazine.org/issue/who-judge.

201 Note, however, that in the roughly contemporaneous Constitutions of Melfi of Frederick II, governing Aquinas' own home region, the power to interpret the law is partly separated from governing power at lower levels of the system; legal

interpretation is vested in courts whose judges may not also be bailiffs, and from which an appeal lies ultimately to the Emperor. *See* Liber Augustalis 32 (Title XXXI), 39 (Title LXXI) (1231), translated in The Liber Augustalis; or Constitutions of Melfi Promulgated by the Emperor Frederick II for the Kingdom of Sicily in 1231 (James M. Powell, trans., 1971). The best analogy to this in our system is probably the internal structure of many federal agencies. In a typical scheme, there is a separation of adjudicative functions from prosecutorial and rulemaking functions at the lower levels of the agency, with adjudication entrusted to independent, tenured Administrative Law Judges. But the agency itself in the strict legal sense – the top-level commissioners or Cabinet secretary or other decision-maker – combines all functions in one set of hands at the highest level; it enacts regulations, can direct the prosecution of cases, and is the ultimate court of appeal within the agency for the decision of those very cases and the interpretation of law.

202 Peter Paul Koritansky, *Thomas Aquinas and the Late Justice Scalia: A Response to Fr. Giambrone*, First Things (Apr. 20, 2016), https://www.firstthings.com/blogs/firstthoughts/2016/04/thomas-aquinas-and-the-late-justice-scalia-a-response-to-fr-giambrone (emphasis in original).

203 *See* Antonin Scalia & Bryan A. Garner, Reading Law 234–39 (2012) (endorsing and explaining the canon); Green v. Bock Laundry Mach. Co., 490 U.S. 504, 527–30 (1989) (Scalia, J., concurring in the judgment).

204 Aquinas, note 3 above, at pt. II-II, q. 120, art. 1, ad. 2.

205 508 U.S. 223 (1993).

206 18 U.S.C. § 924(c)(1).

207 *Smith*, 508 U.S. at 241–47 (Scalia, J., dissenting).

208 574 U.S. 528 (2015).

209 Ibid. at 531 (plurality opinion).

210 Ibid. at 549.

211 Tennessee Valley Auth. v. Hill, 437 U.S. 153 (1978).

212 See Encyclical Letter of the Holy Father Francis Laudato Si,

ON CARE FOR OUR COMMON HOME, paragraphs 156ff, https://www .vatican.va/content/francesco/en/encyclicals/documents/papa-fr ancesco_20150524_enciclica-laudato-si.html.

213 *Compare, e.g.,* John F. Manning, *Textualism and the Equity of the Statute*, 101 COLUM. L. REV. 1 (2001) *with* William N. Eskridge, Jr., *All About Words: Early Understandings of the "Judicial Power" in Statutory Interpretation, 1776–1806,* 101 COLUM. L. REV. 990 (2001).

214 Jacobson v. Massachusetts, 197 U.S. 11, 22 (1905) (quoting Sturges v. Crowninshield, 17 U.S. (4 Wheat.) 122, 202 (1819) (Marshall, J.)).

215 *See* RICHARD EKINS, THE NATURE OF LEGISLATIVE INTENT 275 (2012). For the role of international law as an influence on the interpretation of federal statutes in the U.S. legal system, see Murray v. The Charming Betsy, 6 U.S. (2 Cranch) 64 (1804) ("an act of Congress ought never to be construed to violate the law of nations, if any other possible construction remains"); CURTIS L. BRADLEY & JACK L. GOLDSMITH, FOREIGN RELATIONS LAW: CASES AND MATERIALS 529–39 (7th ed. 2020).

216 DIG. 1.3.17 (Celsus, *Digest* 26) (A. Watson, trans., 2009).

217 Riggs v. Palmer, 22 N.E. 188, 188–89 (N.Y. 1889).

218 Ibid. at 189.

219 Ibid. at 190.

220 Ibid.

221 Ibid.

222 Ibid.

223 *Riggs*, 22 N.E. at 191 (emphasis added).

224 Ibid. at 192–93.

225 299 U.S. 304 (1936).

226 Ibid. at 312–14.

227 Ibid. at 318.

228 Ibid. at 320.

229 Ibid. at 315–17 (emphasis added).

230 Ibid. at 318.

231 United States v. Lara, 541 U.S. 193, 201 (2004).

232 *Curtiss-Wright*, 299 U.S. at 318 (emphasis added).

233 Louis Henken, Foreign Affairs and the United States Constitution 19–20 (2d ed. 1996).

234 Adrian Vermeule, *Echoes of the Ius Commune*, note 23 above.

235 *Curtiss-Wright*, 299 U.S. at 318.

236 Ibid. at 322–29.

237 Bracton on the Laws and Customs of England, 33 (Samuel E. Thorne, trans., 1968) (thirteenth century).

238 *See generally* The Invention of Tradition (Eric Hobswan & Terence Ranger, eds., Canto Classics ed. 2012).

239 *See generally* Eric J. Segall, Originalism as Faith (2018).

240 *See generally, e.g.,* Jack M. Balkin, *Abortion and Original Meaning*, 24 Const. Comment. 291 (2007).

241 *See* Jutta Schickore, *Scientific Discovery*, Stan. Encyclopedia Phil. (Mar. 6, 2014; rev. ed. June 5, 2018), https://plato.stanford.edu/entries/scientific-discovery/#DisBetConDisConJus. In what follows, I trace originalism in its modern form back to theorists like Bork writing in the 1970s. In a different account, the origin story should be located farther back, in opposition to the civil rights movement of the 1950s and 1960s. See Calvin Terbeek, *"Clocks Must Always Be Turned Back": Brown v. Board of Education and the Racial Origins of Constitutional Originalism*, 115 American Political Science Review 821 (2021). That story is entirely compatible with my own – if anything, it reinforces it – and in any event the difference between them makes no difference for the points I make. Originalism, as a full-fledged constitutional theory and legal movement, is a relatively recent innovation.

Originalists sometimes attempt to blur this fact by pointing to older cases and commentary that employed arguments from original meaning or, more often, intention. *See, e.g.,* South Carolina v. United States, 199 U.S. 437, 448–49 (1905) (basing its discussion on the most clearly proto-originalist decision, Dred Scott v. Sandford, 60 U.S. (19 How.) 393 (1857)). Of course it is true that more than zero instances of originalist-like utterances can be detected across the vast landscape of our legal history. Law being messy, it is always possible to find some material or other to support a thesis. But originalist artifacts do not add up to originalism as it is today, the dominant ideology of the conservative legal movement. "Unlike their ideological descendants . . . these actors did not understand themselves as self-consciously setting forth a 'theory.' Such as it was, the intent construct was invoked at a high level of generality." Terbeek, above, at 825. Those examples as a class are thus unlike modern originalism. *See* ibid. at 824 n. 10. They tend to speak of the framers' intentions rather than the original meaning as understood by the ratifiers. *See* South Carolina v. United States, 199 U.S. at 456. As such they embody a version of originalism that few currently defend. Furthermore, they usually show only a weak form of respect for the original aims of the lawmaker, one that appears alongside other modalities of interpretation. In that sense they are entirely compatible with the role of positive law in the classical legal tradition, as we will see. Overall, the originalism of the period after World War II emerges, especially in the work of Robert Bork, as a full-blown, theoretically elaborated interpretive framework, claiming to be the exclusive valid approach. It is that sense of originalism that matters, and it is that sense that is my subject here.

242 *See generally* Campbell, note 143 above.

243 People v. Ruggles, 8 Johns R. 290 (N.Y. 1811).

244 Tyler Dobbs, Note, *Blasphemy as Unprotected Speech: The Original Meaning of the First Amendment*, 134 Harv. L. Rev. (forthcoming 2021) (unpublished manuscript on file with author).

245 District of Columbia v. Heller, 554 U.S. 570 (2008).

246 See Lawrence B. Solum, *Originalism and Constitutional Construction*, 82 Fordham L. Rev. 453–537 (2013).

247 See the brilliant treatment by David Kenny, *Politics All the Way Down: Originalism as Rhetoric*, 31 DPCE Online 660 (2017), http://www.dpceonline.it/index.php/dpceonline/article/view/439.

248 Dworkin, *Bork's Jurisprudence*, note 14 above.

249 Ronald Dworkin, *Comment,* in Scalia, A Matter of Interpretation, note 190 above, at 115.

250 Dworkin, *Bork's Jurisprudence*, note 14 above, at 668–74.

251 Balkin, note 240 above.

252 *See generally, e.g.,* Steven G. Calabresi & Julia T. Rickert, *Originalism and Sex Discrimination*, 90 Tex. L. Rev. 1 (2011).

253 *See* Balkin, note 240 above; Steven G. Calabresi & Hannah M. Begley, *Originalism and Same-Sex Marriage*, 70 U. Miami L. Rev. 648 (2015).

254 Nelson Lund, *Living Originalism: The Magical Mystery Tour*, 3 Tex. A&M L. Rev. 31, 37, 39 (2015).

255 Jack M. Balkin, Living Originalism, 115–16 (2011). The sardonic observation that even Dworkin can in a sense himself be described as an originalist – *see* Jeffrey Goldsworthy, *Dworkin as an Originalist*, 17 Constitutional Commentary 49 (2000) – underscores a problem for originalism, not for Dworkin. Originalism stakes itself to the claim that it can exclude convergence of this sort with non-originalist modes of constitutional interpretation, the very modes it was formulated to combat. Originalism claims to have something distinctive to say. If it cannot even distinguish itself from its antagonists, then the question arises, what good is it exactly?

256 140 S. Ct. 2183 (2020).

257 Ibid. at 2211 (stating holding).

258 Ibid. at 2202–03.

259 Ibid. at 2203–04.

260 Ibid. at 2243 (Kagan, J., concurring in the judgment with respect to severability and dissenting in part).

261 Ibid. at 2243–44 (internal citations omitted).

262 *Seila Law*, 140 S. Ct. at 2190.

263 *See* John Manning, *Separation of Powers as Ordinary Interpretation*, 124 Harv. L. Rev. 1939 (2011).

264 *Seila Law*, 140 S. Ct. at 2205.

265 140 S. Ct. 2316 (2020).

266 Ibid. at 2320.

267 *"We Are All Originalists,"* Mitch McConnell: Republican Leader (Oct. 13, 2020), https://www.republicanleader.senate.gov/newsroom/research/we-are-all-originalists-barrett.

268 *Seila Law*, 140 S. Ct. at 2326 (quoting NLRB v. Noel Canning, 573 U.S. 513, 557 (2014)).

269 Ibid. at 2326.

270 Ibid. (quoting The Pocket Veto Case, 279 U.S. 655, 689 (1929)).

271 J. F. Stephen, *The Federalist*, JAMES FITZJAMES STEPHEN (Oct. 11, 2016), fitzjames-stephen.blogspot.com/2016/10/the-federalist .html, originally published in THE SATURDAY REVIEW, Mar. 26, 1864.

272 THE FEDERALIST NO. 68 (Alexander Hamilton).

273 THE FEDERALIST NO. 64 (John Jay).

274 1 MAX FARRAND, THE FRAMING OF THE CONSTITUTION OF THE UNITED STATES, 175 (1913).

275 *Seila Law*, 140 S. Ct. at 2326.

276 *Confirmation Hearing on the Nomination of Elena Kagan to be an Associate Justice of the Supreme Court of the United States: Hearing Before the S. Comm. on the Judiciary*, 111th Cong. 61–62 (2010) (testimony of Elena Kagan).

277 140 S. Ct. 1731 (2020).

278 Ibid. at 1737.

279 Ibid. at 1738.

280 Ibid. at 1741.

281 Ibid.

282 Ibid. at 1745 ("none of these contentions about what the employers think the law was meant to do . . . allow us to ignore the law as it is").

283 Steven D. Smith, *Law Without Mind*, 88 MICH. L. REV. 104 (1989).

284 *Bostock*, 140 S. Ct. at 1822–37 (Kavanaugh, J., dissenting).

285 Ibid. at 1824.

286 Ibid. at 1755 (Alito, J., dissenting).

287 *Bostock*, 140 S. Ct. at 1750–51.

288 Ibid. at 1751.

289 Ibid.

290 *See, e.g.,* the sophisticated treatment in LEE J. STRANG, ORIGINALISM'S PROMISE: A NATURAL LAW ACCOUNT OF THE AMERICAN CONSTITUTION (2019). *See also,* on a more popular level, Josh Hammer, *Common Good Originalism*, AM. MIND (May 6, 2020), https://americanmind.org/features/waiting-for-charlemagne

/common-good-originalism; Josh Hammer, *Common-Good Originalism: Our Tradition and Our Path Forward*, 44 Harv. J. L. & Pub. Pol'y 917 (2021). I have offered a brief response to these views which I still think suffices, so I will not rehash it at length here. See Adrian Vermeule, *On "Common-Good Originalism,"* https://mirrorofjustice.blogs.com/mirrorofjustice/2020/05/com mon-good-originalism.html.

Two points deserve special mention. First, this sort of view yields only an ersatz form of respect for the natural law. One obeys the natural law only insofar as it happens to be picked up by an originalist command (a form of soft positivism), not because it has binding force as natural law in its own right. But it is intrinsic to the natural law that it should be followed for its *own* binding force, not merely because some incumbent ruler commanded that it be followed. The natural law isn't truly followed at all if it isn't followed *as* natural law.

Second, Hammer and others argue that the constitutional oath somehow requires an originalist methodology of constitutional interpretation. In itself, however, swearing to respect "the Constitution and laws," or any similar vow, does not say anything about how the Constitution should be interpreted; thus the constitutional oath merely poses, rather than resolving, the interpretive question. The argument for positivism and originalism from the constitutional oath is transparently circular, however elaborate the efforts to infuse it with methodological content. Any such argument is always parasitic on independent assumptions. It is immaterial whether those assumptions are made explicit or left implicit and smuggled in. In either case, the oath by itself is simply incapable of doing the work that originalist proponents hope to force it to do.

Indeed, the constitutional oath argument for originalism is self-refuting, for the same reason originalism generally is self-refuting: as has always been clear, and as recent scholarship has underscored (*see, e.g.,* Gienapp, note 4 above), *the framers and ratifiers themselves were not originalists.* They were classical lawyers. (Note that trying to change the subject from the original to the amended Constitution, for example by focusing on the Reconstruction Amendments, does not save originalism in this regard. It is an open question whether the ratifiers of 1868 were any less classical than the founding generation, and even if they were, the Reconstruction Amendments left untouched the great bulk of the structural constitution and the Bill of Rights, at least as applied to the federal government.)

291 *See generally* Jeffrey A. Pojanowski, *Why Should Anyone Be an Originalist?*, 31 Diritto Pubblico Comparato de Europeo Online 583 (2017); Jeffrey A. Pojanowski & Kevin C. Walsh, *Enduring Originalism*, 105 Geo. L.J. 97 (2016). For brevity, I will refer simply to "Pojanowski" in the text.

292 A wrinkle is that Pojanowski and Walsh explicitly deny that they have – as of yet – offered a theory of adjudication in particular, as opposed to interpretation in general. See Pojanowski and Walsh, note 291 above, at 146. And yet, confusingly, Pojanowski and Walsh trade on terms, like "originalism," that are usually offered as centrally relevant to adjudication. To the extent possible, I will sidestep this problem by confining my remarks to problems that might afflict any interpreter. As I shall also suggest, however, this hesitation to complete the theory may be no accident. Specifying the theory to the setting of adjudication would raise, and force the authors to confront, a serious dilemma about whether to disrupt existing non-originalist precedents decided over the course of our legal development. Embracing this disruption would undermine the claim of the theory to promote stability over time; not doing so would undermine the claim of the theory to promote a form of originalism. The existence of this dilemma, in my view, underscores that originalism is in itself a disruptive approach, as discussed below.

293 *See* Ronald Dworkin, Justice in Robes (2008); Holberg Prize, *Holberg Prize Symposium 2007: Law and Political Morality*, YouTube (June 4, 2012), https://www.youtube.com/watch?v=D8 D5aIOHRNI.

294 For elaboration of this point, see Dworkin's powerful response to

Jeremy Waldron at the Holberg Prize Symposium on Dworkin's work, https://youtu.be/FL8U5J7vh30.

295 Pojanowski, note 291 above, at 587.

296 *See* Walter Sinnott-Armstrong, *Consequentialism*, STAN. ENCYCLOPEDIA OF PHIL. (June 3, 2019), https://plato.stanford.edu/entries/consequentialism/#ConWhaRigRelRul.

297 *See generally, e.g.,* W.J. Waluchow, *Democracy and the Living Tree Constitution*, 59 DRAKE L. REV. 1001 (2011).

298 *See generally* David A. Strauss, *Common Law Constitutional Interpretation*, 63 U. CHI. L. REV. 877 (1996).

299 Trop v. Dulles, 356 U.S. 86, 101 (1958).

300 *Cf.* JOHN HENRY NEWMAN, AN ESSAY ON THE DEVELOPMENT OF CHRISTIAN DOCTRINE 40 (14th ed. 1909).

301 576 U.S. 644 (2015).

302 Ibid. at 652.

303 Ibid. at 712 (Roberts, C.J., dissenting).

304 Vermeule, *Liturgy of Liberalism*, note 85 above.

305 *See* Little Sisters of the Poor Saints Peter and Paul Home v. Pennsylvania, 140 S. Ct. 2367, 2372–79 (2020) (describing the years-long litigation).

306 *See* Aquinas, note 3 above, pt. I-II, q. 95 art. 2.

307 *Cf.* BRIAN Z. TAMANAHA, LAW AS A MEANS TO AN END: THREAT TO THE RULE OF LAW (LAW IN CONTEXT) (2006).

308 Gladden Pappin, *Toward a Party of the State*, 3 AM. AFFAIRS 149 (2019), https://americanaffairsjournal.org/2019/02/toward-a-party-of-the-state.

309 *See* Newman, note 300 above, at 206.

310 272 U.S. 365 (1926).

311 Annex to the Letter Dated 2 December 2020 from the Permanent Representative of the United States of America to the United Nations Addressed to the Secretary-General: Geneva Consensus Declaration on Promoting Women's Health and Strengthening the Family, U.N. Doc. A/75/626 (Dec. 2, 2020), https://documents-dds-ny.un.org/doc/UNDOC/GEN/N20/344/30/PDF/N2034430.pdf?OpenElement. President Biden, however, signaled his intent to withdraw US support for the agreement shortly after

his inauguration. Joseph R. Biden, Jr., *Memorandum Protecting Women's Health at Home and Abroad*, DAILY COMP. PRES. DOCS. 100 (2021), https://www.govinfo.gov/content/pkg/DCPD-202100 100/pdf/DCPD-202100100.pdf.

312 Newman, note 300 above, at 170, 178, 185, 189, 195, 199, 203.

313 Brendan Murphy, *The Development of Doctrine*, SIMPLY CATHOLIC, https://www.simplycatholic.com/the-development-of-doctrine.

314 *See* A. Vermeersch, *Modernism*, in 10 THE CATHOLIC ENCYCLOPEDIA (Charles G. Herbermann, ed., 1911), made available online by NEW ADVENT, https://www.newadvent.org/cathen/10415a.htm.

315 272 U.S. 365 (1926).

316 Ibid. at 388.

317 Ibid. at 388–89.

318 Ibid. at 387 (emphasis added).

319 *See, e.g.,* Kim Lane Sheppele & Laurent Pech, *What Is Rule of Law Backsliding?* VERFASSUNGSBLOG ON MATTERS CONSTITUTIONAL (Mar. 2, 2018), https://verfassungsblog.de/what-is-rule-of-law-backsliding.

320 Selmouni v. France 1999-V Eur. Ct. H.R. 149, 183 ("[T]he increasingly high standard being required in the area of the protection of human rights and fundamental liberties correspondingly and inevitably requires greater firmness in assessing breaches of the fundamental values of democratic societies").

321 U.S. CONST. amend. V. ("nor shall private property be taken for public use, without just compensation").

322 Kelo v. City of New London, 545 U.S. 469, 482–83 (2005).

323 See note 186 above.

324 JAMES FITZJAMES STEPHEN, LIBERTY, EQUALITY, FRATERNITY 25–28, 49 (Stuart D. Warner, ed., Liberty Fund 1993) (1873).

325 R.H. Coase, *The Market for Goods and the Market for Ideas*, 64 AM. ECON. REV. 384, 384 (1974).

326 Village of Euclid v. Ambler Realty, Co., 272 U.S. 365, 387 (1926).

327 *See generally* LEONARD FRANCIS TAYLOR, CATHOLIC COSMOPOLITANISM AND HUMAN RIGHTS (2020).

328 *See* Mary Ann Glendon, *Reclaim Human Rights*, FIRST THINGS

(Aug. 2016), https://www.firstthings.com/article/2016/08/reclaim-human-rights; *De Nicola Ctr. for Ethics & Culture, Authority, Rights, and Responsibilities – FC2018*, YOUTUBE (Nov. 9, 2018) (including Professor Glendon's remarks entitled "Can the Modern Human Rights Project Be Saved?"), https://youtu.be/5l YbawIHOSA.

329 *See, e.g.,* Gregor Puppinck, *Abortion and the European Convention on Human Rights*, 3 IRISH J. LEGAL STUD. 142 (2013); *Reproductive Rights*, EUR. CT. OF H.R., PRESS UNIT 1–2 (Feb. 2021), https://www.echr.coe.int/documents/fs_reproductive_eng.pdf.

330 Schalk and Kopf v. Austria; 2010-IV Eur. Ct. H.R. 409; Hämäläinen v. Finland, 2014-IV Eur. Ct. H.R. 369; and Chapin and Charpentier v. France, App. No. 40183/07 (June 9, 2016), https://hudoc.echr.coe.int/eng#{"itemid":["001-163436"]}.

331 Lautsi v. Italy, 2011-III Eur. Ct. H.R. 61.

332 Annex, note 311 above (listing signatories).

333 Ibid.

334 576 U.S. 644 (2015).

335 Ibid. at 664–65.

336 338 U.S. 1 (1967).

337 Ibid. at 2–3.

338 434 U.S. 374 (1978).

339 Ibid. at 377.

340 482 U.S. 78 (1987).

341 Ibid. at 82.

342 *Obergefell*, 576 U.S. at 657, 668.

343 Ibid. at 664 ("The nature of injustice is that we may not always see it in our own times").

344 See DIGEST OF JUSTINIAN 23, 2, 14, 2 ("in regard to the regulations for entering into matrimony, natural law and decency must also be considered").

345 Ibid. at 700 (Roberts, C.J., dissenting).

346 "Marriage, or matrimony, is the union of a man and a woman, committing them to a single path through life." JUSTINIAN'S INSTITUTES 1.9.1 (Peter Birks & Grant McLeod, trans., 1987). On this account, there is a serious claim that it would be arbitrary

and contrary to natural law for a state to *allow* same-sex civil marriage. For now, however, it is unnecessary to resolve that further question to appreciate that *Obergefell* was entirely wrong to override, as a matter of federal constitutional law, states that wished to preserve the traditional definition.

347 Ibid. at 738 (Alito, J., dissenting).

348 DIG. 1.1.7 (Papinian, Definitions 2) (A Watson, trans., 2009).

349 RAFAEL DOMINGO, ROMAN LAW: AN INTRODUCTION 121 (2018).

350 DIG. 1.1.8 (Marcian, Institutes 1) (A. Watson, trans., 2009). *See* the fascinating discussion in Franciszek Longchamps de Bérier, *The Praetor as a Promoter of Bonum Commune*, 3 LEGAL ROOTS 217 (2014).

351 *See* Cass R. Sunstein, *Is Tobacco a Drug? Administrative Agencies as Common Law Courts*, 47 DUKE. L. J. 1013, 1055–63 (1998).

352 I discuss the development of this regime at length in Vermeule, note 24 above.

353 *See* Rafael de Arizaga, *Jurisprudence as a Subaltern Science*, IUS & IUSTITIUM (Sept. 7, 2020), https://iusetiustitium.com/jurisprudence-as-a-subaltern-science.

354 As in, for example, Dworkin, note 15 above.

355 5 U.S.C. § 500ff.

356 DIG. 1.1.1 (Ulpian, Institutes 1) (A. Watson, trans., 2009).

357 The administrative state, of course, long predates the Progressive Era; indeed, it develops right from the beginning of our constitutional order. *See generally* JERRY MASHAW, CREATING THE ADMINISTRATIVE CONSTITUTION: THE LOST ONE HUNDRED YEARS OF AMERICAN ADMINISTRATIVE LAW (2012) (showing that the US Congress delegated vast discretion and authority to administrative officials during the first century after the Constitution was adopted). As to the crucial topic of delegation to agencies, see Nicholas Bagley & Julian Davis Mortenson, *Delegation at the founding*, 121 COLUM. L. REV. 277 (2021).

358 *See* MORTON HORWITZ, THE TRANSFORMATION OF AMERICAN LAW 1870–1960, 219 (1992) ("Pound, who had singlehandedly proclaimed 'social engineering' and 'sociological jurisprudence' as the twin goals of earlier Progressive reform, was devoting

himself to denouncing the dangers flowing from 'administrative absolutism.' 'The reader of Pound's earlier writings,' Judge Jerome Frank observed, 'rubs his eyes' upon encountering Pound's recent denunciations and asks: 'Can this be the same man?'" (footnotes omitted)).

359 My focus here is on judicial review. I will not discuss law within the executive branch, such as the executive orders governing agency rulemaking, but I believe a parallel argument could be made about the important and arguably increasing role of high-level principles within that body of law as well. Two examples, one from each of the two most recent presidential administrations: (1) in President Obama's Exec. Order No. 13563, 76 Fed. Reg. 3821 (Jan. 18, 2011), an important provision authorizes agencies "[w]here appropriate and permitted by law . . . [to] consider (and discuss qualitatively) values that are difficult or impossible to quantify, including *equity, human dignity, fairness, and distributive impacts*" (emphasis added); (2) President Trump's Exec. Order No. 13892, 84 Fed. Reg. 55239 (Oct. 9, 2019), states that "[w]hen an agency takes an administrative enforcement action, engages in adjudication, or otherwise makes a determination that has legal consequence for a person, it may apply only standards of conduct that have been publicly stated in a manner that would not cause *unfair surprise*" (emphasis added). The latter is a prime example of the sort of procedural principles discussed, in judicial review settings, in Sunstein and Vermeule, note 25 above.

360 Here and throughout this chapter, I draw upon Sunstein & Vermeule, note 25 above.

361 Roscoe Pound, *The Growth of Administrative Justice*, 2 Wis. L. Rev. 321 (1924).

362 *See generally* Gerald J. Postema, Bentham and the Common Law Tradition (2d ed. 2019) (explaining Bentham's critique of the English common law).

363 Pound, note 361 above, at 334.

364 Ibid.

365 Lord Hewart of Bury, The New Despotism (1929).

366 Friedrich A. Hayek, The Road to Serfdom (1944).

367 Carl Schmitt, *The Plight of European Jurisprudence*, 83 Telos 35, 53 (G.L. Ulmen, trans., 1990) (translating an essay that originally appeared as Carl Schmitt, *Die Lage der Europäischen Rechtswissenschaft (1943/44)*, *in* Verfassungsrechtliche Aufsätze aus den Jahren 1924–1954: Materialien zu einer Verfassungslehre 386 (2d ed. 1973)).

368 Ibid. at 52–54 (internal footnotes omitted).

369 See Dworkin, note 15 above; *see also* Holberg Prize, *Holberg Prize Symposium 2007: Justice in Robes: Integrity and the Rule of Law*, YouTube (June 4, 2012), https://www.youtube.com/watch?v=FL8U5J7vh3o&feature=youtu.be [https://perma.cc/6YRP-Q72P] (providing a discussion between Dworkin and Jeremy Waldron).

370 Holberg Prize Symposium, note 369 above.

371 Dworkin, note 15 above, at 182.

372 Ibid. at 212.

373 *See generally* Dan Ernst, Tocqueville's Nightmare: The Administrative State Emerges in America, 1900–1940 (2014) (showing that judges came to view the administrative state as acceptable and within the bounds of law as long as agencies followed the fundamentals of due process); Adrian Vermeule, *Portrait of an Equilibrium*, The New Rambler (Mar. 4, 2015), https://newramblerreview.com/images/files/Vermeul-Review-of-Ernst.pdf [https://perma.cc/Q8YU-BJCQ] (reviewing Ernst's book). For the regulative ideal of keeping "government, overall and on average, tolerably with the bounds of law," see Richard H. Fallon Jr., *Some Confusions About Due Process, Judicial Review, and Constitutional Remedies*, 93 Colum. L. Rev. 309, 311 (1993).

374 *See, e.g.,* Roscoe Pound, Administrative Law: Its Growth, Procedure, and Significance (1942).

375 5 U.S.C. § 551(4) (2018) (emphasis added).

376 5 U.S.C. § 706 (2018) ("The reviewing court shall . . . hold unlawful and set aside agency action, findings, and conclusions found to be – arbitrary, capricious, an abuse of discretion, or otherwise not in accordance with law").

377 5 U.S.C. § 553(b)(3)(B) (2018).

378 Adrian Vermeule, *Our Schmittian Administrative Law*, 122 Harv. L. Rev. 1095, 1107 (2009).

379 See Wolfgang Waldstein, note 10 above (discussing natural law codes).

380 339 U.S. 33 (1950).

381 Vermont Yankee Nuclear Power Corp. v. Nat'l Res. Def. Council, Inc., 435 U.S. 519 (1978).

382 *Wong Yang Sung*, 339 U.S. at 40–41 (emphasis added).

383 *See* Dworkin, Law's Empire, note 9 above, at 225–75 (1986).

384 *See* Motor Vehicle Mfrs. Ass'n v. State Farm Mut. Auto. Ins. Co., 463 U.S. 29, 51 (1983).

385 *See* FCC v. Fox Television Stations, Inc., 556 U.S. 502, 515 (2009) (finding that an agency must explain its departure from past positions when it contradicts earlier factual findings or when reliance interests are implicated); *cf.* Dep't of Homeland Sec. v. Regents of the Univ. of California, 140 S. Ct. 1891, 1915 (holding that the agency must assess potential reliance interests when repealing a discretionary nonenforcement policy).

386 *See* Dep't of Commerce v. New York, 139 S. Ct. 2551, 2576 (2019).

387 *See* Arizona Grocery v. Atchison, Topeka & Santa Fe Ry., 284 U.S. 370, 390 (1932).

388 SEC v. Chenery Corp., 332 U.S. 194, 196–97 (1947).

389 *See* Portland Audubon Soc'y v. Endangered Species Comm., 984 F.2d 1534, 1546 (9th Cir. 1993); *cf.* Myers v. United States, 272 U.S. 52, 135 (1926) ("[T]here may be duties of a quasi-judicial character imposed on executive officers and members of executive tribunals whose decisions after hearing affect interests of individuals, the discharge of which the President cannot in a particular case properly influence or control").

390 In addition to the examples in the text, consider the fundamental principle of *resource allocation*: agencies have discretion to allocate resources across programs and activities in whatever way they deem necessary to promote their missions, and judges will broadly defer. *See, e.g.,* Massachusetts v. EPA, 549 U.S. 497, 527 (2007) ("As we have repeated time and again, an agency

has broad discretion to choose how best to marshal its limited resources and personnel to carry out its delegated responsibilities"); Lincoln v. Vigil, 508 U.S. 182, 192 (1993) (invoking the resource allocation principle to find non-reviewable an agency's allocation of funds under a lump-sum grant). There is no enacted text that creates such a principle; it is extrapolated by judges from the political roles and political morality of agencies and their duties. In one of his few direct forays into administrative law, Dworkin addressed the procedural due process calculus of *Mathews v. Eldridge*, 424 U.S. 319 (1976), arguing that the Court's analysis was flawed by a misconception of the nature of the harm to claimants. *See* RONALD DWORKIN, *Principle, Policy, Procedure*, in A MATTER OF PRINCIPLE 99–103 (1985). In Dworkin's view, claimants erroneously denied benefits would suffer not only the "bare harm" of failure to obtain the benefit but also the conceptually distinct "moral harm" of being denied a rightful entitlement. This is plausible, but only part of the picture, because when there is a fixed share of social resources available for a benefits program, the erroneous grant of a benefit to one claimant means that some other claimant(s) with valid entitlements will have to be denied, threatening *them* with "moral harm." In these settings, one way of understanding the principle of resource allocation is that it allows agencies to make difficult normative judgments about where the risk of moral harm should fall. The principle of resource allocation, in other words, is no mere managerial privilege; it is itself possessed of important moral significance.

391 Dworkin, note 15 above, at 325.

392 *See* Ernst, note 373 above, at 51–78 (describing this as the basic equilibrium reached by the Hughes Court).

393 5 U.S.C. § 701(a)(2) (2018). For an excellent treatment of the relevant issues, see Peter Karanjia, *Hard Cases and Tough Choices: A Response to Professors Sunstein and Vermeule*, 132 HARV. L. REV. F. 106 (2019).

394 *See* Citizens to Preserve Overton Park, Inc. v. Volpe, 401 U.S. 402, 410 (1971).

395 *See* Ronald M. Levin, *Understanding Unreviewability in Administrative Law*, 74 M ɪɴɴ. L. Rᴇᴠ. 689, 708 (1990).
396 Webster v. Doe, 486 U.S. 592, 608 (1988) (Scalia, J., dissenting).
397 Ibid. at 608–10 (citations omitted).
398 *Cf.* Withrow v. Larkin 421 U.S. 35, 51–55 (1975) (declining to establish a *per se* rule against the combination of prosecutorial and adjudicative functions in agencies as a matter of due process, because "the growth, variety, and complexity of the administrative processes have made any one solution highly unlikely").
399 A corollary of increasing complexity is that, under some conditions, judicial deference has itself become a legal principle, indeed in some sense the organizing principle around which many doctrines of administrative law are arranged. *See generally* Vermeule, note 24 above (explaining how lawyers and judges came, by internal legal argument, to qualify or abandon crucial elements of the classical framework of *de novo* judicial review). This is not at all to say that courts are always obliged to defer. It is commonplace that legal principles have both scope and weight; they are both limited and, in certain cases, overridable by other considerations. But it does mean that courts doing administrative law always have to consider not only the content of the law, but the question of the institutional allocation of primary authority to determine that content. As the law has evolved over time to make second-order principles of deference increasingly central to our law, courts apply first-order principles with a strong margin of deference for the discretion of public authorities, in what is simultaneously an abnegation and a fulfillment of the legal project. *See generally* ibid. (detailing how the logical implications of legal principles pointed to abnegation as the judiciary's wisest course of action). I add here that the omnipresence of deference principles in administrative law results from the increasing complexity of the administrative state; it is thus, itself, an example of the triumph of jurisprudential principle, for basically the reasons Dworkin gave.
400 Schmitt, note 367 above, at 54.

401 *See generally* Jack Goldsmith & John F. Manning, *The President's Completion Power*, 115 YALE L. J. 2280 (2006).

402 See Vermeule, *Rationally Arbitrary Decisions*, note 27 above.

403 556 U.S. 502 (2009).

404 Ibid. at 515.

405 Helmholz, Natural Law, note 2 above, at 47–48.

406 Adrian Vermeule, *Deference and Due Process*, 129 HARV. L. REV. 1890 (2016).

407 *See* Citizens to Preserve Overton Park, Inc., v. Volpe, 401 U.S. 402, 416 (1971).

408 For a discussion of courts' general approach and a defense of it, *see generally* Richard J. Pierce, Jr., *What Factors Can an Agency Consider in Making a Decision?* 2009 MICH. ST. L. REV. 67 (2009).

409 572 U.S. 489 (2014).

410 Ibid. at 519.

411 *See* James B. Thayer, *The Origin and Scope of the American Doctrine of Constitutional Law*, 7 HARV. L. REV. 129, 143 (1893).

412 WILLIAM SHAKESPEARE, MEASURE FOR MEASURE act 2, sc. 2.

413 Using this term in the political theory sense, not the legal sense. In the former sense, the family, the locality, and the professional association all count as "corporations."

414 For explanation of the "state of exception," or the emergency situation that calls for going beyond the bounds of normal legal rules, *see* Lars Vinx, *Carl Schmitt*, STAN. ENCYCLOPEDIA PHIL. (Aug. 29, 2019), https://plato.stanford.edu/entries/schmitt (citing CARL SCHMITT, POLITICAL THEOLOGY: FOUR CHAPTERS ON THE CONCEPT OF SOVEREIGNTY 5, 13 (1922) (G. Schwab, trans., University of Chicago Press 2005)).

415 Compendium, note 18 above, at ¶ 188 (2004) (emphasis in original; internal quotation omitted).

416 CHARLTON T. LEWIS & CHARLES SHORT, *Subsidium*, A LATIN DICTIONARY (1879), http://www.perseus.tufts.edu/hopper/text?do c=Perseus:text:1999.04.0059:entry=subsidium.

417 *Cf.* CARL SCHMITT, DICTATORSHIP: FROM THE ORIGIN OF THE MODERN CONCEPT OF SOVEREIGNTY TO THE PROLETARIAN CLASS STRUGGLE (M. Hoelzl & G. Ward, trans., Polity Press 2014) (1921)

(distinguishing the restorative and protective functions of the Roman commissarial dictatorship from the sovereign dictatorship, which founds a new legal order).

418 Messner, note 10 above, at 214.

419 Compendium, note 18 above (emphasis in original).

420 Michael P. Moreland, *The Pre-History of Subsidiarity in Leo XIII*, 56 J. Cath. Legal Stud. 63, 70 (quoting Pope Leo XIII, Encyclical Letter *Rerum Novarum* ¶ 36 (1891)). Professor Moreland rightly calls attention to the neglected positive aspect of subsidiarity.

421 Messner, note 10 above, at 215.

422 *See* Andrew Lintott, The Constitution of the Roman Republic 109–13 (1999).

423 Edward L. Rubin & Malcolm Feeley, *Federalism: Some Notes on a National Neurosis*, 41 UCLA L. Rev. 903 (1994).

424 Ibid. at 914–26.

425 *See* ibid. at 941.

426 Ibid. at 950–51.

427 *See, e.g.,* Ernest A. Young, *The Puzzling Persistence of Dual Federalism*, in Federalism and Subsidiarity: NOMOS LV 34 (James E. Fleming & Jacob T. Levy, eds., 2014).

428 *See generally* Adrian Vermeule, Mechanisms of Democracy: Institutional Design Writ Small (2007).

429 *See generally* Sunstein and Vermeule, note 25 above.

430 5 U.S.C. § 706 (2018).

431 Pub. L. No. 104–4, 109 Stat. 48 (codified in scattered sections of 2 U.S.C.).

432 Vermeule, note 428 above, at 228.

433 There is some confusion about this in the literature. For a clear explanation of the Act's point-of-order mechanisms and its limits, *see* Cong. Research Serv., R40957, Unfunded Mandates Reform Act: History, Impact, and Issues (2020), https://fas.org/sgp/crs/misc/R40957.pdf.

434 576 U.S. 473 (2015).

435 Ibid. at 483.

436 Ibid. at 484–98.

437 Ibid. at 498–518 (Scalia, J., dissenting).

438 545 U.S. 1 (2005).

439 Ibid. at 5–8, 19.

440 Ibid. at 33.

441 McCulloch v. Maryland, 17 U.S. (4 Wheat.) 316, 421 (1819) ("[T]he sound construction of the constitution must allow to the national legislature that discretion . . . which will enable that body to perform the high duties assigned to it").

442 567 U.S. 709 (2012).

443 18 U.S.C. § 704 (2012).

444 535 U.S. 234 (2002).

445 For an excellent series of videos on the topic, see *The Common Good Project*, YouTube, https://www.youtube.com/channel/UCq 25IwskSdpq7FNZWSThrVA.

446 Hervada, note 10 above.

447 I draw here on several excellent accounts. See Dominic Legge, O.P., *Do Thomists Have Rights?*, 17 Nova et Vetera 127 (2019); R.H. Helmholz, *Natural Human Rights: The Perspective of the Ius Commune*, 52 Catholic University Law Review 301 (2003); Brian Tierney, The Idea of Natural Rights: Studies on Natural Rights, Natural Law and Church Law 1150–1625 (1997). Stated in brief, the crucial contrast is that rights under the *ius commune* were real legal entitlements that supported legal claims, but were justified by reference to, and adjusted to fit, "the objective needs of society," the common good, rather than on the basis of individual autonomy. Helmholz, *Natural Human Rights* above, at 325.

448 *See, e.g.,* The Religious Freedom Restoration Act's standard for burdening free exercise rights at 42 U.S.C. § 2000bb-1.

449 *See* Gerards, note 37 above, at 198–99 (2019).

450 Jud Campbell, *The Emergence of Neutrality*, Yale L.J. (forthcoming), at 1, available at https://papers.ssrn.com/sol3/papers.cfm ?abstract_id=3898663&dgcid=ejournal_htmlemail_legal:histor y:ejournal_abstractlink. *See also* Campbell, note 143 above.

451 Campbell, note 143 above, at 253 (footnotes omitted).

452 *See* the sources cited in note 63 above.

453 567 U.S. 709 (2012).

454 Ibid. at 713–14 (Kennedy, J., plurality opinion).

455 Ibid. at 723.

456 Ibid.

457 Ibid. at 726–28.

458 *See generally* Garrett Hardin, *The Tragedy of the Commons*, 162 SCIENCE 1243 (1968).

459 535 U.S. 234 (2002).

460 Ibid. at 239–40, 58.

461 Ibid. at 236.

462 Mill argued that the proper scope of human liberty "requires liberty of tastes and pursuits, of framing the plan of our life to suit our own character, of doing as we like, subject to such consequences as may follow, without impediment from our fellow creatures, so long as what we do does not harm them, even though they should think our conduct foolish, perverse, or wrong." JOHN STUART MILL, ON LIBERTY 12 (Elizabeth Rapaport, ed., Hackett 1978) (1859).

463 Dobbs, note 244 above (internal citations omitted).

464 *See generally* ENCYCLICAL LETTER OF THE HOLY FATHER FRANCIS LAUDATO SI, note 212 above.

465 504 U.S. 555 (1992).

466 *See, e.g.,* ibid. at 562–68.

467 U.S. CONST. art. III, § 2.

468 *Lujan*, 504 U.S. at 577 (quoting Allen v. Wright, 468 U.S. 737, 760 (1984)).

469 See Cass R. Sunstein, *What's Standing After Lujan?*, 91 MICH. L. REV. 163, 166 & n. 15 (1992).

470 *See* U.S. CONST. art. II, § 1 ("The executive Power shall be vested in a President of the United States of America").

471 *Lujan*, 504 U.S. at 580 (Kennedy, J., concurring in part and concurring in the judgment).

472 As indicated in, for example, Vermont Agency of Natural Resources v. United States ex rel. Stevens, 529 U.S. 765 (2000) ("This is not to suggest that Congress cannot define new legal rights, which in turn will confer standing to vindicate an injury caused to the claimant"); Massachusetts v. EPA, 549 U.S. 497, 516–17 (2007).

473 549 U.S. 497 (2007).

474 Ibid. at 505.

475 Ibid. at 517–19.

476 *See* Vermont Agency of Nat. Res. v. U.S. ex rel. Stevens, 529 U.S. 765, 773–74 (2000).

477 United States v. Richardson, 418 U.S, 166 (1974) (quoting Ex parte Le vitt, 302 U.S. 633, 634 (1937)) (citing Laird v. Tatum, 408 U.S. 1, 13 (1972)).

478 J. INST. 2.1.1.

479 U.S. CONST. amend. V; ibid. art. XIV § 1; for the public use requirement, *see, e.g.,* Kelo v. City of New London, Conn., 545 U.S. 469 (2005).

480 Joseph R. Biden, Jr., *Memorandum on Modernizing Regulatory Review*, DAILY COMP. PRES. DOCS. 1 (2021), https://www.whiteh ouse.gov/briefing-room/presidential-actions/2021/01/20/moder nizing-regulatory-review (emphasis added).

481 488 U.S. 204 (1988).

482 Ibid. at 471. For the standpoint of the classical law, *see* Patrick J. Smith, *The Moral Rule Against Retroactivity*, https://iusetiustiti um.com/the-moral-rule-against-retroactivity.

483 483 U.S. 435 (1987).

484 Ibid. at 436, overruling O'Callahan v. Parker, 395 U.S. 258, 274 (1969).

485 *Solorio*, 483 U.S. at 450 (internal quotation omitted). *See also* United States v. Dixon, 509 U.S. 688, 711–12 (1993), which overruled Grady v. Corbin, 495 U.S. 508 (1990) as a departure from prior precedent.

Index

Legal Process school 2
legal progressivism 119, 120
"legislate morality" 37, 180, 181
legislatures 48
legitimate development 123–4
lex 3–4, 18, 19
  definition 4
liberal constitutional theory 165
liberal theory 50–1, 166
liberalism of fear 49
liberals 13
libertarian constitutionalism 92
libertarians 13, 14, 67
liberty 14, 37–8, 39, 50, 65
Little Sisters of the Poor 119–20
living constitutionalism 85, 87–8
living originalism 97–9, 105, 106,
  110–11
Lochner v. New York (1905) 21, 52,
  60–7
logical sequence (Newman's
  doctrine) 123
Loving v. Virginia (1967) 131
Lujan v. Defenders of Wildlife
  (1992) 174
Lund, Nelson 98

mala fides 65
Manning, Dean John 79, 102
Marcian 137
margin of appreciation 20
marketplace of ideas 127–8
marriage 131–3, 218–19n346
Marshall, Chief Justice 62
Massachusetts v. EPA (2007) 175
Mathews v. Eldridge (1976)
  223n390
McCulloch v. Maryland (1819) 33,
  40, 62
meaning
  ordinary 78, 96
  in originalism 91, 92, 94–6, 97,
    106, 107, 110–11
  public 95
medical marijuana 163

Messner, Johannes 157
Mill, John Stuart 171, 228n462
modernism 67, 122, 124
monstrous government 27–8
morality 37
motorized lawmaking 142, 145
Mugler v Kansas (1887) 32, 60,
  62–3
municipal law 54, 64
municipal positive law *see ius civile*
Munn v. Illinois (1876) 32, 33, 60
"murdering heir" statutes 80

natural justice 181
natural law 4, 19, 20, 55, 56,
  188n10, 214n290
  agencies and 152–3
  discretionary determination
    45–6
  fundamental fairness 60
  general precepts 46
  general principles of 153
  marriage 132
  positive law and 44–5, 58
  primary role 59–60
  stability 113–14
Natural Law in Court (Helmholz)
  44, 55
natural liberty 64
natural rights 54, 56–7, 167–8
New Deal 40
Newman, St. John Henry 23, 118,
  123–4
nirvana fallacy 113
"no law to apply" test 149–50
no-backsliding principle 126
non-originalist constitutionalism
  122
Novak, William 55, 203n136

Obama administration 119–20
Obergefell v. Hodges (2015) 23,
  118–19, 120, 122–3, 131–3
objective natural morality 8
obscenity 170–2